Contents

Introduction

The terms "post-colonialism" and "post-modernism" have become increasingly important ones for the discipline of literary studies over the past decade. This is the first book to seek to characterise post-modernist and post-colonial discourses in relation to each other, and to chart their intersecting and diverging trajectories.

Definitions of post-modernism are necessarily wide-ranging, and such definitions explicitly or implicitly form or inform the subject matter of many of the essays in this volume. Behind the usage of the term "post-modern," as Robert Wilson notes, "are two distinct archives, two sets of relevant primary and secondary texts." While the first "archive" constructs post-modern as a period, the second is "a highly flexible analytic-descriptive term capable of isolating conventions, devices and techniques across the range of all the cultural products (though architecture, painting and fiction seem privileged) that can be caught in a widely-flung transnational net" (113).

Post-colonialism too, might be characterised as having two archives. The first archive here constructs it as writing (more usually than architecture or painting) grounded in those societies whose subjectivity has been constituted in part by the subordinating power of European colonialism—that is, as writing from countries or regions which were formerly colonies of Europe. The second archive of post-colonialism is intimately related to the first, though not co-extensive with it. Here the post-colonial is conceived of as a set of discursive practices, prominent among which is *resistance* to colonialism, colonialist ideologies, and their contemporary forms and subjectificatory legacies. The nature and function of this resistance form a central problematic of the discourse.

As a number of these essays note, however, there is a good deal of formal and tropological overlap between "primary" texts variously categorised as "post-modern" or "post-colonial." Salman Rushdie's *The Satanic Verses*, or his earlier *Midnight's Children* provide classic examples of works which have been so appropriated. Very often it is not something intrinsic to a work of fiction which places it as post-modern or post-colonial, but the way in which the text is discussed. But if there is overlap between the two discourses in terms of "primary" texts—to continue with Robert Wilson's distinction—there is considerably less in the "secondary" category. It is thus in the selection and the reading of such "primary" texts, and in the contexts of discussion in which they are placed, that significant divergences between post-colonialism and post-modernism are most often isolated. The contemporary relationship *between* the two critical and theoretical practices thus becomes a further complicating factor. For although post-colonial theory and criticism ground themselves in texts produced by formerly colonised peoples, so increasingly does contemporary post-structuralism (the theoretical and critical practice intrinsically interwoven with post-modernism) but in a very different way. This relationship, as W.J.T. Mitchell's account implies, is of a depressingly familiar kind, one in which the "colonies" again provide the "raw materials" for a Euro-American critical and theoretical industry which arrogates to itself rights of truth and judgement:

> The most important new literature is emerging from the colonies — regions and peoples that have been economically or militarily dominated in the past — while the most provocative new literary criticism is emanating from the imperial centres that once dominated them — the industrial nations of Europe and America.

> Horace noted long ago that the transfer of empire from Greece to Rome (the translatio imperii) was accompanied by a transfer of culture and learning (a translatio studii). Today the cultural transfer is no longer one-way. But what is the nature of the transference going on between the declining imperial powers and their former colonies, and between contemporary literature and criticism? (B-1)

What Mitchell's comment attests is that this relationship is a deeply political one, and it is to questions of politics both *within* and *between* these two discourses that many of the writers here turn.

In various ways, both discourses share a problematic political relationship with modernism. Post-modernism constituted as a period term determinedly rejects, while it paradoxically reinscribes modernism. Post-colonialism, as Hena Maes-Jelinek points out, derives in part from the spread of European modernist texts and contexts to colonial areas, and post-colonial responses to modernism are necessarily linked to it, even as post-colonials point out the partial geneses of both modernism and post-modernism in the European encounter with "other" cultures. But words like "spread" and "encounter" elide the politics of repression and the very real hegemonies of Euro-representation, blurring the relation between object and subject, and eliding the *direction* of appropriating "gaze."

Post-modernism, whether characterised as temporal or topological, originates in Europe, or more specifically, operates as a Euro-American western hegemony, whose global appropriation of time-and-place inevitably proscribes certain cultures as backward and marginal while co-opting to itself certain of their cultural "raw" materials. Post-modernism is then projected onto these margins as normative, as a neo-universalism to which "marginal" cultures may aspire, and from which certain of their more forward-looking products might be appropriated and "authorised." In its association with post-structuralism, post-modernism thus acts, as Barbara Christian has noted, as a way of depriving the formerly colonised of "voice," of, specifically, any theoretical authority, and locking post-colonial texts which it does appropriate firmly within the European episteme. Post-modernism as mode is thus exported from Europe to the formerly colonised, and the local "character" it acquires there frequently replicates and reflects contemporary cultural hegemonies. Writing on the Futur* Fall Conference held in Australia in 1984, Robert Wilson notes that the Australian brand of post-modernism was Europe-descended, Europe-orientated, and thus apocalyptic, while the Canadian was more concerned with specific textual analysis, reflecting United States proclivity and practice (35, 38).

All the contributors to this volume, with one exception, come from, or live and work in countries formerly colonised by Britain. It is thus not surprising that the neo-colonising role of post-modernism in post-colonial areas underpins or forms the subject of discussion in a number of the essays. For if "modernism" was imposed by England through colonial education systems, post-modernism and post-structuralism have followed, less openly perhaps, and therefore more insidiously, in its wake. The result, as Kumkum Sangari notes, is that

> on the one hand, the world contracts into the West; a Eurocentric perspective . . . is brought to bear upon 'Third World' cultural products; a 'specialized' skepticism is carried everywhere as cultural paraphernalia and epistemological apparatus, as a way of seeing; and the postmodern problematic becomes the frame through which the cultural products of the rest of the world are seen. On the other hand, the West expands into the world; late capitalism muffles the globe and homogenizes (or threatens to) all cultural production — this, for some reason, is one 'master narrative' that is seldom dismantled as it needs to be if the differential economic, class, and cultural formation of 'Third World' countries is to be taken into account. The writing that emerges from this position, however critical it may be of colonial discourses, gloomily disempowers the 'nation' as an enabling idea and relocates the impulses for change as everywhere and nowhere . . . Such skepticism does not take into account either the fact that the postmodern preoccupation with the crisis of meaning is not everyone's crisis (even in the West) or that there are different modes of de-essentialization which are socially and politically grounded and mediated by separate perspectives, goals, and strategies for change in other countries. (183–84)

Post-modernism is Europe's export to what it regards as "margins." By contrast, post-colonial writing ("primary" and "secondary") moves from colonised, formerly colonised, and neo-colonised areas — from African countries, Australia, Canada, the Caribbean, India, New Zealand — towards Europe, or more recently, towards the United States. While there are a number of prominent post-colonial critics (the term here being used as in its second archive) based in Europe, their critical and theoretical practice is more strongly influenced by post-colonial (used in the sense of the first archive) writings than by European post-modernist and post-structuralist frameworks. The slowly increasing institutionalisation of the teaching of post-colonial literatures and post-colonial theory in both Europe (and to a lesser degree the United States) has more often derived from post-colonial and national practices, than from the contemporary post-structuralist interest in "Third World" texts.

Of course the intersections of post-modernism and post-colonialism are far more complex than this account suggests, but nevertheless, two hazardous generalisations might be made: post-colonialism is more overtly concerned with politics than is post-modernism; and, secondly, the post-modern (in conjunction with post-structuralism) has exercised and is still exercising a cultural and intellectual hegemony in relation to the post-colonial world and over post-colonial cultural productions.

Thus while certain conventions, devices, techniques of writing variously characterised as "post-colonial" or "post-modern" often appear similar, indeed indistinguishable, the uses to which such devices are put, or seem to be put, and the direction of their political valency are very different, often reflecting the unequal power-relationships between the two discourses, and in the field of literary studies generally. Moreover, specific tropes may take on very different meanings and vectors depending on the cultural context of their production and the ways in which they are understood by particular audiences. As Lorraine Weir, in a passage quoted by Linda Hutcheon in her essay here notes, irony,

> in the hands of those who exercise genuine power is very different from the same device in the hands of those classified as powerless. Among those whose basic communication may frequently depend upon the skilled use and reception of ironic utterance—that is, among the powerless—irony will be all the more powerful. The Irish, as is commonly known, are masters of irony and invective; so is the primary community of women. (67)

Discontinuity, polyphony, parodic form, and in particular the problematisation of representation and the fetishisation/retrieval of "difference," take on radically different shape and direction within the two discourses. While post-modernism has increasingly fetishised "difference" and "the Other," those "Othered" by a history of European representation can only retrieve and reconstitute a post-colonised "self" against that history wherein an awareness of "referential slippage" was inherent in colonial being. While the disappearance of "grand narratives" and the "crisis of representation" characterise the Euro-American post-modernist mood, such expressions of "breakdown" and "crisis" instead signal promise and decolonisation potential within post-colonial discourse. Pastiche and parody are not simply the new games Europeans play, nor the most recent intellectual self-indulgence of a Europe habituated to periodic fits of languid despair, but offer a key to destabilisation and deconstruction of a repressive European archive. Far from endlessly deferring or denying meaning, these same tropes function as potential decolonizing strategies which invest (or reinvest) devalued "peripheries" with meaning.

Again, however, such distinctions are not really as clear-cut as this. Hena Maes-Jelinek argues that post-colonialism has not been sufficiently prepared to acknowledge its positive debt to European modernism, while Simon Gikandi's re-interpretation of literary history in the Caribbean places male writers like Cesaire,

Lamming and V.S. Naipaul within a Euro-modernist framework, with contemporary feminist writing revisioning and challenging this patriarchal tradition through "post-modernist narrative strategies."

As these essays suggest, the problematic connections between post-modernism, post-colonialism, and the "national" and "international" are crucial to any consideration of the relationship between the two discourses, and such questions thus form the subject matter of a number of the essays. Part of post-modernist "author/ity" derives from its claims to an "internationalism" which can loftily eschew the claims of "narrow" and "essentialist" nationalisms. Yet, the cultural and institutional authorization so apparently derived, is demonstrably grounded to European ontologies and epistemologies, and its power intimately bound up with imperialist relations—both old and new—between nations and cultures. The post-modernist project as it operates within the world, thus apparently runs counter to its own ideology. As Elizabeth Ferrier notes

> In spite of the identification of post-modernism with difference, discontinuity and fragmentation, it tends to be marketed globally as a general movement which addresses global concerns. . . . [This] perpetuates an emphasis on 'global culture' masking European and American metropolitan biases even as they describe this culture as de-centred, fragmented and marked by difference in opposition to the totalizing culture of modernity. (17)

Post-colonial *readings* of post-modern discourse can compensate for this emphasis on the global by focussing on local historical and geographical specificities, situating post-modernism in relation to these practices rather than the other way round. They direct our attention to cultural difference and local productions which resist or transform imperialist cultural forms (Ferrier 15). Graham Huggan, in discussing the persistent cartographic tropes in Australian, Canadian and more generally post-colonial writing suggests that this

> cannot be solely envisaged as the reworking of a particular spatial paradigm, but consists rather in the implementation of a series of creative revisions which register the transition from a colonial framework within which the writer is compelled to recreate and reflect upon the restrictions of colonial space to a post-colonial one within which he or she acquires the freedom to engage in a series of "territorial disputes" which implicitly or explicitly acknowledge the relativity of modes of spatial (and, by extension, cultural) perception. (134)

But post-colonialism's relationship with the local, with the "regional" or "national" is also problematic. The institutional genesis of post-colonial discourse has frequently been in national or regional challenges to European or Euro-American claims to centrality, to the "normative." Increasingly, however, national literary studies and post-colonial theory have begun to part company, particularly in Africa and Australia.

Some African critics and theorists distrust the cross-cultural valency of post-colonialism, attacking its comparative basis in colonised cultures *both* white and black, settler-invader and indigenous as replicating imperialist politics and neglecting the very real differences between cultures and kinds of imperialist oppressions. Like African critics, some Australian commentators have rejected the comparatist base, preferring to consider Australian culture as a unique phenomenon best considered exclusively in local terms. Post-colonial theorists, on their part, have critiqued this position for both its national/nationalist slippage (and the often imperialist and racist essentialisms it replicates locally) and for apparent inability to perceive that the old, if cryptic comparison—with Britain and Europe—thus remains authorised within both national cultural institutions and within the academy.

Taking up this sort of debate, Diana Brydon questions Linda Hutcheon's reading of post-colonialism as neo-imperialism, asserting that responsible post-colonial critique has always attended to cultural difference—indeed is committed to and founded upon it—and that distinctions not just between, but *within* post-colonial societies—for instance that between settler-invader and indigenous populations—are crucial in any theorization of the post-colonial. Hutcheon challenges post-colonial theory for its comparative frame, claiming that only indigenous Canadian populations, not settler-invader ones, can rightly be regarded as "post-colonial." Using the concept of "contamination as literary strategy," Brydon challenges the idea of authentic indigenity on which Hutcheon's critique of post-colonialism is based, arguing that post-modernism's fetishisation of simulacra inevitably sponsors a counter "cult of authenticity." The effect of such a "cult" in Brydon's view, is "to defuse conflict, denying the necessity of cultural and political struggle and suggesting that tourism is probably the best model for cross-cultural interaction" (195). While she recognizes the right and the strategic political value of such claims to authenticity on the part of native peoples themselves, Brydon warns that a total investment in "authenticity" in the contemporary world may prove self-defeating.

⤙ Simon During's essay is also concerned with questions of simulacra and authenticity and with the ironies generated and politics energised by their intersection within post-modern and post-colonial discourse. During's exploration of the question ranges from Johnson and Boswell's tour of the Hebrides in 1773 to Carol O'Biso's travelling *Te Maori* exhibition of the 1980s. His concern with the function and place of the "sacred" in both indigenous and contemporary Euro-descended discourses leads him to consider the reception of Rushdie's *The Satanic Verses* and to a critique of James Clifford's "post-culturalism," a theory which *potentially* by-passes some of the problems for cultural theory raised by the intersections of the post-colonial and the post-modern.

Questions of authenticity and simulacra on which During's and Brydon's arguments revolve are closely related to the issue of representation, and like indigenity and authenticity, representation becomes a key discussion point for any investigation of post-colonial and post-modern intersections. The politics of representation are at issue in the essays by Gikandi, Huggan, Srivastava and Hutcheon, and the so-called post-modern "crisis of representation" forms the basis of the argument in the essays by Stephen Slemon and Ian Adam. Slemon isolates an important difference between the two discourses in post-colonialism's inescapable and *originary* "awareness of referential slippage," and like Gikandi and Adam, he characterises a post-colonial writing practice as one which works *towards* realism within this awareness, developing strategies for "signifying through literature an order of mimesis." Ian Adam discusses works by Carey and Birney in the context of the philosophy of Charles Sanders Peirce, "the foundation of whose project is an assault on the scepticism of that European Cartesianism whose legacy is still manifest in post-structuralist theory" (86). Birney's language in "David" is founded on the modernist faith that "something like total referentiality" is possible, but its narrative allegorically undermines that foundation, an undermining whose final resolution, however, lies not in linguistic scepticism but in the provisionality of post-colonial practice, anticipated in Peirce's semiotic. Post-colonial cultures, conscious from the beginning of textual overdetermination, thus manifest, in Slemon's formulation, a *dual* agenda, where, for instance, a work like Neville Farki's *The Death of Tarzana Clayton*, which apparently offers all the "tropological pyrotechnics" of the post-modernist paradigm, nevertheless retains "a recuperative impulse towards the structure of 'history' and manifests a Utopian desire grounded in reference" (6). There is thus a dual agenda within post-colonial literary reiteration whose consequence is a "bifurcation in referential strategy."

Questions then of the national, the international, the transnational; of authenticity and simulacra; of representation and referentiality provide focal areas in the consideration of post-colonialism and post-modernism. Underlying all are questions of politics, both within and between the two discourses, and all the essays in this volume are to varying degrees concerned with politics and textuality within post-modernist or post-colonial frameworks. Graham Huggan discusses the politics of cartography and the implications of post-modernist (post-structuralist) readings of post-colonial worlds and texts. Aruna Srivastava considers the politics of Rushdie's *Shame* and *Midnight's Children* within the context of colonialist history. Robert Wilson finds political purchase in the writings of Angela Carter after a tour de force of post-modernist playfulness, and both Stephen Slemon and Linda Hutcheon distinguish between the post-modern and the post-colonial on the grounds of political motivation and valency.

Gareth Griffiths considers Kosinsky's *Being There* and Malouf's *An Imaginary Life* as examples of, respectively, post-modernist and post-colonial texts, and begins his analysis by quoting Caribbean writer and political activist Jacques Stephen Alexis on the difference between Haitian "marvellous realism" and what Alexis referred to in 1956 as "the cold-blooded surrealistic researches" and "analytical games of Europe" (153). For Alexis (and Cesaire) as Griffiths notes, art and political activism were inextricably interwoven, and it is to theory and politics, specifically post-structuralism and black South African art and activism that Annamaria Carusi turns in her essay.

Carusi argues that post-modernist and post-structuralist discourses can have revolutionary potential in "a context of urgent cultural contestation," and that a post-colonial "liberation literary discourse" gains from such inter-articulation through countering the reactionary tendencies implicit in any type of nationalism, while continuing to use its ideologies for strategic effect. She notes however, that her own theoretical discourse has its place in a particular institution. "Grassroots activists in the townships do not need Foucault, or any theorist to tell them this, but academics working in university institutions perhaps do. There is a rupture between what we do in universities and what activists are doing, but this is not necessarily unhealthy" (105–6).

John Frow in his essay reminds us of both the extra-literary genesis and range of the post-modern, and warns against the dangers—particularly for an active post-colonialism—of conflating the cultural and the political with the economic. Writing from a post-modernist perspective, he considers the global implications of a rampant international capitalism for cultural production. Here "post-modern" and "post-colonial" are conceived of not in terms of their difference from or their difficult and ambivalent resistance to modernity, but as themselves framed within capitalist extra-territorialisations:

> The result of this new speed and flexibility of capital is neither a colonial order of direct domination nor a neo-colonial order of indirect domination of one nation state by another, but a world system which we might call precisely "post-colonial"—in which dominance is exercised by international capital through the agency of dominant nation-states and regions, but in large part independently of their control. (149)

Frow's essay is entitled "What *was* Post-Modernism" (emphasis added) and for Stanley Fish, amongst others, the term has become "somewhat old-fashioned." Nevertheless the politics of its intersection with post-colonialism, as this volume indicates, takes many forms. European and Euro-American institutional and cultural hegemonies are protean. Post-modernism's most persuasive institutional legacy is post-structuralism, and post-colonial texts, as Mitchell noted, are increasingly being appropriated to and read within its *potentially* neo-colonising agendas. In Wole Soyinka's view,

> [We] have been blandly invited to submit ourselves to a second epoch of colonisation—this time by a universal-humanoid abstraction defined and conducted by individuals whose theories and prescriptions are derived from the apprehension of *their* world and *their* history, *their* social neuroses and *their* value systems. (x)

Increasingly the tensions between the post-modernist (and post-structuralist) and the post-colonial have become a central problematic of post-colonial discourse itself. Gayatri Spivak and Homi Bhabha, whose post-structuralist practice might be more accurately characterised within the broad range of the post-colonial as an imperial or colonialist critique, focus their attention on the texts of the imperialist, and on the inevitable dismantling of their authority at the colonial periphery through—to take Bhabha's formulation of ambivalence and mimicry. Within post-colonialism this practice thus remains deconstructive rather than positivist, and its purchase lies in the dismantling of imperial fictions and colonialist ideologies.

But as Benita Parry has argued, although deconstructive work on the discourse of colonialism has succeeded in reversing an implicit collusion between criticism and colonial power, deconstruction's necessary privileging of the imperial text as the object of critical attention amounts discursively to an erasure of the anti-colonialist 'native' voice and the limiting of the possibility of native resistance. (Parry 34). And as Stephen Slemon argues in this volume, a purely deconstructive theory cannot account for the "dual agenda" he finds characteristic of the post-colonial text.

Whatever the fate of textual/literary studies in the twenty-first century, post-modernism, or specifically post-structuralism in *alliance* with post-colonialism has determinedly and successfully eroded the centrality of British literature and canon-based studies within academic institutions. But as well as the positive effects of this alliance, we must also understand the tensions and stresses, the power relations within and between the two discourses if we are to chart the course of literary history and its relationship to world cultures and politics this century.

Helen Tiffin

WORKS CITED

Christian, Barbara. "The Race for Theory," *Cultural Critique* 6 (1987): 51–64.

During, Simon. "Postmodernism or Postcolonialism?" *Landfall* 39.3 (1985): 366–80.

Ferrier, Elizabeth. "Mapping the Space of the Other: Transformations of Space in Postcolonial Fiction and Postmodern Theory." Unpublished PhD dissertation, U Qld, 1990.

Mitchell, W.J.T. *The Chronicle of Higher Education* 19 April 1989: B1–3.

Parry, Benita. "Problems in Current Theories of Colonial Discourse." *Oxford Literary Review* 9. 1–2 (1987): 27–58.

Sangari, Kumkum. "The Politics of the Possible." *Cultural Critique* 7 (1987): 157–86.

Soyinka, Wole. *Myth, Literature and the African World*. Cambridge: CUP, 1976.

Weir, Lorraine. "Toward a Feminist Hermeneutics: Jay Macpherson's *Welcoming Disaster*." *Gynocritics: Feminist Approaches to Canadian and Queluec Women's Writing* ed. Barbara Godard. Toronto: ECW P, 1987. 59–70.

Wilson, Robert. "Playpens for Leviathan: Canadian Uses of 'Postmodern' " *Australian-Canadian Studies* 8.1 (1990): 35–46.

This book has been published with the assistance of a grant from the Alberta Foundation for the Literary Arts.

Modernism's Last Post

STEPHEN SLEMON

"The remedy for decadence is a journey to the frontier."
DAVID TROTTER, "Modernism and Empire"

Perhaps the only point of consensus in the debate over "post-modernism" is that the defining term of this apparently contemporary phenomenon inherently posits for Euro-American culture some kind of radical break from the discourse of "modernism" as it developed at the end of the nineteenth century (Jameson 53). The accuracy of this hypothesis in nomenclature, the cultural specificity of this semiotic "break," the discursive and ideological purchase of this new social episteme — these, of course, are immense issues, and they furnish an exciting theatre for the spectacle of critical disagreement within Western intellectual practice. An important consequence of this debate, however, is that the narrow and prevailing idea of "modernism" itself is at last being systematically reworked to reveal a foundation for contemporary First World representation not simply in a radically vanguardist and anti-bourgeois movement (Wortman 175), but rather in the wholesale appropriation and refiguration of non-Western artistic and cultural practices by a society utterly committed to the preservation of its traditional prerogatives for gender, race and class privilege. In its debate over the genealogy of the post-modern problematic, Western culture is coming to understand that — as Ashis Nandy puts it (xiv) — the "armed version" of modernism is colonialism itself, and that modernism's most heroically self-privileging figurative strategies — its "fragmentation of textual unity," its "play of contradictory genres," its anti-normative aestheticising impulse (Frow 117) — would have been unthinkable had it not been for the assimilative power of Empire to appropriate the cultural work of a heterogeneous world "out there" and to reproduce it for its own social and discursive ends.[1]

It would seem natural, therefore, that the two critical discourses which today constitute themselves specifically in opposition to this historical conjunction would have forged for themselves a strong affiliative network of methodological collaboration. But except for the general project of anti-colonialist critique as it is taken up by post-structuralist or new historicist theorists — the most well known of whom are Gayatri Chakravorty Spivak, Homi Bhabha, Peter Hulme, and Stephen Greenblatt — post-modernist theory and post-colonial criticism have remained more or less separate in their strategies and their foundational assumptions. Why these two critical projects should remain asymmetrical is thus a matter of great interest, and what I would like to do in this short paper is attempt to situate at least one of the major fault-lines that runs between them. Needless to say, the astonishing variety in critical activity taking place *within* each of these two projects means that any such attempt will necessarily overreach itself. I proceed in the understanding that what follows is at best a form of critical piece-work: provisional, interrogative, and most of all, motivated within an ongoing critical struggle over the political terrain of textual interpretation.

As almost all commentators like to point out, definitions of post-modernism tend to situate the "phenomenon" somewhere between two absolute positions, the first of which understands post-modernism as a culturally specific historical *period*, and the second of which understands it as a *style* of representation that runs, albeit with important differences, across various artistic media. In the first camp are theorists such as Fredric Jameson, for whom "post-modernism" signifies the pastiche energetics of Western society under late capitalism, where a "new depthlessness" in representation — one grounded in the fetishization of the image as simulacrum — marks off a profoundly ahistorical drive which seeks to efface the past as referent and leave behind itself nothing but texts (53–66). In the second camp are theorists such as Ihab Hassan or Michael Newman, for whom the "post-modern" can be captured in a catalogue of figurative propensities (indeterminacy, multivalence, hybridization, etc.) whose ludic celebrations of representational freedom — as J.G. Merquior points out (17) — are grounded in a "dubious analogy" between artistic experimentation and social liberation. My reading in the post-modern debate is limited, but to my mind the most interesting theorist to take on the conjunction between these two general approaches is Linda Hutcheon, who rejects not only the assumption that post-modern representation provides in any simple sense "the background hum for power" (see Kariel 97) as the first camp would argue, but also the assumption that post-modernism can accurately "describe an international cultural phenomenon" (4), as the second camp seems to imply.

For Hutcheon, post-modernism is a "problematizing force" in Western society (xi) which, far from expressing a straightforward "incredulity with regard to the master narratives" of dominant culture, as Lyotard would have it (Jardine 65), paradoxically inscribes *and* contests culturally certified codes of recognition and representation. Post-modern culture, art, and theory, for Hutcheon, is inherently contradictory, for it both "uses and abuses, installs and then subverts," the "conventions of discourse" which it sets out to challenge (xiii, 3). As it does so, post-modernism discloses a "contradictory dependence on and independence from that which temporally preceded it and which literally made it possible" (18). Post-modernist discourse, that is, *necessarily* admits a provisionality to its truth-claims (13, 23) and a secondary (or allegorical) foundation to its referential sweep. As Hutcheon sees it, this inherently quotational or reiterative grounding of post-modernism issues into a dominant signifying practice whose central rhetorical strategy is intertextual parody. Post-modern parody, Hutcheon explains, functions "as repetition with critical distance that allows ironic signalling of difference at the very heart of similarity" (26). It "paradoxically enacts both change and cultural continuity" (26). And as it *uses* the strategies of dominant culture to challenge its discursive processes from within (20), post-modern parody *also* reveals its "love of history by giving new meaning to old forms" (31).

Hutcheon's framing of the post-modern field is important, for the general textual practice she defines here resembles — at least on the surface — the kind of reiterative textual energy which for a number of critics marks out an especially interesting moment within a broadly post-colonial literary activity. Definitions of the "post-colonial," of course, vary widely, but for me the concept proves most useful not when it is used synonymously with a post-independence historical period in once-colonized nations but rather when it locates a specifically anti- or *post*-colonial *discursive* purchase in culture, one which begins in the moment that colonial power inscribes itself onto the body and space of its Others and which continues as an often occulted tradition into the modern theatre of neo-colonialist international relations. A post-colonial *critical* discourse is therefore never wholly absent from colonial culture: there is always at work in the discourses of the colonized a network of disidentificatory traditions which J. Michael Dash has eloquently labelled a "counter-culture of the imagination" (65). But this critical discourse is never fully present as unmediated resistance. Simon During suggests that the "post-colonial" can be located in "the survival of residual forms of economic life" in colonial societies, the "need for an identity granted not in terms of the colonial power, but in terms of themselves" (369); and to the extent that During's definition identifies for colonial subjects what Richard Terdiman has called a "counter-discourse" I agree with it. But whereas During posits a radical split between "post-colonizing" and "post-colonized" forms of a heterogeneous discourse and argues that unreconstituted white settler cultures have no recourse to an "effective post-colonised discourse" (371), I would want to preserve for "post-colonialism" a specifically anti-colonial counter-discursive energy which *also* runs across the ambivalent space of what Alan Lawson has called "second world" societies — a discursive energy which emerges *not* from the inherent cultural contradiction that necessarily marks transplanted settler societies but rather from their continuing yet subterranean tradition of refusal towards the conceptual and cultural apparatuses of the European imperium.[2]

As During points out, a post-colonial "affect" needs always to be specified in relation to, and within, each post-colonial society (369). But in general terms, a post- or anti-colonial critical or disidentificatory discourse can be seen to energize an enormously heterogeneous set of social and representational practices from within a large number of post-colonial (and sometimes, latently, within colonialist) social configurations. *Part* of this larger, differential post-colonial discourse, I would argue, resides in the contemporary post-structuralist project of anti-colonialist critique; another part — the part that concerns me here — operates within post-colonial literary activity. And *one* of the heterogeneous modalities of this post-colonial discourse within post-colonial literary writing is the figuration of a reiterative quotation, or intertextual citation, in relation to colonialist "textuality." This counter-discursive intertextuality in post-colonial literary writing is in some important ways different from the writing practice that Hutcheon usefully locates at the centre of the post-modernist project; and in order to specify that difference I want now to turn to post-colonial critical practice, and to how it seeks to establish a specific matrix of cultural resistance within the rhetorical play of the post-colonial text.

It has often been noted (see, for example, Viswanathan) that one of colonialism's most salient technologies for social containment and control is the circulation within colonial cultures of the canonical European literary text. Mediated through the colonialist educational apparatus, the European literary text becomes a powerful machinery for forging what Gramsci called cultural domination by consent; and in recognizing this, post-colonial critical discourse seeks to position the oppositional and reiterative textual responses of post-colonial cultures in dialectical relation to their colonialist precursors. Far from articulating a simple "anxiety of influence," however, this post-colonial textual reiteration is heard to be speaking directly to the struggle within colonialist ideology. Post-colonial criticism's key beginning point here, then, is that a "parodic" repetition of imperial "textuality" sets itself specifically in opposition to the interpellative power of colonialism — a power which interweaves itself throughout colonial societies, making the imperial culture appear referentially seamless and the colonial culture appear radically fractured — outside the scope of literary "realism" (Bhabha) and incapable of being "represented" through the imported or imposed structures of transplanted European language. Post-colonial literary reiteration — or parody, or intertextuality, or quotation — is thus seen to be challenging directly a colonialist textual function; and this colonialist textual function is *not* seen as being coterminous with the circulation of textual images in other cultural locations, which are of course in their own ways produced and consumed ideologically.

There is no single mode for signalling this counter-discursive energy within post-colonial literary writing. In fact, as post-colonial critical work continues, it is discovering an enormously differential and thorough infusion of disidentificatory reiteration across the various national post-colonial literatures. The most visible area of this reiterative practice takes place in the post-colonial project of rewriting the canonical "master texts" of Europe — most notably *The Tempest* and *Robinson Crusoe* — in ways that expose their residual colonialist politics and that refigure their narratives to a new ideological vector.[3] Another highly salient practice of this kind involves the figurative invocation of colonialist notions of "history" — as in texts such as George Lamming's *Natives of My Person* or Patrick White's *A Fringe of Leaves* — and the juxtaposition of the imperialist "pretext" with a dis/placive "historical" narrative that, as Helen Tiffin points out (31), functions both to interrogate the politics of narrative production within colonial society and to effect a purgative energy (reiteration as a modality of expulsion) against that version of history which implicitly inscribes European hierarchical values into colonial and post-colonial codes of recognition. Christopher Miller has recently brought to light a much less visible mode of this post-colonial counter-discursive activity at work in Yambo Ouloguem's *Le devoir de violence*. Here, Miller argues, Ouloguem's excessive plagiarizing strategy operates as an anti-colonialist assault on European assumptions about originality and mimcry, working against the pretextual domain of "authorial" European writing to raise questions about why, when a unified Western voice is said to "own" language, the colonized subject becomes implicitly constituted within the fracturing semiotics of Empire as a multiple, dipersed copyist, a *nègre* or "ghostwriter." And to offer a final example: Ketu H. Katrak has recently argued that a counter-discursive "tactical" assault on colonialist assumptions about representation is at work in the Sistren Collective's use of a West Indian creole or nation language. The linguistic assault in this practice, Katrak argues, needs to be explained in a comprehensive theory of linguistic decolonization; and decolonization, as Fanon has pointed out, needs to be grounded in a practice of *violent* discursive resistance.

It is not hard to see that these post-colonial textual strategies bear a close relation to the principle of intertextual parody which Hutcheon defines for post-modernism. But the first difference here, as I have been arguing, is that the location of textual power as an especially effective technology of colonialist discourse means that post-colonial reiterative writing takes on a discursive specificity. This specificity is important for how we attempt to "theorize" the work of the text, for it leads on to a second difference between a post-modern and post-colonial reading of the text. Whereas a post-modernist criticism would want to argue that literary practices such as these expose the constructedness of *all* textuality and thus call down "the claim to unequivocal domination of one mode of signifying over another" (Johnson 5), an *interested* post-colonial critical practice would want to allow for the positive production of oppositional truth-claims in these texts. It would retain for post-colonial writing, that is, a mimetic or referential purchase to textuality, and it would recognize in this referential drive the operations of a crucial strategy for survival in marginalized social groups.

This referential assumption would appear to make what I am calling a post-colonial criticism radically fractured and contradictory, for such a criticism would draw on post-structuralism's suspension of the referent in order to read the social "text" of colonialist power and at the same time would reinstall the referent in the service of colonized and post-colonial societies. The especial valency of textuality within colonialist discourse, however, means that the "referent" simply cannot be totalized; for if the question of representation really is grounded in a "crisis" within post-modern Western society under late capitalism, in post-colonial critical discourse it necessarily bifurcates under a dual agenda: which is to continue the resistance to (neo) colonialism through a deconstructive reading of its rhetoric *and* to retrieve and reinscribe those post-colonial social traditions that in literature issue forth on a thematic level, and within a realist problematic, as principles of cultural identity and survival. Here is how Craig Tapping describes the second principle in this dual agenda:

> despite theory's refutation of such absolute and logocentric categories as these — "truth" or "meaning," "purpose" or "justification" — the new literatures . . . are generated from cultures for whom such terms as "authority" and "truth" are

6   STEPHEN SLEMON

empirically urgent in their demands. Land claims, racial survival, cultural revival: all these demand an understanding of and response to the very concepts and structures which post-structuralist academicians refute in language games, few of which recognize the political struggles of real peoples outside such discursive frontiers.

This dual — and perhaps theoretically contradictory — agenda for post-colonial criticism is grounded, I would argue, in the dual function of post-colonial reiterative texts themselves in the area of cultural work, and in order to establish this point I want to turn briefly to a text which articulates this duality with unusual clarity: *The Death of Tarzana Clayton* by the Jamaican writer Neville Farki.

Post-modernism's catalogue of rhetorical features describes a good deal of Farki's tropological pyrotechnics in this novella, which as the title makes clear is a parodic retelling of Edgar Rice Burroughs's paradigmatically racist fable. *Tarzana Clayton* is fundamentally fragmented and hybridized; it engages overtly in a decentring and decanonizing labour; it is enormously self-reflexive and ironic; it draws obviously and excessively on the devices of "fiction" to demystify imperialist versions of "history"; it "uses and abuses" the received codes of popular culture in order to effect a serious intervention in the production and circulation of majority opinion.

But at the same time — and here Farki's text departs from the post-modernist paradigm — *Tarzana Clayton* retains a recuperative impulse towards the structure of "history" and manifests a Utopian desire grounded in reference. The reiterative portion of the novella is framed by the narrator's account of how the Tarzan story in fact predates its historical moment of fictionalization by Burroughs, and how the struggle against colonialism — the ideology that is embedded within Tarzan aesthetics — has been continued by historical figures such as Kwame Nkrumah and thus carried forward into the present. And within the reiterative portion of the text, much of Farki's energy is directed towards the re-insertion into history of those acts and figures of anti-colonialist resistance that imperialist forms of representation have systematically left out — at one point in the narrative, for example, Hamum, Farki's exemplary colonial "subject," travels to New York where he hears Marcus Garvey speak. Far from calling down the idea of "history" itself, then, Farki's text works to map over colonialism's false historicism with a reconstituted, "decolonised" sense of historical event, the result being that the apparently anti-referential display of tropological excess in the narrative is grounded to what I see as an underlying post-colonial realist script. Farki — in opposition to the anti-foundational claims of post-modern logic — is concerned with the production of an alterior "knowledge" for post-colonial cultures, a knowledge of historical agency in colonized subjects and an awareness that the lived experiences of the Others of Empire offers a thematic touchstone for a continuing resistance to colonialism's power. And so, as the following passage makes clear, the project of reiterating the colonialist "pretext" not only involves the figuration of textual resistance but also the recuperation — the remembering or relearning — of "the role of the native as historical subject and combatant, possessor of another knowledge and producer of alternative traditions" (Parry 34). Needless to say, the encounter taking place on the character level in this passage is an allegory of the struggle between colonizer and colonized. And the "fiction" being constituted here is both a figuration of a recovered realism and a gesture towards the question of how a "history" of the colonized past might come to be rewritten in the future:

> Tarzan inflicted many wounds on Hamum with the dagger and when he threw the wounded Ashanti to the ground, he bared his teeth as he moved towards his adversary for the kill. Hamum had learnt that an overly angry or confident attacker was apt to make the fatal mistake of underestimating a cornered enemy. Hamum played limp and completely helpless as Tarzan raised his hand to plunge the long bloodstained blade into his enemy's chest. But Hamum . . ., moving with great agility rose, and like a fleetfooted gazelle, leaped and grasped Tarzan in a fatal hold around his neck. He held his neck with one hand and with the other he held Tarzan's hand with the dagger, thrusting it into the whiteman's stomach several times. As Hamum released his hold slowly, Tarzan's body fell on its face in the road. It was not to be buried and was left as meat for scavengers from the forest and the sky. This was the end of Tarzana Clayton. (62)

I want to stress the proliferation of this dual agenda within post-colonial literary reiteration, and its consequent bifurcation in referential strategy, for it is here, I think, that Western post-modernist readings can so overvalue the anti-referential or deconstructive energetics of postcolonial texts that they efface the important recuperative work that is also going on within them. As post-colonial writers and critics have always pointed out, the assumption of "natural" seamlessness within language has never taken hold within colonized territory; for when colonialism transports a language, or imposes it upon a differential world, a fracturing, indeterminate semantics becomes the *necessary* medium for verbal and written practice. Although Euro-American writing is at last waking up to the fundamental conditionality of language and is thrashing through the theoretical implications of this realization within a debate over the "crisis of representation," post-colonial cultures have a long history of working towards "realism" within an awareness of referential slippage, and they have developed a number of strategies for signifying through literature *an* "order of mimesis." *Tarzana Clayton* provides us with a highly visible site in which this reach for a positive (post-colonial) referentiality operates alongside a counter-discursive parodic energy — one which a post-modernist methodology would at least notice if not always specify. But in a number of post-colonial texts — especially those texts which post-modernism has managed to canonize for itself — the referential purchase is not always so visible, at least not to readers from outside the culture. And this can result, within the post-modernist problematic, in a critical reading which is radically skewed.

To give just one example: post-modernist explorations of Salman Rushdie's *Midnight's Children* have proved extremely useful in locating the way in which the novel problematizes the question of authorship and calls down the structures of "history." They have also been useful in establishing the way in which a dysfunctional, excessive typology infuses the text and thus puts the question of cultural coding itself into play. But post-modernist readings have not taken seriously the typologically obvious but "realist" suggestion that *Midnight's Children* positively reinscribes cultural coding through the Vedantic thematization of its "creator" as listener or reader: that is, as Padma (or Laksmī), the lotus goddess, who embodies the creative power of māyā and who even at the text's moment of seemingly total cultural dissolution may be "writing" the text of a post-colonial future not through the indeterminacies of interpretive slippage and "freedom" but from a solid grounding in pre-colonized cultural and religious agency.

Meaghan Morris has made the point that feminist politics have no *necessary* argument with "post-modernism," but rather that the real problem in the intersection of these two projects is the post-modernist *debate*. She looks specifically at the bibliography of Jonathan Arac's introduction to his collection *Postmodernism and Politics,* and points out that although post-modernism *requires* the work of feminist writers of literature to "frame" its discourse, it has consistently erased the work of feminists from its "pantheon" of theorists (seven women out of more than seventy entries).

A similar erasure seems to be happening, I think, in the intersection between post-colonial cultural work and the debate over post-modernism. It seems impossible, for example, that a conceptual framework for post-modernism could have emerged without the assimilation of South American "boom" fiction. But as Katrak has noted (158), the First World debate over the semiotics of difference has systematically ignored the "theoretical" work of Third World and post-colonial subjects, often because that "theory" presents itself *in* literary texts and *as* social practice, not in the affiliative theoretical language of Western intellectual institutions. Even when post-colonial work actually presents itself *as* theory, it seems to be overlooked by post-modernists — as is very obviously the case with Wilson Harris's important work on the question of representation. By excluding this post-colonial theoretical work from the debate, and by overlooking the cultural specificity of so many of the literary texts it has otherwise read with reasonable accuracy, the "post-modernist" phenomenon — for all its decentring rhetoric — has paradoxically become a centralizing institution, a Western problematic whose project in the cross-cultural sphere has become the translation of differential literary and social "texts" into philosophical questions and cultural attitudes whose grounding in Western culture is too rarely admitted, let alone significantly addressed.

For as Kumkum Sangari has noted, "the postmodern preoccupation with the crisis of meaning is not everyone's crisis (even in the West)," and "there are different modes of de-essentialization which are socially and politically grounded and mediated by separate perspectives, goals, and strategies for change in other countries" (184). The fact that a great deal of the work going in the post-modernist debate remains more or less unaware of these "different modes" is perhaps contributive to post-modernism's overwhelming tendency to present itself — as During explains (368) — as a crisis, a contradiction, an "apotheosis of negativity." But from a post-colonial perspective, notes During, post-modernism "can also be thought of as the apotheosis of cultural confidence and of economic strength. Power has become so centered, so organised that it no longer needs notions of organic totality" to effect the strategic containment of its Others when it appropriates their cultural work. The universalizing, assimilative impulse that carries itself forward in the name of post-modernism is certainly not the only political tendency within this broad cultural movement, but for many post-colonial critics and theorists it appears to be becoming the dominant one: and it is here, I think, in this residual impulse, that post-modernism joins hands with its modernist precursor in continuing a politics of colonialist control.

Like modernism, post-modernism *needs* its (post-) colonial Others in order to constitute or to frame its narrative of referential fracture. But it also needs to exclude the cultural and political specificity of post-colonial representations in order to assimilate them to a rigorously Euro-American problematic. This, it could be argued, is a typically self-sustaining post-modern contradiction; and yet in this contradiction there could perhaps reside a fissuring energy which could lay the foundation for a radical change of tenor within the post-modern debate. For if the modernist ethos is coming to be re-read not simply as the manifestation of an historical period or style but also as the representational marker of a *crisis* within European colonialism — as Edward Said has recently suggested (222–23) — it may well be that the post-modernist debate can become one of the key sites upon which the Anglo-American West, if it is to unravel its own moment of cognitive and cultural aporia, finds itself *forced* to take the representational claims of the post-colonial world seriously (Said 223). At its best, the debate over post-modernism constitutes a theatre of exchange in which dominant Western culture attempts to understand artistic and intellectual activity as a militant set of practices in the project of social change, but too often the very real *crisis* of post-modernism is lost to a blandly self-reflexive methodology which forgets its own genealogy and its cultural and geographical place. As post-colonial discourse continues to negotiate the relationship between colonialist power and the possibilities for post-colonial freedom, however, it may yet come in for some serious attention within post-modernism and assist it in rediscovering its cultural location. Perhaps also, post-modernism may yet find a way to join with, not assimilate, post-colonial critical discourse in the necessary post-modernist work of decolonizing Western culture — decolonizing it, that is, from a residual modernism, which continues to mark for Western culture its relations with the world.[4]

NOTES

1.   For an amplification of this conjunction between modernism and colonialism, see Said (222–23) and Trotter, *passim*.

2. Diana Brydon in "Myths That Write Us" makes an important argument against an overly binarized concept of colonialism and for preserving the cultural work of settler colonies within contemporary post-colonialism.

3. The critical work on this body of literature is much too long to cite here, but a useful analysis of the refigurations of *The Tempest* in Canadian and Caribbean literature is provided in Brydon, "Re-writing *The Tempest*."

4. Discussions with various colleagues — among them Helen Tiffin, Diana Brydon and Bill New, members of the Research Unit on Post-Colonial Writing at the University of Queensland, and members in my study group at the University of Alberta — assisted my thinking on this topic. A hallway discussion with Robert Wilson contributed to the formulation of this paper's title. My thanks to all.

WORKS CITED

Bhabha, Homi K. "Representation and the Colonial Text: A Critique of Some Forms of Mimeticism." *The Theory of Reading*. Ed. Frank Gloversmith. Brighton: Harvester, 1984. 93–112.

Brydon, Diana. "Re-writing *The Tempest*." *World Literature Written in English* 23.1 (1984): 75–88.

———. "The Myths That Write Us: Decolonising the Mind." *Commonwealth* 10.1 (1987): 1–14.

Dash, J. Michael. "Marvellous Realism — The Way Out of Negritude." *Caribbean Studies* 13.4 (1973): 57–70.

During, Simon. "Postmodernism or Postcolonialism?" *Landfall* 39.3 (1985): 366–80.

Farki, Neville. *The Death of Tarzana Clayton*. London: Karnak House, 1985.

Frow, John. *Marxism and Literary History*. Oxford: Blackwell, 1986.

Hassan, Ihab. "Pluralism in Postmodern Perspective." *Critical Inquiry* 12.3 (1986): 503–20.

Hutcheon, Linda. *A Poetics of Postmodernism: History, Theory, Fiction*. New York and London: Routledge, 1988.

Jameson, Fredric. "Postmodernism, or The Cultural Logic of Late Capitalism." *New Left Review* 146 (1984): 53–92.

Jardine, Alice A. *Gynesis: Configurations of Woman and Modernity*. Ithaca and London: Cornell UP, 1985.

Johnson, Barbara. *A World of Difference*. Baltimore: Johns Hopkins UP, 1987.

Kariel, Henry S. *The Desperate Politics of Postmodernism*. Amherst: U of Massachusetts P, 1989.

Katrak, Ketu H. "Decolonizing Culture: Toward a Theory for Postcolonial Women's Texts." *Modern Fiction Studies* 35.1 (1989): 157–79.

Lawson, Alan. " 'There is Another World But It is This One': A Cultural Paradigm for the Second World." Paper delivered Badlands Conference, U of Calgary, August 1986.

Merquior, J.G. "Spider and Bee: Towards a Critique of the Postmodern Ideology." *ICA Documents* 4–5 (1986): 16–18.

Miller, Christopher. *Blank Darkness: Africanist Discourse in French*. Chicago and London: U of Chicago P, 1985.

Morris, Meaghan. *The Pirate's Fiancée: Feminism, Reading, Postmodernism*. London: Verso, 1988.

Nandy, Ashis. *The Intimate Enemy: Loss and Recovery of Self under Colonialism*. Delhi: OUP, 1983.

Newman, Michael. "Revising Modernism, Representing Postmodernism: Critical Discourses of the Visual Arts." *ICA Documents* 4–5 (1986): 32–51.

Parry, Benita. "Problems in Current Theories of Colonial Discourse." *Oxford Literary Review* 9. 1–2 (1987): 27–58.

Said, Edward. "Representing the Colonized: Anthropology's Interlocutors." *Critical Inquiry* 15.2 (1989): 205–25.

Sangari, Kumkum. "The Politics of the Possible." *Cultural Critique* 7 (1987): 157–86.

Tapping, Craig. "Literary Reflections of Orality: Colin Johnson's *Dr. Wooreddy's Prescription for Enduring the Ending of the World*." Paper delivered at MLA Convention, New Orleans, December 1988.

Terdiman, Richard. *Discourse/Counter-Discourse: The Theory and Practice of Symbolic Resistance in Nineteenth-Century France*. Ithaca and London: Cornell UP, 1985.

Tiffin, Helen. "Recuperative Strategies in the Post-Colonial Novel." *Span* 24 (1987): 27–45.

Trotter, David. "Modernism and Empire: Reading *The Waste Land*." *Critical Quarterly* 28.1 & 2 (1986): 143–53.

Viswanathan, Gauri. "The Beginnings of English Literary Study in British India." *Oxford Literary Review* 9.1 & 2 (1987): 27–58.

Wortman, Marc. Review of Charles Newman, *The Post-Modern Aura: The Act of Fiction in an Age of Inflation. Telos* 71 (1987): 171–78.

Narration in the Post-Colonial Moment: Merle Hodge's *Crick Crack Monkey*

SIMON GIKANDI

1. *Writing After Colonialism*

Merle Hodge, whose novel *Crick Crack Monkey* marks a crucial transition from nationalist discourse to post-colonial writing in the Caribbean, has written on how colonial education, by presenting the lived experiences of the Caribbean people as invalid, negated the very subjectivity of the colonized by taking them away from their "own reality": "We never saw ourselves in a book, so we didn't exist in a kind of way and our culture and our environment, our climate, the plants around us did not seem real, did not seem to be of any importance — we overlooked them entirely. The real world was what was in books" (quoted in Dabydeen 78). If existence and significance are defined by the texts we write and read, as Hodge seems to suggest here, then the absence of female texts in the Caribbean canon meant that political independence had not restored speech to the Caribbean female subject. If independence represented the triumph of modernist forms, it had legitimized a situation in which the lives of Caribbean women were still surrounded by a veil of silence perpetuated by a male-dominated discourse. For this reason, the current outpouring of Caribbean women's writing can clearly be seen as the first major challenge to the project of modernity initiated by the colonizer.

Caribbean women writers such as Hodge, Zee Edgell and Michele Cliff do not appear to be sympathetic to post-modernism in the way it has been defined by Lyotard — as the rejection of those metanarratives that legitimize "knowledge and its institutions" (Lyotard 37). As a matter of fact, these women writers are involved in the quest for narrative forms that might recover, and hence legitimize, the experiences of Caribbean women within the unstable contexts of ideology and power in the modern Caribbean. As Ford-Smith of the Sistren Theatre Collective has aptly put it, "[T]here exists among the women of the Caribbean a need for a naming of experience and a need for communal support in that process. In the past silence has surrounded this experience" (Sistren 22). Narratives like those of the Sistren Collective are indeed some of the most important ways in which Caribbean women devise what Pat Ellis aptly calls "strategies to overcome the obstacles that threaten to curtail their freedom" (1); in this sense, these texts seek to establish the authority of metanarratives.

And yet these narratives cannot be defined by the modernist paradigms which have hitherto defined the texts of major Caribbean male writers such as Cesaire, Lamming and V.S. Naipaul, to name just a few. For if the doctrine of modernity transfers the authority of power and utterance in the Caribbean from the colonizer to the black male, then a feminist renaming of experience implies the revision of modernism, even the outright rejection of its totalizing tendencies.[1] Thus, although the ideologies of post-modernism may not appeal to these Caribbean women writers, they increasingly fall back on post-modernist narrative strategies — such as temporal fragmentation, intertextuality, parody and doubling — to devalorize the modernist project.[2] Moreover, by positing gender differences as a site for representing and reconstructing new identities (in narrative and semiotic terms), these writers establish what de Laurentis calls "the conditions of existence of those subjects who are muted, elided, or unrepresentable in dominant discourse" (9).

In a sense, for post-colonial Caribbean women writers to reconfigurate modernist discourse, and to unmask its function as an instrument of male domination, they invent strategies of representation which reject the notion of a subject that is defined, and fixed by, the dominant patriarchal culture. As I will show in my reading of Hodge's *Crick Crack Monkey*, Caribbean women writers are concerned with a subject that is defined by what de Laurentis calls "a multiple, shifting, and often self-contradictory identity, a subject that is not divided in, but rather at odds, with language" (9). In this context, then, language and subjectivity challenge the assumption that modernism and modernization necessarily liberate the Caribbean subject from the tyranny of tradition. For the kind of modernist discourse we have witnessed in Caribbean male writing must be seen, like its European counterpart, as a symptom of what Andreas Huyssen calls "a crisis both of capitalist modernization itself and of the deeply patriarchal structures that supported it" (58). As the Sistren Theatre Collective from Jamaica has reminded us, narration in the post-colonial moment questions the liberating claims of modernization; it suggests "an altering or redefining of the parameters of political process and action; this revision in turn signalizes factors which would otherwise disappear or at least go far underground" (4), including the voice and identity of the subaltern.

2. *Narrative and the Recovery of Voice*

Merle Hodge's *Crick Crack Monkey* was the first major novel by a post-colonial West Indian woman writer to problematize and emphasize questions of difference and the quest for a voice in a social context that denied social expression to the colonized self and hence cut it off from the liberating forms of self-expression which define the Caribbean narrative. For Hodge, this emphasis on voice as a precondition for black subjectivity in a colonial situation was necessitated by both ideological and technical reasons. First of all, in the plantation societies of the Caribbean, the voices of the oppressed and dominated slaves and indentured labourers survived against the modes of silence engendered by the master class. For these slaves and labourers, then, the preservation and inscription of a distinctive voice would signify the site of their own cultural difference and identity. Second, the voice was, in radically contrasting ways, an instrument of struggle and a depository of African values in a world in which the slaves' traditions were denigrated and their selfhoods repressed (Brathwaite; Glissant). In terms of narrative, the recovery of voice becomes one way through which unspoken and repressed experiences can be represented.

In Merle Hodge's novel, then, the voice is a synecdoche of the unwritten culture of the colonized, the culture of Aunt Tantie and Ma, and its privileging in the text signifies an epistemological shift from the hegemony of the written forms; alternatively, the negation of the spoken utterance through education and assimilation is a mark of deep alienation. When Tee opens her retrospective view of her childhood at the beginning of *Crick Crack*, she discovers that the past cannot be narrated without a cognizance of the voices that defined it. The voice is shown to be both central to the subject's conception of her past and as a paradigm that defines the context in which her multiple selves were produced. At the opening of the novel, a moment in which the birth of a new baby is superseded by the death of the mother, the world appears to Tee merely as a relationship of voices: "a voice like high-heels and stocking, an old voice . . . wailing, Some quavery voices, a grumble of men's voices" (2). Tee's subsequent alienation in the colonial world is prefigured by her inability to identify with these fetishized voices as easily as she identifies with the voice of Tantie and Ma.

In addition, Tee's alienation as a narrating subject is obvious in the way her authority of representation is propped up and denied at the same time. At the opening of the narrative, the narrator is not placed in the position of innocence and the absence of consciousness which is such a common tradition in the Caribbean *Bildungsroman*. True, Tee has already placed herself on a pedestal — "We had posted ourselves at the front window, standing on a chair" (1) — from where she represents her own experience with ostensible authority, controlling the reader's response to her context. However, on closer examination, the reader discovers that what Tee represents is not her unique "reading" of phenomena, but her reproduction of the views and opinions of adult figures, and that what appears to be a clear perception of things (from her position) is hazy and ill-defined (2–3). The reader knows that Tee's mother and the new baby are dead and her father has left the country, but the narrator's limited knowledge is obvious in her conclusion that Papa "had gone to see whether he could find Mammy and the baby" (3).

In a sense, then, Hodge's narrative develops along what appear to be contradictory lines: the subject is privileged in the discourse, but this privilege is undercut by her function as the reporter of other's speech, or by her limited perspective. This is an important strategy for showing not only how the subject develops in multiple and contradictory ways, but also the extent to which a unique sense of self is often produced by a painful struggle with the discourse of others. We have moved away from trying to invent a new language of self to a recognition of Bakhtin's famous assertion that "language, for the individual consciousness, lies on the borderline between oneself and the other. The World in language is half someone else's" (293).

But even as she reproduces other people's words and views, Tee still struggles to establish the integrity of her voice and her privileged position as an observer and narrator; she seeks strategies of expressing things "otherwise," or of endowing received discourse with what Bakhtin would call her "semantic and expressive intention" (293). For example, while her mother lies dying, Tee, who is only aware of the original reason for the mother's hospitalization (the birth of a baby) sits watching at the window, "struggling to keep my eyes open," her words expressing her now belated expressive intention and expectation: "There were fewer people going past now, so that I all but fell asleep between each set of footsteps. But I always revived to see if it was them, and if not to shout 'We gettin a baby!' to whoever it was" (2). And yet, her attempt to evoke an authority of narration which is built on her position as an observer — that is, an eyewitness account — is immediately shown to be seriously flawed because she is not privy to the knowledge of death and suffering which, at this point in the story, is shared by the adults. At this junction, Tee's voice and perspective are overwhelmed by a multiplicity of other, adult voices, disconcerting and estranged from their speakers, prefiguring her later alienation in the language of the school and Aunt Beatrice. Her own semantic and expressive intentions become secondary.

Still, there is greater tension in the novel between what we may call "objective reality" — the unmediated, non-projected experience — and the subject's self-representation in images and spectacles. For Tee, the self has the power to put the primary claims of experience into question, for it is only when the self has recreated reality in its own image, or evoked that reality as a projection of its desires, that self-representation (and hence narration) become possible:

> At the shed there was usually a fringe of children hanging about, and they let us shake the chac chac; there were some little boys who were regular pan-men and who even got to beat a pan on the road at Carnival. The players felt about idly and aimlessly on their pans for a long spell until without one noticing the sounds had converged into order. So close to the band that the bass-pans thudded through your belly, and the iron-section with the sounds crashing out from the touch of the tiny stick on the anonymous piece of engine entrails was your teeth clashing together in time with the beat. (6)

The passage began with a general description of the steelband shed, but as it progresses, we notice how the dichotomy between subject and object is narrowed; the narrator/character internalizes the objects (the bass-pans thud in her belly) and eventually merges the external with the internal so that at the end of the quotation she cannot tell the difference between the sounds from the iron-section and the clashing of her teeth. In essence, experience has value insofar as it is projected as a spectacle which the self itself has created. External reality is populated, to use Bakhtin's words, with the speaker's intention (293).

There is another sense in which the above shift from an "objective" to a "subjective" form of representation brings out the ambivalence which characterizes, indeed produces Tee, as a colonial subject: the author needs to maintain a disjunction between Tee's functions as a narrator and a character, and this necessitates not only the doubling of the self but also its alienation in the very strategies it develops to represent its doubleness. For if Tee were just to tell her story from the (ostensibly) non-problematic perspective of a child (compare Anthony's *The Year in San Fernando*), the author might succeed in maintaining the integrity of the narrating self, but this unity would lead to the negation of her primary thematic concern — the alienation of this subject through language. On the other hand, if she were to narrate this story from the vantage point of the adult, then the representation of the subject's alienation could only be achieved by the erasure of the important illusion of integrity and unity we associate with the childhood narrator. This illusion is of utmost importance in the Caribbean text because it prefigures the collective desire for wholeness which motivates cultural production in the islands. Thus, although Hodge's goal is to thematize alienation, she operates from the premise that childhood holds the utopian possibility that Tee can exist, to quote Thorpe, "in complete harmony with her environment" (32).

Furthermore, to understand the conditions in which the character becomes alienated, we must also be in a position to read the gap that separates childhood from adulthood: as a character, Tee becomes alienated almost without her knowledge and consent; as an adult narrator, she posits self-representation in dominant discourse as a form of alienation which she has mastered through narration. In his introduction to *Crick Crack Monkey*, Narinesingh argues that the reader of Hodge's text is "made to share in the diversity and richness of Tee's experience without being able to discern at times where the child's voice with a child's perception of things slides into the adult voice and vision of the omniscient author" (vii). Now, while it is true that there are instances when the child vision and the adult vision seem to be indistinguishable, a more attentive reading of the text will surely highlight the differences between these two voices or call attention to their paradoxical relationship. For it seems to me that Hodge's intention is to expose the illusionary nature of Tee's desire for assimilation by highlighting the gap between her as a child and as an adult narrator. In other words, the narrator draws our attention to the divisions and separations the child goes through in its struggle to become the "other" and measures its loss against the narrating self which has, presumably, overcome its alienation by mastering its history through narration.

What this adds up to, everything else aside, is that there is no authentic subject before its representation in language; the pleasure of writing is inherent in the search for a language which will recover the fragments of a past life and turn it into a spectacle. After all, before the writing of *Crick Crack Monkey*, who was Tee except the projection of other people's desires and intentions — Aunt Tantie, Ma, Beatrice, the colonial school? The value of the juvenile perspective lies precisely in its capacity to show how Tee was colonized by the utterances of other subjects. And in significant ways, a return to childhood does not establish a metaphorical relationship between the child and her landscape; what she hears, and often appropriates, are the "disembodied voices" of others: "Women going past walked a gauntlet of commentary on their anatomy and deportment. And for Mrs Hinds in particular they had no mercy. Like any proper lady (it seemed to me) she had a high, stiff, bottom and spectacles and stockings" (7). Here we not only have the narrator representing the child's perspective of the boys' comments on Mrs. Hinds, but also using a parenthesis to make a distinction between how things seemed to Tee then, suggesting that she knows better now. Between the boys' commentary, Tee's juvenile view, and the narrator's qualifier, can we ever identify an original experience? Isn't the loss of original experience — a loss which becomes more and more apparent as Tee moves away from the "organic" worlds of Tantie and Ma and enters Beatrice's colonial orbit — what generates the autobiographical text?

3. *Narration and the Mask of Language*

Tee's identity is, of course, constructed by her shifting speech or language communities: she moves to and fro between the universes defined by Tantie, Ma, Aunt Beatrice, and the colonial school. The important point, though, is that she belongs to all of them, and to none; in reality, she is consumed and confused by all of them; the narration of her confused identities is an excellent example of how language both masks and unmasks the subject's conditions of possibility. For instance, what appeared at the beginning of the novel to be Tee's vantage position, a position of mastery and insight, is an adult position that conceals the uncertainty of the little girl. Similarly, Tee's apparent security in the world of Tantie and Ma conceals, as does her later involvement with Beatrice's middle-class culture, the state of anxiety and unbelonging in which she lives.

My argument here runs contrary to Thorpe's influential reading of *Crick Crack Monkey*, where she casts the novel in a structural opposition in which Tantie's creole world represents "belonging and security" while Beatrice's colonial world stands for "alienation and displacement" (37). Admittedly, these binary oppositions can be sustained if we approach the text through the eyes of Tee, the narrator: after her exile in Europe, the narrator is strongly nostalgic and appreciative of the creole world she had been displaced from by the colonial culture. But from the perspective of Tee the child, there is a strong ambivalence toward oppositions such as alienation/security, Beatrice/Tantie; in none of these worlds can she posit herself as a subject. In Tantie's world, what Tee echoes and repeats is her aunt's language and views (12); after she has lived with Beatrice for some time, her utterances now reflect the language and ideology of the colonized bourgeoisie (85). In none of these cultural universes can the child appropriate a language to designate herself as a self that is not the effect of the other's language system; she cannot choose one entity as a way of overcoming her alienation because the moment she does so, she will become entrapped in another language system.[3]

So, the value of Hodge's text does not lie in any resolution to the cultural dichotomies we have discussed so far. On the contrary, I want to suggest, the value of this novel lies in the author's capacity to sustain both the creole and colonial cultures as opposed sites of cultural production which the "modern" Caribbean subject cannot transcend entirely, nor reconcile. Although Tee feels at home in Tantie's creole world, she is also aware of its incompleteness, of its marginalization in the colonial economy; her desire is hence for the scriptural universe of the colonial school:

> I looked forward to school. I looked forward to the day when I could pass my hands swiftly from side to side on a blank piece of paper leaving meaningful marks in its wake; to staring nonchalantly into a book until I turned over the page, a gesture pregnant with importance for it indicated that one had not merely been staring, but that that most esoteric of processes had been taking place whereby the paper had yielded up something or other as a result of having been stared at. (20)

Here, the school and writing are posited as both mythological practices (an "esoteric process") and as forms of empowerment. In retrospect, however, literacy is a form of mastery that is achieved at the expense of the self which, as we have already seen, becomes alienated in the modes of representation which were supposed to empower it:

> My reading career also began with A for Apple, the exotic fruit that made its brief appearance at Christmas time, and pursued through my Caribbean Reader Primer One the fortunes of two English children known as Jim and Jill, or it might have been Tim and Mary. (25)

Paradoxically, this alienation becomes a precondition for the colonial subjects accession into the language and discourse of colonialism.

Tee's cultural alienation is built around a crucial chiasmic reversal: the tangible reality of the creole culture is dismissed as an unreal construct, while the fictions promoted by the colonial textbook are now adopted as the "real" Caribbean referent:

> Books transported you always into the familiar solidity of chimneys and apple trees, the enviable normality of real Girls and Boys who went a-sleighing and built snowmen, ate potatoes, not rice, went about in socks and shoes from morning until night and called things by their proper names. . . . Books transported you into Reality and Rightness, which were to be found abroad. (61)

The colonial library, represented here by the book van — which Tee awaits every Saturday "with the greatest of impatience" — is a mirage which has become a tangible reality in the girl's imagination. The world of the ordinary is denied referentiality because as Thorpe notes, it is the exact opposite of, indeed contradicts, "the values of the former colonial masters" — the realm of colonial desire (34).

It is in this context that Tee, in an attempt to deal with her dualities and crisis of identity, begins to apprehend herself as the other: she invents a double, a mirror image of herself, who is, nevertheless, white and thoroughly colonial, one who doesn't have to negotiate the dangerous chasm between creole and colonial, self and other because she is ideal—

> Thus it was that I fashioned Helen, my double. She was my age and height. She spent the summer holidays at the sea-side with her aunt and uncle who had a delightful orchard with apple trees and pear trees in which sang chaffinches and blue tits, and where one could wander on terms of the closest familiarity with cowslips and honeysuckle. . . . Helen entered and ousted all the other characters in the unending serial that I had been spinning for Toddan and Doolarie from time immemorial. (61–62)

Indeed, in Tee's imagination, Helen is more than a double: she has usurped the subject's identity — "She was the Proper Me. And me, I was her shadow hovering about in incompleteness" (62).

In the Lacanian notion of the "mirror stage" (Lacan 2), the colonial subject has recognized itself in an ideal I, but this form of identification is also a misrecognition because the externalized image is achieved only at the cost of self-alienation, and the subject can never assimilate this idealized image because it has no existence except in the imaginary. However, the mirror image which cannot be assimilated, is, as Kaja Silverman has succinctly noted, the object in relation to which the subject defines herself: "As a consequence of the irreducible distance which separates the subject from its ideal reflection, it loves the coherent identity which the mirror provides. However, because the image remains external to it, it also hates that image" (158). Tee does not express any overt hate for Helen, but there is obvious recognition (from the narrator) that there were profound tensions between the two characters. This tension is clearly brought out in an important passage in the novel when the narrator explains the social and historical conditions that necessitated a double:

> For doubleness, or this particular kind of doubleness, was a thing to be taken for granted. Why, the whole of life was like a piece of cloth with a rightside and a wrongside. Just as there was a way you spoke and a way you wrote, so there was the daily existence which you led, which of course amounted only to marking time and makeshift, for there was the Proper daily round, not necessarily more agreeable, simply the valid one, the course of which encompassed things like warming yourself before

a fire and having tea at four o'clock; there were the human types who were your neighbours and guardians and playmates—but you were all marginal together, for there were the beings whose validity loomed at you at every book, every picture.... (62)

Tee is structured by a set of oppositions, none of which offer her true identity: her creole world is makeshift and marginal; her desired colonial universe is artificial. When she recognizes the sources of marginality and the nature of artifice, then she will outgrow Helen "in the way that a baby ceases to be taken up with his fingers and toes" (62). Herein lies the value of narration in the post-colonial moment: as the adult narrator of her own experiences and subjectivity, Tee will not need external mediators molded in the image of the colonizer; having discovered that idealized images are unreal and that the colonial subject cannot adopt the colonizer's discourse for her new identity, the narrator will write about her past to exorcise the ghost of colonialism and to challenge the assumption — often sustained by the neo-colonial elite — that independence is the native's way of appropriating the modernity project initiated by the colonizer.[4]

NOTES

1. My premise that post-modernism is a revision of, rather than a break with, modernism, is indebted to the works by Huyssen and Laclau. From a post-colonial perspective, there is great suspicion that the so-called post-modernist breakthrough still sanctions Western hegemony. As Miyoshi and Harootunian have aptly observed, by tolerating post-industrial capitalism, "postmodernism ends up consenting to the first world economic domination that persists in exploiting the wretched of the earth" (388).

2. For a comprehensive study of theories of narrative in the post-modernist tradition, see Hutcheon.

3. For another view of *Crick Crack Monkey* see Lawrence.

4. There is no greater indication of how the colonization of the Caribbean initiated the project of Western modernity than Christopher Columbus's famous claim that the "discovery" of America ushers in "that time so new and like no other" (see Todorov 5).

WORKS CITED OR CONSULTED

Anthony, Michael. *The Year in San Fernando*. London: Heinemann, 1970.

Bakhtin, M.M. Discourse in the Novel. *The Dialogic Imagination: Four Essays*. Austin: U of Texas P, 1981. 259–422.

Brathwaite, Edward. *History of the Voice*. London: New Beacon, 1984.

Dabydeen, David. *A Handbook for Teaching Caribbean Literature*. London: Heinemann, 1988.

de Laurentis, Teresa. "Feminist Studies/Critical Studies: Issues, Terms, and Contexts." *Feminist Studies/Critical Studies*. Ed. Teresa de Laurentis. Bloomington: Indiana UP, 1986. 1–19.

de Man, Paul. The Rhetoric of Temporality. *Blindness and Insight: Essays in the Rhetoric of Contemporary Criticism*. Introd. Wlad Godzich. 2nd ed., revised. Minneapolis: U of Minnesota P, 1983. 187–228.

Ellis, Pat. "Introduction — An Overview of Women in Caribbean Society." *Women of the Caribbean*. Ed. Pat Ellis. London: Zed, 1986.

Glissant, Edourdo. "Free and Forced Poetics." *Ethnopoetics*. Ed. Michel Benamou and Jerome Rothenberg. Boston: Alcheringa, 1976. 95–101.

Hodge, Merle. *Crick Crack Monkey*. 1970. Introd. Roy Narinesingh. London: Heinemann, 1981.

Hutcheon, Linda. *A Poetics of Postmodernism: History, Theory, Fiction*. New York: Routledge, 1988.

Huyssen, Andreas. *After the Great Divide: Modernism, Mass Culture, Post-modernism*. Bloomington: Indiana UP, 1986.

Lacan, Jacques. *Écrits: A Selection*. Trans. Alan Sheridan. New York: Norton, 1977.

Laclau, Ernesto. "Politics and the Limits of Modernity." *Universal Abandon?: The Politics of Postmodernism*. Ed. Andrew Ross. Minneapolis: U of Minnesota P, 1989. 63–82.

Lawrence, Leota S. "Merle Hodge." *Fifty Caribbean Writers*. Ed. Daryl Cumber Dance. Westport, CT: Greenwood Press, 1986. 224–28.

Lyotard, Jean-François. *The Postmodern Condition: A Report on Knowledge*. Trans. Geoff Bennington and Brian Massumi. Foreword by Fredric Jameson. Minneapolis: U of Minnesota P, 1984.

Miyoshi, Masao, and H.D. Harootunian. Introduction. *Postmodernism and Japan*. Spec. issue of *South Atlantic Quarterly* 87.3 (1988): 387–400.

Narinesingh, Roy. Introduction. Hodge vii-xiv.

Silverman, Kaja. *The Subject of Semiotics*. New York: Oxford UP, 1983.

Sistren, with Honor Ford Smith. *Lionheart Gal: Life Stories of Jamaican Women*. Toronto: Sister Vision, 1987.

Thorpe, Marjorie. "The Problem of Cultural Identification in *Crick Crack Monkey*." *Savacou* 13 (Gemini 1977): 31–38.

Todorov, Tzvetan. *The Conquest of America*. Trans. Richard Howard. New York: Harper, 1984.

Waiting for the Post: Some Relations Between Modernity, Colonization, and Writing

SIMON DURING

In the West no concept has been more entrenched than that of the "modern." The West? The peculiar force of the idea of the modern is such that in this context one can qualify that clumsy, spatializing metonymy only by the adjective "modern" itself. Once again an equation that came effectively to propel European expansionism is spelled out: the West is modern, the modern is the West. By this logic, other societies can enter history, grasp the future, only at the price of their destruction. Today, however, the power of this logic is waning, and a new set of still hazy and abstract oppositions (including those between cultural and the post-cultural, the modern and post-modern) are coming into view. This essay aims to explore these remarks — though it begins with a distant event that occurred at the threshold of the modern idea of the "modern."

In 1773 Dr. Johnson and James Boswell travel through the Hebrides, a poor country defeated by a metropolitan power in a brutal war thirty years before. They are not, in today's sense, sightseers. Indeed their trip has no definite purpose: Boswell wants to see how Dr. Johnson, the famous man of letters, will respond to a country in a state of "grossness and ignorance" (Johnson 80). They both expect to find an example of an order that they call "patriarchy" but it is rare that Johnson can exclaim, as he does at Rasay, "this is truly the patriarchal life: this what we came to find!" Rare, because the people they meet surprise them. The English speakers have often read Johnson's books, particularly his Dictionary; while the peasantry, speaking a declining language — Erse — can barely be communicated with at all. Both kinds of "natives" (as the travellers call them) are, however, unwilling to submit themselves to an examination producing the kind of "truth" that Johnson wishes to find. Boswell laboriously keeps a journal mainly about his friend's responses to the country, which Johnson corrects, admires and wishes were worth publishing. Encouragement enough for Boswell. Soon Johnson decides to publish his tour too, making his decision seated at a bank "such as a writer of Romance might have delighted to feign" (35) and remarking, wistfully, that he could have made a "very pretty book" of the Indians had he gone to America (Boswell 245). The purpose of the trip becomes clear: it is undertaken to be turned into writing. It is not a surprising decision, especially when we discover that Johnson only

23

really enjoys the journey when he is close to roads along which he can post a stream of letters back to the capital.

What makes accounts of this tour worth publishing is the interplay between those who write and those who are written about. The Hebrides's poverty, superstition and ignorance; its being controlled by genealogy, revenge and clans to use terms that came easily to the travellers — are subject to observation by these models of modernity and learning. Boswell is the son of a man who helped deprive the Hebridean lairds of their private prisons and jurisdiction over their kin. As a lawyer himself, he fights cases he knows to be false, an activity he defends to the locals who, accustomed to a different kind of justice, remain suspicious of dissimulated advocacy. Further still from the customs and values of the Highlanders (as they are also, confusingly, called), Johnson is self-made, a man without ancestors whose thoughts turn into written words with incredible rapidity: the gap between the spoken and the written is narrower in him than in anyone. During his tour he argues incessantly — both with Boswell and the educated Highlanders, evincing "an uncommon desire to be always in the right" (252). Where need be, he browbeats his opponents as, for instance, he defends literary copyright against those who, like Lord Monboddo, hankering for oral culture, believe that to learn a book by heart is to own it too, or as he attacks patronage, or as he declares that people are malleable, only education and training making them different from one another. Behind these enlightened views lies the urban claim to reach his own opinion through discussion. Yet despite all this, he is sympathetic to those he considers ignorant precisely because he is anxious about his own enlightened modernity. He fears the loss of faith and certainty implicit in his own position, based on his disrespect for untested opinions. Thus he craves transcendental possibilities, signs of living hierarchies. He admires the genealogical "patriarchy" that he encounters in the Highland chiefs. He is authoritatively and arbitrarily open-minded towards an order he believes to be disappearing — approving of the Christian ministry's "extirpation" of folkloric beliefs ("sturdy fairies," and Greogach, the old man with the Long Beard) while refusing to discount the possibility of "second sight."

Johnson and Boswell's tour, neither simply an example of a larger formation nor an origin, can be read either as a moment in the development of cultural imperialism, or as a moment in the emergence of the tourist industry (Boswell pleads for more guidebooks so that travellers in future will know what monuments to visit), or even as a threshold at which private travelling transmutes into a rudimentary ethnography (after all, Johnson is concerned to record and turn into truth the manners and customs of those he encounters). More to the point, however, the journey brings into view that crucial but extraordinarily elusive difference between what I am calling, skeptically, the modern and the nonmodern. Skeptically because, as their tour shows, that difference is simultaneously undisplaceable and uncontainable: any attempt to fix it is doubtful. Here it is certainly not a difference between cultures for instance — Johnson and Boswell have no concept of "culture," so they can deplore the Highlanders' "ignorance" and "superstition" without relativist qualifications. Nor do they have any notion that the bodies of those they are visiting have a specific biology — the difference here is not racial. They do not have any evolutionary schema by which the Highlanders might be called "primitive" either. Nor do they regard the locals, however "archaic" they may think them, as existing in the proximity of a primordial nature. Nor, finally, do they have a strong political or economic sense of the difference: for Johnson and Boswell, the Hebrides' poverty is merely the result of its inhabitants' "laziness." The difference between the travellers and the locals functions more as the product of a desire to maintain a past considered to be doomed. It is as if it were too much a commodity (a spur to publication), too important in constructing hierarchies, to disappear. The difference, however, is produced in the very act of its representation — to generalize about it is at once to be placed on the side of the modern. Which means that it does not belong to any single place or time — the Highlanders and the American Indians are joined in single dying order named "patriarchy." Yet the modern does not simply cease where the nonmodern begins. For the difference to be represented, a complex technological and infrastructural system must exist — transport routes, postal systems and legal edicts — most of which converge on the metropolis, London, and which, at least potentially, the locals are formed by too.

What can be found on one side can also be found on the other. As Johnson moves through the Highlands he engages in a particular discursive practice, characteristic of the articulation of enlightened knowledge. First he "accurately" inspects, then he "justly" represents (44). In doing so, however, he unknowingly finds himself imitating those whom he observes. After meeting a local who cannot give him the information he wants, despite the fact that the Highlander had lived in a period when "the mountains were yet unpenetrated, no inlet was opened to foreign novelties" (57), Johnson immediately declares: "In nations, where there is hardly the use of letters, what is once out of sight is lost for ever. They think but little, and of their few thoughts, none are wasted on the past . . ." (58). How does this stand beside his opinion recorded a few pages previously: "They who consider themselves as ennobled by their family, will think highly of their progenitors, and they who throughout successive generations live always together in the same place, will preserve local stories and hereditary prejudices. Thus every Highlander can talk of his ancestors . . ." (42) so that indeed "Everything in those countries has its history" (44)? Nothing but history, and no history: two contradictory propositions side by side. Johnson incessantly complains that the North-erners are "at variance with themselves" (45), but his own truth procedures lead to similar contradictions. An effect of repetition has broken through the modernist difference — which also reproduces itself within the zones that it separates. For instance, Johnson's own authority is connected to his extraordinary capacity for boredom and consumption. With patriarchal *hauteur*, he demands food, drink, thoughts and events to discourse upon. Thus Boswell:

> I must take some merit from my assiduous attention to him, and from my contriving
> that he shall be easy wherever he goes, that he shall not be asked twice to eat or drink
> any thing . . . and many such little things, which, if not attended to, would fret him. I

also may be allowed to claim some merit in leading the conversation: I do not mean leading, as in an orchestra, by playing the first fiddle; but leading as one does in examining a witness, — starting topics, and making him pursue them. He appears to me like a great mill, into which a subject is thrown to be ground. It requires, indeed, fertile minds to furnish materials for this mill. I regret whenever I see it unemployed; but sometimes I feel myself quite barren, and having nothing to throw in. (338–39)

This highly metaphorical passage travels through a series of schematized analogies and displacements: it is as mobile as its authors' tour. First of all, Johnson's lordship is situated in his bodily appetites which are equivalent to his mind and its hunger for ratiocination. That capacity for analysis is also reified as a process of mechanical production, the Mill. From the other side, Boswell, as assiduous servant, provides for and leads his master so that his own fertility is constantly threatened with depletion. The image of a barren, deferential Boswell anthropomorphizes the desolated colonized country they are touring. The relations between these travellers, the way they fashion themselves, play out the difference they have come to inspect and represent.

                              *   *   *

For a long time, to be modern was to be ordered by, to have access to, universals, to be *rational*. Dr. Johnson himself tried to shout down the universalisms that were already being given value around him; in fact his antagonism to them helped draw him to the Hebrides, where the local and the chiefly presided. Modern universalism takes many, and conflicting, forms — those theories of natural law, human and civil rights and the primordial social contract which variously support the revolutions of the late eighteenth century and continue to legitimate democracy; German idealist theories that place universal duty in a continuum leading back to the formal pre-conditions of perception and understanding; Benthamite principles of utility which partially under-pin statism in Britain and the imperial administration of India; theories of an invisible hand that orders a market without formal barriers to entry; even the humanist marxian critique of formalist universalisms is itself a universalism, for it anticipates a time when the substance of the individual, the productive being, will be drawn into a noncoercive legal and economic apparatus available to all.

In modernity, one concept in particular — culture — stands against these con-flicting notions. Not that the concept originates in a struggle against rationality: indeed the great counter to universalisms begins in universalism. The notion of "culture" appeared in order to answer the question: "What customs are general to all com-munities?" This is too universalist a question for Johnson to pose in a systematic fashion, but his contemporary, Giambattista Vico does — and finds three: marriage contracts, burial and religion. Vico regards these as essential to human nature, not as necessary conditions for justice, order or knowledge. Gradually language, music, production of artifacts, rituals, and so on come to be similarly conceived of as expressions of human nature and, grouped together, are regarded as grounding *cultural* identities. The customs destroyed by modernity are no longer veiled (at best) in the haze of Gothic nostalgia: their loss appears tragic and irreversible. These relations are complex then: cultures are both vulnerable to enlightenment and specific to communities, though their specificity is an essential expression of a universal human nature; modernity decultures by universalizing and forgetting (so culturalists claim) that meanings, norms, values, ideals, only have substance in lived expressive practices. After Johnson the unnameable difference imposed by the death of the old order hardens into an opposition between enlightenment and culture. It would be tempting to say that "we" do not think — or live — in terms of this harsh opposition. It would be tempting to suppose that we belong either to the order of the "post-modern" with its suspicion of progressive narratives of history whose end is one universalism or another or to what can be called the "post-cultural" with its sense that cultural products are not essentially bound to the life-world that produced them.[1] But in nations like New Zealand, Australia, Canada and South Africa (which should not, perhaps, be named in a single breath) it is especially difficult to place oneself in those "posts." Not all of the communities in our countries have passed through the threshold of modernity: some are maintained, some wish to maintain themselves, at the far side of the difference. Where colonizers continue to enrich themselves more or less indirectly by claiming modernity, the elusive difference is construed not so much as cultural but as racial — located in the body. Yet where the difference is most fetishized, the benefits of universal modernity seem most worth fighting for.

So it comes as no surprise that the most charismatic living figure of the enlightenment is a black South African: Nelson Mandela. In his essay "In Admiration of Nelson Mandela or the Laws of Reflection," Jacques Derrida suggests that Mandela attracts our admiration because of what Derrida calls "the force of reflection" (454). Derrida suggests that Mandela is admirable both because he himself admires so intensely — in the spirit of the Enlightenment he admires that universal Law which applies to all and which makes all equal — and because he is so careful, so reflective. He is reflective even in his advocacy of violence: for him violence stands in the place of those rights that are disallowed him so that Mandela's violence is more like discourse than terror. Derrida's admiration is a moment in a play of mirrors, as for both Derrida and Mandela, the universal Law has no ontological basis. Mandela sees what few others see, a long continuity threading the stories that the elders of his tribe in the Transkei told him about "the good old days, before the democratic rule of their kings and their *amapakati*" (149) to its "council variously called Imbizon, or Pitso, or Kgota [that] was so completely democratic that all members of the tribe could participate in its deliberations" (150). By mirroring and inverting, Mandela's memory attaches these strands of mythology to "the tales of wars fought by our ancestors in defence of the fatherland, the acts of valor performed by generals and soldiers during those epic days" (149), and finally to the political struggle towards a state in which "all South Africans are entitled to live a free life on the basis of fullest equality of the rights and opportunities in every field, of full democratic rights, with a direct say in the affairs of the government" (150).

So Mandela is addressed by the Law almost as the Prophets were once addressed by God; others are not called in this way. His Law, when practiced, is unlike Boswell's dissimulated advocacy, a force that makes it a duty for an "attorney worth his salt" (as Mandela puts it) to serve his people in defiance of the state's legal apparatus. And not one but two laws: Mandela's ideal law and that of the South African state. Thus in his speeches, two implied audiences: those present and those who will listen when the two laws are less far apart. Imprisoned, living at the borders of the West, Mandela reflects the West too in the sense that he has had to "interiorize the Occidental principle of interiority" (Derrida 465). As a man of the law deemed outside the law, the object of so much scrutiny and repression, he has had to hug the law to himself, to enter it not as a profession but as a vocation. He must enact it. For Derrida, the Law — with a capital L — exists in the circulation between Mandela's imprisoned self and his ancestral past, the development of democratic structures, the European enlightenment and so on, all of which are far removed from his local situation and none of which themselves adequately express the Law. In this act of interiorization which keeps the law in circulation, Mandela becomes symbolic of the struggle for freedom, losing his individuality in his very individual toughness. But, as Derrida suggests, Mandela reflects the West most powerfully in that he shows how the universals that have come to operate as signifiers of, and laws for, occidental identity undo the boundaries of their place of origin; they do not simply belong to the West — or even to modernity. Not only can they not be spatialized or temporalized, they speak with greatest force to those, like Mandela, from whom the West withholds the Law. They *require* that some stand outside the Law. In sum: Mandela disrupts the unnameable difference, first by positing continuities from the pre-colonial/non-modern to the post-colonial/modern (reflecting the present lack on the past and vice versa), then by demonstrating that enlightenment fascinates and seduces by its very power of reflection and subjectification, its power to unsettle boundaries and given identities.

An enlightenment without a simple frame or ground, this is what Derrida finds in Mandela. Traditionally universalism has come under attack because for it the local merely exists as a placeholder for a general right or responsibility. Both Derrida and Mandela turn that to their advantage. Universalisms are necessarily directed towards limits and identities that they cannot take account of. Arguments for democracy, for instance, cannot of themselves point to those who deserve democratic privileges. Not just everybody? But why just nationals of a particular state? Why those over 21? Why not those in prison or mental institutions? It is Derrida's particular contribution not to construe these limits as a crippling contradiction but as the condition of possibility for the articulation of a double-jointed universalism, one which is performed as much as obeyed and which, as we need no reminding, has real force in repressive conditions. Universalism can advance the struggle of the colonized against those who would limit access to the Law while it opens out to a deconstruction that would resist the closures of rationality. Yet the limits to enlightened universalism cannot simply be considered as aporias that enable most to admire it and some to live it out. Mandela himself belongs to social formations that have little connection with enlightenment. Although Derrida does not mention it, he belongs to the global imaginary, he is an excuse for a rock concert, an image bounced off satellites to all nations. It is true that he would not belong to this imaginary were he not also to embody enlightenment, but, on the other hand, he would not embody enlightenment if his image were not so often transmitted through the international communication networks. Derrida's complex play of reflection is also entwined within the flow of the imaginary. For the world outside his home country at least, Mandela is precisely a representation without an original. That the original is imprisoned and silenced, physically absent from the public sphere, is what propels him into the post-modern, permits him to exist as a charismatic and broadcasted image and name. This is worth saying because it is often assumed that there are no interactions between enlightened universalism and the order of the post-modern. But of course not everything does enter into relation with universals. Black South Africans can embrace the enlightenment all the more readily because, forming the national majority, democracy will help them control their own destiny. Their identity is consolidated by those oppressive apparatuses that, using racist and culturalist discourse, discriminate against — and fix them — as black. The seductiveness — or necessity — of universals leads to problems of analysis: the "black consciousness" movement may be widely regarded as peripheral in South Africa, but is class or race to be the privileged term for thinking about its past and future? Currently the important question for those working in the liberation struggle is the degree to which the ANC will urge a programme of state socialism in order to prevent the market from executing apartheid's work once the latter has been formally abolished. This problematic is much less relevant in countries in which the colonized form a minority, however large, to whom democracy offers little.

In such states a politics of identity replaces the politics of enlightenment. There the project of the colonized peoples becomes preservation of a cultural identity (supposedly) grounded in the era before the modern to which current needs and wants attach. And New Zealand, "exceptional in many ways" as Donald Denoon notes, stands as the paradigmatic instance of such states, because (for reasons that will be clarified) it is there that the border which divides and joins the politics of enlightenment to the politics of cultural identity is most fiercely contested (206). In her book *Maori Sovereignty*, Donna Awatere, a Maori activist, expresses such a programme thus:

> The aim is to redesign the country's institutions from a Maori point of view. The aim
> is to reclaim the land and work it from a Maori point of view. . . . To forge a distinct
> New Zealand identity from a Maori point of view. (32)

And she states the question of identity that she faces by appealing to the notion of time:

> The Maori use of time differs from that of British culture. To the whites, the present
> and the future is all important. To the Maori, the past is the present is the future. Who

I am and my relationship to everyone else depends on *Whakapapa* [genealogy], on
my language, on those from whom I am descended. . . . (54)

These two passages lead in different directions but it is clear from her book as a
whole that the Maori point of view is something only a Maori speaking the Maori
language, living in Maori time, has access to. Indeed that follows from what a Maori,
for Awatere, is. She defines the Maori, not in racist or culturalist discourse, but by
their possessing a *whakapapa*. For her, the relation between the past and the present
is a matter of preserving the *mana* of one's ancestors and observing *tapus*. To describe
what Johnson called one's "progenitors" negatively, for instance, is impossible within
Maori traditions because that would reduce ancestral *mana*. Thus even Pakeha
historians who feel intense sympathy for Maoris, and who have desired to record their
past in writing have come under increasing attack. ("Pakeha" is the received New
Zealand word for whites.) The historian Michael King, for instance, recounts how he
was asked by a member of the Ngata family to expunge references to his ancestor,
Ropata Wahawaha, who, fighting with the British, had shot one hundred Maori
prisoners then pushed their bodies over a cliff (153). Little dialogue is possible across
the difference between the Maori and Pakeha when it is supposed that Maori identity
is still grounded in the aura of a time which is not yet historical, still sacred.
Nonetheless the loss of sacred, genealogical thinking and structures helped the whites
to act extraordinarily unscrupulously and viciously even by their own values. No future
generations would ever *fight* for their reputation; no ancestral spirit was judging them.

Post-colonial identity politics tend towards paradox and irresolution because, with
the coming of Europeans, the narratives, signifiers and practices available to Maoris
(for instance) to articulate their needs and wants are at once inscribed within
Eurocentric modernity — and vice versa. The moment of arrival opened out into a
scene of forgetting and (mis)recognition. Forgetting: the crucial signifiers of pre-
colonial Maori language began to lose their meaning until no consensus remains as to
what certain words "mean." (Is "*atua*" to be translated as "god," "devil" or "spirit"?)[2]
The reason for this is, of course, that their sense depended upon practices that European
settlement disrupted. (Mis)recognition: the whites and their ships triggered an orgy of
metaphoricization by the Maori. They were apparently recognized as "*tupua*" (a word
sometimes translated as "gnomes"), "*atua*," whales, floating islands and so on in a
linguistic mobility that is the obverse of the loss of "meaning" of the words (Best
362–67). The locals, of course, were (mis)recognized as "cannibals," "savages." In
colonial history (at least, until the post-cultural moment) each side has, however,
solidified *and* dismantled the other's image, disavowing *and* discovering — at different institutional and social sites — the rhetorical strategies, amnesia and misrecog-
nitions by which identity is produced.[3] Yet even the first moment of forgetting and
misrecognition does not simply obey the modernist paradigm. When, for instance, the
missionaries expressed their own quasi-sacred horror at Maori cannibalism they were
drawn into a debate which, on utilitarian grounds, they could only lose (Wilson 136).

After all, there are no "rational" reasons why warfare's victims should not be eaten —
here the Maori is more "modern" than the Pakeha.

These not unfamiliar points require extensive examplification. Identity construction begins to work at the level of the proper name: "Maori" is a metonymy — it was
an adjective meaning something like "usual" before the Pakeha arrived — the locals
having no identity as a group at all. The signifier "Pakeha" — by which New Zealand
whites now know themselves is most probably a transliteration into Maori of the
English "Bugger you" as used by early whalers and sealers.[4] So too the proper name
"Aotearoa," to which great pathos now attaches (it being regarded as the "original
Maori" name for New Zealand) probably first named only the North Island (Taylor
25).[5] Furthermore: the myths which today underpin Maori identity (above and against
that of individual *whakapapas*) were articulated in complex interrelations with
Pakehas that will never be unfolded in a scholarly true story.[6] One of the most powerful
such mythemes runs like this: the Maoris first arrived in Aotearoa in a fleet of seven
canoes from a place called "Hawaiki"; they displaced an earlier race of inhabitants,
each living tribe being descended from one of these canoes. This little narrative, whose
central propositions are unhistorical but to whose elaborations Maori identity remains
bound (it informs the discourse of the central character in Witi Ihimaera's novel *The
Matriarch*, for instance), belongs neither to the Maori nor to the Pakeha. The story —
which doubles that of European arrival — has been produced, unconsciously and over
time, in exchanges and conflicts between both. To use a Derridean concept: it is
counter-signed.

Nowhere is this effect of the counter-signature more apparent than in the text
which is sometimes referred to as the origin of the legend: Sir George Grey's
*Polynesian Mythology, and the Ancient Traditional History of the New Zealand Race,
as furnished by their priests and chiefs* (1855) which first implies that seven canoes
left Hawaiki at the same time (Orbell 41). Grey was the colony's Governor at the time
he wrote his book — a compilation of Maori legends in the style of the contemporary
"folk lore" movement. Its purpose was explicitly political. As a recent biographer has
noted, Grey's administrative project was to replace Maori practices by British law,
turn the Chiefs and their *mana* into a "form of salaried Government officials" as well
as to make all territory available to surveys, military roads and so on (Rutherford 206).
(The Maori resisted this project in the first of the various "New Zealand Wars.") When
dealing with the resistant Maori (in Grey's words "the oldest, least civilized and most
influential Chiefs in the Islands"), he noticed that their letters often referred to "an
ancient system of mythology" that his interpreters could not understand and to which
no current publication alluded (Grey, *Polynesian* ix-x). Thus "fully and entirely to
comprehend their thoughts and intentions" so as to "control and conciliate" them, he
began to learn Maori and, with the help of informants (the most important of whom
was Wiremu Maihi Te Rangikaheke) he collected and wrote up their myths. Some of
these, he claimed, were told to him only because of his own *mana*. Grey's political
purpose falls back on three crucial theoretical and two historical presuppositions: first,

that the enunciating subject of these narratives is the "Maori" rather than particular individuals or *iwi* (tribes); second (in the terminology of Austinean speech act theory), that the Chief's utterances were constative rather than illocutionary; and third, that their propositions referred to a coherent body of esoteric knowledge. Against the Colonial Office and the metropolitan Press of the time it also rested on the belief that the Maoris were *not* doomed to extinction as a race, that extreme form of the modernist paradigm. Finally, against both eighteenth-century opinion and recent ethnographical theorists (e.g. Jack Goody), it supposed that oral cultures, being static, reproduce their myths and genealogies without variation across time (Goody). Under demands driven by these assumptions and under political/cultural pressure, Maori individuals began to turn both the discursive elements of their rituals and the more or less fragmentary and shifting narratives entangled around their genealogies, into "myths and legends." Perhaps this process did help Grey "know" and "control" the Chiefs — to resist the project that Grey (and his predecessors) were carrying out, the Maoris crowned their own "King," miming an imperialist institution. Grey's compilations of Maori lore implicitly brand such a strategy as nonauthentic. They framed the Maori as "pre-modern" in modern terms. These discursive moves, which freeze the Maori into a genuine pastness, continued after Grey: the major collection of myths — that of John White in six volumes — was financed and published by the government during the 1880s basically to provide information with a potential administrative use-value.[7] And in the first decade of this century Elsdon Best compiled his more ethnographic and sympathetic work, *Tuhoe: Children of the Mist*, in explicit reaction against the political messianic movements which had falsified the "true" Maori heritage by hybridizing Christianity. He speaks contemptuously of "that ruffian Te Kooti" who, after the Kingite movement, had fought the British during the 1860s (and whom, as Best notes, the Tuhoe still believed to have been "protected by the Gods"). Te Kooti is the most important of those anti-settlement warriors who claimed to be prophets of the God of the Old Testament (for the earlier but connected Pai Marire cult, in the shape of the snake). But Best's real scorn is directed at the active Rua, living and preaching against the Pakehas as he wrote; his sympathy and admiration for the "old" Maori, and his recording or reconstruction of their authentic mythology, is aimed against the major figure of their current struggle (Best 666).

By those who collected and published it, Polynesian lore is regarded as simply belonging to the Maori. Yet this limit is not absolute. In an academic paper delivered to the Ethnological Society in London in 1870, Sir George Grey found exact homologies between Polynesian myths and English poetry. This poetry was not the poetry of modern "civilization" but, very oddly, that of Edmund Spenser. "Spenser must have stolen his images and language from the New Zealand poets, or . . . they must have acted unfairly by the English bard," he writes, anticipating a certain contemporary literary theoretical trope (Grey, "Inhabitants" 362). This bears the logic of the modernist paradigm: Spenser and the Maoris create in the era before modernity, their shared constraints are those of a bare "human imagination" as opposed to the boundless and developed power of civilization. (In the paper, Grey's transcription of a Maori narrative — told to him by a Christianized *tohunga* [spirit medium] — is obviously modernized: it contains pieces of information of anthropological interest only, its structure is that of a European romance.) The point of this strategy is clear enough: that the Maoris share Europe's past implies that they are fated not only to repeat the West's historical trajectory but to be absorbed by its Enlightenment. And, in Grey's case at least, the modernist paradigm can also encompass an affirmative interpretation of Maori resistance (like Mandela): he can appeal to their "ancient democracy" which European settlement at first destroyed, but will strengthen with the coming of the Law.

Almost immediately the early records of the Maori's past way of life are used as prescriptions for the staging of its continuity within the theatre of enlightened modernity. This process works on all forms of traditional Maori practice: for instance, in the 1860s (while war was being waged), a group of Maoris, led by the entrepreneurial William Jenkins, toured England to present their culture to the Mother Country. Their *hakas* (war dances) were checked for their genuineness against a book, probably Charles Davis's *Maori Mementos to Sir George Grey* (Mackrell 28). (Simultaneously, actual hakas were being directed at the British!) Similarly with carving: when, from the 1880s onward, pieces were produced for model villages, museums and collectors, the *whakuiro rakau* (ritual carvers), who had flourished with the coming of metal tools, came under pressure to omit those contemporary motifs that had developed since European contact (as well as to de-sexualize their work). A pseudo-traditional style, largely based on Hamilton's *Maori Art: the Art Workmanship of the Maori Race in New Zealand*, but with strong narrative pictorial elements was substituted for a quite informal and syncretic mode that had earlier evolved in work produced, almost indistinguishably, for Maori and Pakeha, meeting houses and the tourist trade (Neich).

The loop mechanisms that I have been describing were perhaps most fully acted out by Makereti, a member of the Tuhourangi *hapu* (sub-tribe) — who had been better known as Maggie Papakura, a name she had given herself when she worked as a guide at Whakarewarewa, a museumified Maori village in geyser country. The area had been touristified ever since the 1840s, though it had become prominent only after the Duke of Edinburgh visited it, largely to thank the Arawa people for fighting with the British against Te Kooti. The Tuhourangi, the *hapu* most involved in the tourist trade, were well known for their secularization, the incidence of prostitution and venereal diseases among them — and for their entrepreneurial skills, encouraged by the government. Thus in 1909 a model village was constructed, in a move that would culminate in the establishment of a state-backed school for Maori carving in 1927. So when, for instance, the filmmaker Gaston Méliès toured the world in 1912, in order, as he said, to "utilize the natives of regions travelled through [for] cinematography," it was the Tuhourangi who "enacted" his dramas, and the pseudo-traditional model *pa* that provided some of his locations (9). As the author of *Maggie's Guide to the Hot Lakes* and a member of the Arawa genealogy (i.e., of the *waka* constituted by those descended from members of the legendary Arawa canoe), Makereti had shown the Duke of York, later King George V, around the *pa* in 1901; had taken a model village to Crystal Palace for the 1910 Coronation Festival of Empire; had presented Maori songs, dress, artifacts and dance on the British Musical Hall circuit for a year in another "cultural entertainment" group; and finally, after marrying a member of the Oxfordshire gentry, began to study anthropology at Oxford. Her (unfinished) book, *The Old-Time Maori*, was a draft of her B.Sc. thesis. It is not written in the ethnographic present but in the past tense of nostalgia. The book contains little sense of a tragic loss of identity in the passage to modern time, though it does not concede that its "old" era was that of colonial contact rather than of time immemorial. Addressed simultaneously to the Oxford anthropologists and to contemporary Maoris, it contains genealogies, accounts of rituals, precise descriptions of the sites at which her tribe cultivated *kumeras* (sweet potatoes) and so on. On the one hand, her sense of the importance of lineage may well have been internalized from the theoretical biases of the anthropology of her time. (She does cite Grey and Richard Taylor as sources.) On the other hand, her writing did, potentially at least, break *tapu*, and at this point a confident affirmation of the text's syncretism begins to be less convincing. Makereti herself refused to translate the *karakia* (incantations) she included because to do so would be to commit sacrilege against her *tohunga* who alone had access to their "true" meaning (187). To refuse to translate is not sufficient to avoid transgression however: a book can be read and taken anywhere — where food is stored for instance — which matters because to consult a *karakia* in the proximity of stored food would be seriously to break *tapu*. The book may be called *The Old-Time Maori*, and written in the nostalgic past tense, but it was a present source of anxiety to its author. On her death bed, so its posthumous editor tells us, Makereti asked for two *karakia* to be removed, fearing that to publish them would be sacrilegious. As she moved from show-business to anthropology, from native informant to believer in *tapu*, did Makereti live in traditional Maori time, pseudo-traditional Maori time, modern Maori time or occidental time? On what side of these differences? Obviously on all — which means, a little, on none. (In this, of course, she was not alone: Jenkins's earlier touring party had been treated both as honoured state guests — they were introduced to the Queen — and as objects of display in a shabby entertainment.) She had to transgress as she had to act out the role of a genuine Maori caught on the wrong side of modernity, in order to preserve her past, which, in turn, was available only in an already touristified and anthropologized form.

    The easiest notion with which to absorb and control the tensions that Makereti enacts is "post-culturalism." It is a term which, in my usage, refers variously to an event, a programme or a mode of analysis. When one accepts that the construction of a non-modern cultural identity is the result of interaction between colonizer and colonized; when one celebrates the productive energy of mutual misrecognitions and forgettings then one enters post-culturalism. It has its politics too. Somewhat in its spirit, a New Zealand identity can be constructed not simply from a Maori or a Pakeha viewpoint but by Maori-izing Pakeha formations and vice versa. This is an immensely attractive social programme: it counters the Europeanization of the Maori by constructing a non-essentialist unity across a maintained difference. In New Zealand the programme is not utopian: the state has begun to sponsor it. There the Department of Education encourages the teaching of Maori in schools; Maori history is being taught, re-enacted in films, made the subject of television documentaries, so that New Zealanders of all races come to identify their home districts in terms of their pre-colonial tribal connections and the mythic narrative and events attached to them. The work of Sir George Grey, Elsdon Best, Percy Smith and their Maori collaborators, is now, more than ever, having effects of power as Maori and Pakeha art students rework traditional Maori crafts, visit *marae* (meeting places), take part in "newly traditional" ceremonies and festivities and — to take a last instance — as more Maori words are being added to New Zealand English and the anglicized pronunciation of Maori phonemes is disappearing. These reversals and displacements fill the rootlessness both of the heirs of the settlers and the urbanized Maoris.

Today various academic methods and theories assume and legitimize the post-cultural. One thinks here of studies like that of the Tshidi people by Jean Comaroff. Working between ethnography, sociology and narrative history, Comaroff analyzes the continuities and articulations between the pre-colonial and post-colonial (here, apartheid) conditions so that one can no longer assume a hard distinction between the "West" and its others.[8] One also thinks of those more traditional historians who, rejecting the "fatal impact" ideologeme, write from the side of the colonized — for instance, James Belich in his *The New Zealand Wars and the Victorian Interpretation of Racial Conflict* or, in South Africa, Peter Delius's account of Pedi resistance: *The Land Belongs to Us*. Belich, who takes up the old theme of Maori military skill, goes so far as to describe the colonial wars not as a (tragic) triumph for colonizing modernity, but as a stalemated struggle between two "tribal" forces: the British regiment as a "sub-culture" having more in common with their opponents than with the disciplined bodies of industrial factories, for instance. And, of course, the distance between the non-modern and the modern can be contested from the other direction: a book like Vincent Crapanzano's *Waiting: the Whites of South Africa* describes an Afrikaans rural town, using both direct quotations à la Studs Terkel and hermeneutically orientated ethnographical reflections so that the "white tribe of Africa" lose their status as citizens of the modern.

It is James Clifford, however, who is most directly concerned with the broad conceptual and historical shift within which these valuable and politically sensitive studies apply particular methods. In essays, most of which have been collected in his *The Predicament of Culture*, he reads the impact of modernity not as necessarily leading to the demoralization or "deculturation" of the colonized but as offering new opportunities for improvisatory and combinatory responses. Post-culture belongs to the "newly traditionally meaningful in the present-becoming-future" ("Salvage" 127). Such abstract formulations, however, soon strike concrete difficulties. These are apparent as soon as one asks (as we have begun to): do Makereti and the Tuhourangi who entered the world of film, tourism, anthropology and cultural entertainment and who fought with the British, belong to this order? Or does Te Kooti who, insisting on his chiefly authority, appropriated the word of the Christian God against the Pakeha land grab? In citing these names, it is important to remind ourselves that the settlements of those Maori successors to Moses, Christ and Muhammed (of whom Te Kooti was only the most famous) looked quite different from the touristified Whakawerawera. Maungapohatu, in particular, constructed by the prophet Rua in the Ureweras, had a plan and architecture that amalgamated Pakeha and Maori styles in a quite unexpected way (Ward 228ff.). (Its meeting house used the playing card club as a symbol of the Trinity, and was decorated in yellow diamonds and blue clubs.) Against this, the Tuhourangi did not so much amalgamate Maori and European forms as take advantage of the separation between them. Indeed, even in New Zealand, Te Kooti's strategy survives: in the 1970s Eva Rickard gained the return of her ancestral land under the direction of what she called "Maori spooks," as a person in touch with *wairua* — the spiritual world which is watched over by the *tupuna* — the ancestors (Macdonald 136). Here what is "new" in the "newly traditional" is precisely a struggle against the injustice and loss which, in New Zealand as elsewhere, continues into the post-cultural era mainly because inequities in employment, health and education continue to be linked to racial difference. Thus the "Maori culture" built by Maori and Pakeha together in co-operation and conflict, may be turned against the heirs of the colonizers at the very moment that it confines the Maori in an inauthentic authenticity.

Because the idea that the pre-colonial can never be torn free from the post-colonial is becoming an academic (if not quite a governmental or political) orthodoxy, it is important to insist that a post-cultural discourse may legitimize a programme of simultaneous de-politicization and de-sacrilization. The new and the traditional are synthesized when the violence, the power of *mana* and *tapu* can be localized and policed, when anxieties and ambivalences like Makereti's over her book can easily be contained. Although an activist like Eva Rickard, guided by her *tapuna*, can still be successful (and, as David Lan reminds us, Zimbabwe's guerrilla war depended on spirit mediums), under the dispensation of the "newly traditional" the sacred is more likely to figure in accounts like that of Carol O'Biso. She is the American woman who organized the exhibition of Maori carvings and sacred objects that toured America under the title *Te Maori*. This exhibition, which included what O'Biso unconvincingly claims to be "the most important symbol of Maori power and spirituality," was the focus of fierce struggles in the Maori community (75). Should these *taonga* (treasures) be museumified, taken out of the context in which they had had *mana* and a non-aes-thetic function? Or should they be used to communicate Maori skills and traditions to a wider audience? These debates were the more intense because the Mobil Oil Company, the exhibition's sponsors, were hoping to sign contracts to construct a natural gas refinery with the New Zealand government. Clifford, who repeatedly mentions the exhibition to argue, for instance, that "museums shouldn't be destroyed," that there is "no way to escape these processes [of representation and appropriation] into some new non-violent, non-representational, non-hierarchical world," ignores the protests the show excited (Clifford, "Discussion" 150). Had he conceded their exist-ence perhaps he could not so easily have organized his argument into global oppositions: either an absolute purity (of the pre-modern traditions or of absolute justice) or the impure, decontextualized, but productive, world of the "newly traditional." In O'Biso's own account, the demonstrations and practical difficulties (how to insure an object whose value is more magical than economic?) merely form the background for her personal experiences. These mime those of Rickard and Makereti. She photographs a sacred object and the museum's lights mysteriously go out. A communication from the *wairua*? Dr. Johnson, who believed in second sight and ghosts, might have thought so, but O'Biso shows no sign of recognizing the question's profound conceptual and political force, the way it reneges on modernity. Quite the contrary: the incident becomes an item in the exhibition's publicity: its very own "King Tut" effect. (As Billy Wilder showed long ago in his brilliant *Ace in the Hole* [a.k.a. *The Big Carnival*], little appeals to the media more than the uncanny execution of ancient curses.) Makereti, Eva Rickard and Carol O'Biso all operate in terms and in spaces that the post-cultural concept is especially able to recognize and theorize, yet to place them together under terms like the "newly traditional" is to pass over what distinguishes them: the personal and publicity; the conjunction of the sacred and political resistance; the impossible preservation of lost auras. From the distance of the American academy maybe these are easy distinctions to ignore.

To begin to put this in a wider perspective: once New Zealand citizens can each be both Maori and Pakeha then they live in a world in which simulacra replace what I am calling "the sacred." Simulacra constitute a third (very early) order of modernity — not that of its necessary triumph over the pre-modern, or of its universalism, but of "a simultaneous irruption of the Same and the Other" as Foucault puts it in his essay on Pierre Klossowski (xxvi). The order of simulacra knows no origins, no facts anchored in a transparent description of the world, no anchored hierarchies, but rather circulations and aggregations of representations, a "realm of appearance in the explosion of time," as Foucault characteristically phrases it. If one generalizes and historicizes Foucault's exposition of Klossowski one can argue that simulacra come into existence along with a God who can communicate to humanity in a book — as soon as the sacred requires "faith" (so that "conversion" is possible), that is, as soon as the sacred is no longer a horizon of the total social system. But simulacra only begin to be recognized as such when society begins to invent itself, when, refusing to be persuaded, it rejects the authority of what is inherited, framing the past rather than maintaining or obeying it. Then one can enquire, as Locke did in the seventeenth century: "if the strength of persuasion be the light that must guide us, I ask how shall anyone distinguish between the delusions of Satan and the inspiration of the Holy Ghost?" (703–04). The sacred here is separated from power; it no longer connects to the world iconically (in so-called "natural signs"), or indexically (as the hidden cause of actual effects) or allegorically (at an unknowable remove) but in a *logos* always open to interpretation. Locke can put his question because, though formally a "believer," he is confident that "neither God nor Satan ever appear" in his world — another phrase by which Foucault defines the order of simulacra. Locke's question can be updated. Are the sacred sanctions, the aura of chiefs and divines, of kings and classical philosophers, expressions of particular political interests, for instance, or inspired by truth, God? Satanic or Divine? Is the God who uses Gabriel as a messenger to talk to Te Au (Te Kooti's predecessor and the founder of Pai Marire) more "real" than the missionaries' God? If Christianity were not already formed in simulacra, the prophets of the colonized could not appropriate it, though of course they are also drawn to it because this God is, strangely, already a God of the dispossessed. When Christianity arrives split by denominational squabbles its Being-as-simulacra is placed in the foreground. Then the relations between sects can duplicate the relation between the colonizer and the colonized as they did in New Zealand when, at a public debate, a Catholic asked a Protestant missionary to read from the Latin Vulgate (Wilson 137). The latter's abashment repeated that of the Maoris themselves when they first faced print.

Locke's question, particularly if embodied in a fiction, still has enormous force because the move from the sacred as a horizon of social practices to a faith involves the disavowal of the order of simulacrum. To take a recent example: think of the effects of Salman Rushdie's *The Satanic Verses*, a book that describes certain religious authenticities as if they were simulacra and, to reinforce the message, narrativizes attempts to exit from the secular to the transcendental as if they were a form of suicide. No discourse on human rights or democracy could unleash the violence that Rushdie has: his work does not enter debate, it blasphemes. Rushdie imagines an order from which little can escape: the more the Ayatollah Khomeini insisted that he was acting in the spirit of God and the Prophet's Law as uttered in the Qur'an, the more he himself threatened the divine authority of that text. For Rushdie's novel already pictures such protestations as dissimulations, it shows that no human being in touch with the supernatural can tell whether they are being addressed by divine truth or the fallen order of political expediency. (It reminds us that Muhammed, the angel Gabriel's familiar, was a victim of such confusion himself at least at one point of his career.) Was the Ayatollah shoring up the Shi'ites' position? Did Satan whisper in his ear? By representing such possibilities the novel drags its targets into the era of the (post) modern. In its aftermath, the more violence that the Iranians threaten the more wedded to death they seem. Rushdie's novel knows that, from within the zone of simulacra, the only way that a ground can be located is by dealing out death. From the other side however: where simulacra do not exist, there can be no blasphemy — only transgression (like Makereti's) and mistakes. To elaborate on Wittgenstein (and, among others, Evans-Pritchard), outside the modern there can be no trickery or fraud in matters of the sacred. What appears as such now are the techniques for the production of sacred effects and events. Though, of course, these techniques can be applied on inappropriate occasions or by improper persons, and therefore unsuccessfully, anxiously, skeptically — just because the "proper" is in part and in a circle defined by the unpredictable success of these techniques (Wittgenstein; Evans-Pritchard 107–09).

*   *   *

Since the eighteenth century, literature has increasingly been drawn into the task of separating the political and the sacred and of controlling the disorder of representation that follows desacrilization. Fiction has drawn ghosts, second sight, brownies, magic into "nature" and "culture" on the one hand and described them as trickery on the other. The non-modern becomes available for representation by a printed narrative "voice" whose authority absorbs that of the "supernatural." This is quite explicit both in Fielding's narrator and in the Gothic novelists whose ghosts turn out to have rational explanation and whose effect is merely a "sensation." No doubt these fictions have a policing role — they help ensure that the aura of an other world cannot be used against modernity's "law and order." (Just as, from the other direction, frank admission of the order of simulacra threatens messianic fundamentalisms used for political purposes.) Today, when there has been a massive migration of Third World nationals to the First World, when Europe and America are losing their economic dominance, when traditional universalist and secular supports are threatened for reasons as much economic as philosophical, then mimesis ceases either to control the play of the simulacra or to undo the connection between the sacred and the political. Violence, like that directed against Rushdie, can be sparked. And this is why I would like to end this paper by very briefly describing a work that, as its author notes in its Preface, "owes nothing to fiction" and which returns to the border at which modernity divides itself from its other, the point where the Law, simulacra and the sacred encounter one another in no hierarchy. In the post-cultural moment, the desire to return to this border is common enough — in New Zealand so as to (re)invent a national tradition, to rewrite civil war as reassuring fratricide (Benedict Anderson's phrase), that is, to construct a past which has been post-cultural from the beginning.[9] My return to this border works to slightly different ends, though not — quite — to reaffirm the compact between the sacred and the political.

Frederick Maning's *Old New Zealand* was first published anonymously as "by a Pakeha Maori" in 1863. A popular book, in print locally for over a century, it has never been hailed as the national epic of which New Zealanders have often felt the lack. And yet no other book has been so often cited, cut and pasted by later historians and anthropologists. More than any other work, it materially articulates the nation-state's existence as *text*. Maning was a Pakeha Maori, one of those whites welcomed into Maori communities to help them trade with passing Europeans before the coming of the settlers. Many Pakeha Maoris, like Maning himself who lived with the Ngapuhi in the Bay of Islands, married women from their adopted tribe; they lived as close as possible to the threshold across which continuities and violence pass: they did not, like Johnson and Boswell, travel through it. Maning in particular did not write to and for the centre. For him, to write on and of this difference is to be driven back onto himself into self-reflexivity:

A story-teller, like a poet or a pugilist, must be *born* and not *made*, and I begin to fancy I have not been born under a story-telling planet, for by no effort that I can make can

I hold on to the thread of my story, and I am conscious the whole affair is fast becoming one great parenthesis. If I could only get clear of this *tapu* I would "try back." (151)

The Maori signifier controls this passage. Maning is in the grip of a power he cannot control: he is writing about *tapu* and wants to move past the topic, but some force — some *tapu* as the pun in the last sentence permits us to say — moves his pen. We find here a contagion of the *tapu* that the Maoris attached to writing (for the "old" Maori, nothing was more contagious than *tapu*, and the power of writing to communicate across a distance is often given as a cause of Maori "conversion" to Christianity, in particular their sense that "the god of the white man is more powerful than the Maori Gods" [Best 362–63]). Maning finds it hard to make his tale more than a parenthesis because he cannot quite grasp what *tapu* is, how it works, from whence it derives its authority. The movement and energy of *tapu* is as uncontrollable as that of his writing; it does not take the form of a law. So, in Maning, writing comes to enact a continuity across the difference in the very attempt to represent that difference. The way that writing writes itself under the guidance (as it seems) of hidden forces keeps *tapu* alive where it ceases to be an agent of social order.

Maning lives in a state of ambivalence. A *tohunga* invokes a recently dead chief who, the first in his tribe to learn to write, has left behind a notebook full of valuable information. Maning attends the spirit ceremony and asks the Chief's spirit where the book is. He is told, the book is retrieved; but when interrogated further about its contents, the spirit disappears. "The deception was perfect. There was a dead silence — at last. A ventriloquist," said I; "or — or *perhaps* — the devil" (146). The italics inclines his realization that the appearance of a spirit may be feigned back toward a structure in which the supernatural may act directly on the world now. And this inclination orientates his own self-deliverance to the techniques of writing. Writing, unlike speech, can always be revised and reconsidered — which means that its claim to presence is also a ventriloquist's trick, an effort concealing effort. But Maning's book is ventriloquist in a completely opposed sense: as he implies, it contains records preserved in the Chief's gift from the grave. *Old New Zealand* is not wholly Maning's work: the written-about, the off-stage, the dead also write it — from a past in which one could not be confident that Satan or God will never appear. It is as if the devil (*atua?*) slips through the space left open where the two ventriloquisms do not meet.

In respecting *tapu*, the book may possess *mana*.

If ever this talk about the good old times be printed and published, and everyone buy it, and read it, and quote it, and believe every word in it, as they ought, seeing that every word is true, then it will be a *puka puka whai mana*, a book of *mana*; and I shall have opinion of the good sense and good taste of the New Zealand public.

When the law of England is the law of New Zealand, and the Queen's writ will run, then both the Queen and the law will have great *mana*; but I don't think either will ever happen, and so neither will have any *mana* of consequence.

If the reader has not some faint notion of *mana* by this time I can't help it; I can't do any better for him. I must confess I have not pleased myself. Any European language can be translated easily enough into any other; but to translate Maori into English is much harder to do than is supposed by those who do it every day with ease, but who do not know their own language or any other but Maori perfectly. (208–09)

Tapu cannot be fixed because it is in the hands of powers that may or may not simulate and do not simply disappear, but *mana*, though it is bound to whatever has force, is merely an impossible word to translate into European languages across the colonial divide. The word cannot be translated but it can be repeated. Then it performs a trick: the Maori signifier acquires an aura, if not quite a signified. We might even say: in modernity *mana* lives on — if nowhere else — whenever a sign floats between word and concept, between signifier and signified or — to put it another way — wherever the untranslatable flirts with meaning as it does as long as it is circulated. If this book that constantly "uses" the word without controlling it, is published, read, incorporated in other books, then *mana* will survive despite its being a sign of what is absent, an unravelled and displaced signifier. Yet more than mere duplication is required. *Mana* will survive in the book because the book is true, which does not mean that it tells truth. Working on the borders of simulacra, Maning cannot simply discover the truth as Johnson does. The book is true, not fiction, because it has delivered itself up simultaneously to the spell of the spirits, to sheer repetition and to the parenthesis of writing at the cost of feigning an absence of revision and care. It will survive because it disavows and repeats not because it inspects and represents.

Being a Maori Pakeha is impossible, for it demands that one speak in two voices that cancel each other. At the book's end, registering his conflict, Maning can only await violence in a passage that breaks through its patriarchal, musty rebelliousness:

I get so confused, I feel just as if I were two different persons at the same time. . . . I belong to both parties, and I don't care a straw which wins; but I am sure we shall have fighting. Men *must* fight; or else what are they made for? Twenty years ago when I heard military men talking of "marching through New Zealand with fifty men," I was called a fool because I said they could not do it with five hundred. Now I am thought foolish by civilians because I say we can conquer New Zealand with our present available means, if we set the right way about it (which we won't). So hurrah again for the Maori! We shall drive the *Pakeha* into the sea, and send the law after them! If we can do it, we are right; and if the *Pakeha* beat us, they will be right too. God save the Queen! So now, my Maori tribe, and also my *pakeha* countrymen, I shall conclude this book with good advice; and be sure you take notice; it is given to both parties. . . . "Be brave, that you may *live*." (211)

The Maoris will drive the Pakehas into the sea; the Pakehas will conquer New Zealand: whoever wins, wins *mana*. Maning seems at last to wish for a Maori victory as the defeat of the Law and universalism. As the writer that he is, he *must* take that side, because his writing effects a continuity with *mana* and *tapu* in opposition to the Law that maims the English. And the passage ends with another borrowing from the Maoris: Be brave that you may live, translates a famous saying of Hongi Hika, *Kei hea koutou kia toa*, repeated by Hongi Heke when he encouraged the Ngapuhi to fight the British. Maning seems also to have encouraged his people to resist the Pakeha, but in his book he himself is brave and lives because he faces and writes from the border where the tensions between simulacra, the Law and the old order of the Maoris are still active. He does not pretend that there will be no war between those separated by the difference where, as here, it divides a nation firmly in two. For him there is not even any way of finally judging whether the Pakehas or the Maoris *ought* to win. In sum: though he enters the struggle personally, insisting on bravery, his writing is not quite in its service, remaining, on one side its own tricky, multivocal order of practice and, on the other, impotent, *unzeitgemässig*. What Maning seems to know is that when the struggle is over, the difference will remain — at the very least in the unfixable relation between the dead past that is "Old New Zealand" and the traces of that past in *Old New Zealand* (and all the texts that cannibalize it). The book, like all writing, lives in a present which is not that of the "newly traditional" (as matter, it is always the same), nor does it belong to what Rushdie calls "the present moment of the past" (the book *does* try blindly to maintain the pastness of past) nor to "the first moment of the future" (it cannot foresee the future [535]). Between dissimulation, copying and delivering itself to language, it again and again performs the old, old trick of giving dead matter — letters, sounds — a little life and significance. That magic itself does not take or belong to time: there has been no recountable succession of events in which "*mana*" moved from meaninglessness to meaning — or vice versa. So it is writing that can form the border between different orders of time — not writing as such however: only that, like *Old New Zealand*, written at the right time in the right place and, perhaps even destined for channels of distribution that do not travel too far through the postal circuits. For such writing, hugged to the heart of a nation, may create a state as text and help prevent it ever simply from becoming "a poor country defeated in a brutal war by a metropolitan power" or simply available for tours, which is a florid way of saying that without Maning's old book, New Zealand would have a different history, different politics (a different resistance to the great powers), a different *mana*.[10]

NOTES

1. This formulation is borrowed from Clifford. See, for instance, "On Collecting."
2. Compare the discussion of the word *atua* by Wilson 82–86 and F. Allan Hanson and Louise Hanson 40–49.
3. For a Maori account of Cook's 1769 arrival see Hore-ta-te-taniwha's narrative as transcribed by and in White 5.125–24.

4. For a quite early Maori record of this etymology see Makereti 110. For a modern assessment on its probability see Wilson 88.
5. Taylor, the first missionary to publish a book on the Maoris, has the name of the North Island as *Aotea roa*, and the name of New Zealand (as uttered by the mythical Kupe) *Aotea toa*.
6. The best de-mystifying accounts of the construction of Maori mythology is to be found in Sorrenson. See also Simmons, and Sharp's pioneering monograph.
7. See Anderson for a description of White's techniques of compilation. Many of the original compilers were in fact land surveyors also.
8. Comaroff's difficulty is that (partly because the pre-colonial is only available in its textual representations) her story of colonial impact tends to take shape as a description of the transformation of, and continuities between, a formal ethnographic model (a contradiction between agnation and matrilinearity) and a somewhat less formal sociological one (a tension between the proletarianization of the Tshidi under apartheid and the symbolic resistance available in the hybridized rituals of the church of 'Zion').
9. Anderson used the phrase in a paper delivered at the University of Melbourne, August 1987.
10. Versions of this paper were delivered at the SAVAL conference, Potchefstroom, South Africa, in April 1989 and at the University of Auckland in October 1987. As part of the arrangements made during my visit to South Africa it has been made available to COSAW (Congress of South African Writers) to use as they may see fit.

WORKS CITED

Anderson, Johannes C. *White's Ancient History of the Maori*. Wellington: The Beltane Book Bureau, n.d. (1949?).

Awatere, Donna. *Maori Sovereignty*. Auckland: Broadsheet P, 1984.

Belich, James. *The New Zealand Wars and the Victorian Interpretation of Racial Conflict*. Auckland: Auckland UP, 1986.

Best, Elsdon. *Tuhoe: Children of the Mist: A Sketch of the Origin, History, Myths and Beliefs of the Tuhoe Tribe of the Maori of New Zealand with Some Account of Other Early Tribes of the Bay of Plenty*. Wellington: A.H. and A.W.Reed, 1972.

Boswell, James. "Journal of a Tour to the Hebrides." Chapman 159–443.

Chapman, R.W., ed. *Johnson's Journey to the Western Islands of Scotland and Boswell's Journal of a Tour to the Hebrides with Samuel Johnson LL.D*. London: OUP, 1924.

Clifford, James. "Beyond the Salvage Paradigm: Of Other Peoples." *DIA* 18–31.

———. In Discussion. *DIA* 142–51.

————. "On Collecting Art and Culture." *The Predicament of Culture: Twentieth-Century Ethnography, Literature and Art*. Cambridge, Mass.: Harvard UP, 1988. 215–52.

Comaroff, Jean. *Body of Power, Spirit of Resistance: The Culture and History of a South African People*. Chicago: Chicago UP, 1985.

Crapanzano, Vincent. *Waiting: The Whites of South Africa*. New York: Random, 1985.

Delius, Peter. *The Land Belongs to Us*. London: Heinemann, 1984.

Denoon, Donald. *Settler Capitalism: The Dynamics of Dependent Development in the Southern Hemisphere*. Oxford: Clarendon, 1983.

Derrida, Jacques. *Psyché: Inventions de l' autre*. Paris: Galilée, 1987.

DIA Art Foundation Discussions in Contemporary Culture I. Seattle: Bay P, 1987.

Evans-Pritchard, E.E. *Witchcraft, Oracles and Magic among the Azande*. Oxford: OUP, 1976.

Foucault, Michel. The Prose of Acteon. Forward to *The Baphomet*, by Pierre Klossowski. Trans. Sophie Hawkes and Stephen Sartarelli. New York: The Eridanos Library, 1988. xix–xxxviii.

Goody, Jack. *The Interface between the Written and the Oral*. Cambridge: Cambridge UP, 1987.

Grey, Sir George. *Polynesian Mythology, and the Ancient Traditional History of the New Zealand Race, as Furnished by Their Priests and Chiefs*. London: Routledge, 1898.

————. "On the Social Life of the Ancient Inhabitants of New Zealand, and on the National Character it was Likely to Form." *Journal of the Ethnological Society of London* 1/4 (Jan. 1870): 339–80.

Hanson, F. Allan and Louise Hanson. *Counterpoint in Maori Culture*. London: Routledge, 1983.

Johnson, Samuel. "Journey to the Western Islands of Scotland." Chapman 1-150.

King, Michael. *Being Pakeha*. Auckland: Hodder and Stoughton, 1985.

Lan, David. *Guns and Rain: Guerrillas and Spirit Mediums in Zimbabwe*. London: James Curry, 1985.

Locke, John. *An Essay Concerning Human Understanding*. Ed. Peter H. Nidditch. Oxford: Clarendon P, 1975.

Macdonald, Robert. "The Hikoi." *Metro* 28 (May 1989): 133–51.

Mackrell, Brian. *Heriru Wikitoria! An Illustrated History of the Maori Tour of England 1863*. Auckland: OUP, 1985.

Makereti. *The Old-Time Maori*. Auckland: New Women's P, 1986.

Mandela, Nelson. "Black Man in a White Court: First Court Statement (1962)." *The Struggle is My Life: His Speeches and Writings Brought Together with Historical Documents and Accounts of Mandela in Prison by Fellow Prisoners*. New York: Pathfinder P, 1986. 133–60.

Maning, Frederick. *Old New Zealand*. Wellington: Whitcombe and Tombs Ltd.,1906.

Méliès, Gaston. *Le Voyage autour du Monde de la G. Méliès Manufacturing Company*. Paris: Association "Les Amies de George Méliès," 1988.

Neich, Roger. "The Veil of Orthodoxy: Rotorua Ngati Tarawhai Woodcarving in a Changing Context." *Art and Artists of Oceania*. Ed. Sid Mead and Bernie Kernot. Wellington: Dunmore P, 1985. 245–65.

O'Biso, Carol. *First Light*. London: Heinemann, 1987.

Orbell, Margaret. *Hawaiki: A New Approach to Maori Tradition*. Christchurch: U of Canterbury P, 1985.

Rushdie, Salman. *The Satanic Verses*. London: Viking, 1988.

Rutherford, J. *Sir George Grey*. London: Cassell and Co., 1961.

Sharp, Andrew. *Ancient Voyagers in the Pacific*. Wellington: The Polynesian Society, 1956.

Simmons, D.R. *The Great New Zealand Myth: A Study of the Discovery and Origin Traditions of the Maori*. Wellington: A.H. and A.W. Reed, 1976.

Sorrenson, M.P.K. *Maori Origins and Migrations*. Auckland: Auckland UP, 1979.

Taylor, Richard. *Te Ika A Maui or New Zealand and its Inhabitants*. London: Wertheim and Macintosh, 1855.

Ward, Alan. *A Show of Justice: Racial Amalgamation in Nineteenth Century New Zealand*. Auckland: Auckland UP and OUP, 1983.

White, John. *The Ancient History of the Maori*. 6 vols. Wellington: Government Printer, 1888.

Wilson, Ormond. *From Hongi Hika to Hone Heke: A Quarter Century of Upheaval*. Dunedin: John MacIndoe, 1985.

Wittgenstein, Ludwig. *Remarks on Fraser's Golden Bough*. Trans. A.C. Miles. Bedford, Notts.: Brynmill, 1979.

"Numinous Proportions": Wilson Harris's Alternative to All "Posts"

HENA MAES-JELINEK

> A truly creative alchemical response to crisis and conflict and deprivation — a response that engages with formidable myth — may well come from the other side of a centralised or dominant civilisation, from extremities, from apparently irrelevant imaginations and resources. The complacencies of centralised, ruling powers . . . begin to wear thin at the deep margins of being within a multi-levelled quest for the nature of value and spirit.
>
> WILSON HARRIS, "Literacy and the Imagination"

As the century and the millenium draw to a close, the major crisis that beset Western civilization with world-wide repercussions before World War I has not abated, and we seem to approach a new era dangerously poised between a sense of exhaustion and disintegration on one hand and the resurgence of a narrow fundamentalism on the other. Also with the possible exception of the Renaissance, no other period seems to have combined more inextricably man's propensity to tyrannize and destroy with his extraordinary capacity for progress, though on the moral side whatever gains were made are largely cancelled out by losses.

Wilson Harris belongs with those writers who still believe in the moral function of art, a belief actualized, as the quotation above indicates, in a quest for value rather than categorical assertion. His many recent essays on imagination as provider of a genuinely creative response to crisis are proof enough that, in his eyes, art is still *the* major potential carrier of meaning. In the context of the "modernism versus post-modernism" debate this makes him close to modernism, as I think he is, but could disqualify him as a post-colonial writer because modernism has grown out of the liberal humanist tradition whose strategies fed on colonialism and the unacknowledged appropriation by metropolitan centres of cultural features from their heterogeneous colonies (Ashcroft et al. 156–157). I am only making this point to show the kind of contradiction one comes up against as soon as one classifies in a field averse *per se* to categorization. Nor am I denying the impact of so-called "primitive" or "exotic" cultures on modernist art but suggest that the influence worked both ways if at different moments, and that not a few post-colonial writers are direct heirs of what *was* a modernist breakthrough in spite of its political conservatism and sometimes, though not always, unconscious ideological biases.

Before comparing Wilson Harris's work with literary post-modernism, a few preliminary comments are prerequisite if only to make clear what specific features call for comparison. No discussion of post-modernism can avoid remarking on the welter of contradictions it elicits among supporters and detractors or even within each group. Such a lack of consensus reflects on the nature of post-modernism itself for the loss of value and significance it posits has entailed a similar disagreement as to what language means, as evidenced, for example, by the proliferation of "posts" and their personal, contradictory meanings. Some could argue, for instance, that Simon During uses "post-cultural" in a progressive sense and George Steiner in a conservative one. Still what appeared originally as the expression of a liberating pluralism is sometimes turning into an obstacle rather than an auxiliary to the understanding of literature. This may sound like the *querelle des anciens et des modernes* all over again, and a comparison with the French "Battle of the Books" is not so preposterous if one remembers that a major issue in seventeenth-century France was an opposition between cartesianism and non-rationalism (whether in religion or poetry), and between the claim to universality represented by the classics and national subjects or myths. Also, then as now, both sides resorted to cartesian logic in their argumentation but created confusion by using the same terms with different meanings. My own purpose is not to enter the post-modernist controversy but to briefly substantiate Wilson Harris's view that the prevailing alternative to post-modernism is a fall-back on a one-sided tradition which he sees as a given "formula" rather than a genuinely renewed and renewable concept.[1]

To give a few examples, Gerald Graff's analysis of the "post-modernist breakthrough" has the merit of clarifying the issue, though perhaps too systematically. He argues that post-modernism is the "logical culmination" of romanticism and modernism and continues these movements rather than represent a sharp break with them. Eagleton offers a parallel argument when he writes that it was "modernism which brought structuralist and post-structuralist to birth in the first place" (139), and Lentricchia makes a fairly similar point (xiii). But there is a certain irony in Graff's presentation of post-modernism as a "reactionary tendency" (219) for he criticizes it through his essay in the name of rationalism and coherence, basically the values already put forward in the late twenties by Wyndham Lewis against romanticism, the intuitive in Bergson's philosophy as well as against Joyce and Lawrence, all destroyers of the classical ideal, endangering Western civilization by a return to primitivism. It is worth mentioning that for Graff, as indeed for most commentators on post-modernism, the role of imagination is to shape and order rather than discover (237).

In a commonsensical article on the arbitrariness and the motives of the "modernism versus post-modernism" debate, Susan Suleiman argues that it is one of naming rather than content, relevant only in the Anglo-Saxon context (255–270). In the same volume Hans Bertens, one of its editors, offers a well-informed and helpful survey of the characteristics and historical development of post-modernism as term and concept. But in spite of his insistence on the pluralism of the post-modern *Weltanschauung* and of his own approach to it, and apart from a brief allusion to Latin American Magical Realism, he makes no reference whatsoever to phenomena outide Europe and the United States. He shares with Graff and Suleiman, as indeed with most Western commentators for or against post-modernism, a total lack of attention to basic factors which brought about the much emphasized disintegration, decentering (though not loss of power) and disenchantment or bitterness of the West. That this was formerly experienced by colonized peoples is totally ignored, as is the interaction of cultures in a "global" world and the surfacing even in the West of visions and modes of thought alien to its tradition and capable of modifying or renewing it.

The most telling example of this limited outlook in the Fokkema and Bertens volume is the essay by Richard Todd, generally a perceptive critic on British fiction by conventional standards. Todd is intent on proving that there is such a thing as "Postmodernist British Fiction" and he considers it of primordial importance that the writers he has in mind should have become part of the canon. Some of the novels he mentions are indeed by major British writers (Fowles, Murdoch, Golding in *The Paper Men*) but the aspects of their fiction he discusses, such as playfulness, pastiche and parody, are not the only or major criteria one would judge by if prone to canonization, despite Linda Hutcheon's insistence on their creative potential (*Narcissistic Narrative, A Theory of Parody*). Moreover, what Todd sees as the aspiration of British post-modernist fiction towards a pluralistic discourse seems to be of a very limited kind. This also applies to other Western commentators for whom pluralism generally means separate commitments to the "ex-centric" in "class, race, gender, sexual orientation or ethnicity" as opposed to the "homogeneous monolith . . . middle-class, male, heterosexual, white, western" (Hutcheon, *Poetics* 12). Todd refers to the "colonial or imperial past" but significantly mentions Scott and Farrell and seems unaware of experimental post-colonial writing in Britain other than Rushdie's, generally one of the few post-colonial writers worthy of "appropriation" by British critics.

Linda Hutcheon, on the contrary, offers an amazingly inclusive analysis of the many forms of post-modernism and exposes its paradoxes and contradictions, seeing in them a source of power and creative tension as well as the reason for the diverging interpretations it gives rise to (Hutcheon, *Poetics* 47, 222ff.). Above all, she suggests that post-modernism remains partly trapped by that which it challenges and rejects when she writes that "one of the lessons of the doubleness of post-modernism is that you cannot step outside that which you contest, that you are implicated in the value you choose to challenge (223). Truth and reference, she says, have not ceased to exist but have been problematized (223)[2] and the post-modern foregrounds process as opposed to the discovery of total vision even when it does find such a vision (48). One of her recurring arguments against negative comments on post-modernism is that its representatives are aware that their creations are only human constructs, which naturally follows from the negation of a referent. But the impression one often gets is that, within the persisting confines of their tradition, the writers she deals with dismantle and "play" with its building blocks and move them around, but seldom cross its borders except at surface level. Certainly, the self-reflexiveness of much post-modernist fiction has not necessarily entailed a drastic revision of narrative strategies and change in outlook. I would take Fowles's fiction as one example among many. Like Todd, who considers *The French Lieutenant's Woman* as "perhaps Britain's closest approach to the 'canonic' Postmodernist novel" (Todd 112), Hutcheon clearly sees it and *A Maggot* as significant examples of post-modernist fiction. Her analysis of Sarah's role as fiction-maker in the first of these novels is illuminating. But her conclusion is that the creative aspects of parody, allegory and *mise en abyme* which characterize metafiction in this novel are saving techniques for the mimetic genre (*Narcissistic Narrative* 70). If saving the mimetic genre is what matters, and it obviously is since she approves of the novel as "realism redefined" (58), it is difficult to accept that post-modernism has been the genuinely revisionary mode she sees in it. It contradicts what I see as a major feature (and shortcoming) in Fowles's fiction. He is a good storyteller, and the role played by women in his novels as stimulators of male consciousness can be seen as an advance on his predecessors in the realistic tradition. He may even have suggested through Alison, the Australian girl in *The Magus*, that English society needs to be regenerated from the outside. But in spite of the mysterious aura about Sarah in *The French Lieutenant's Woman*, he has repeatedly tried and failed to convey a deeper, mysterious dimension through his narratives. The trials Nicholas is subjected to in *The Magus*, the different versions of the allegorical episode of the cavern in *A Maggot* (which partly mars the *tour de force* achieved by Fowles in his trial narrative, a challenge indeed to historiography [Hutcheon, *Poetics* 106]), are incentives to awareness through a fairly conventional though baroque symbolism and through mechanical devices such as His Lordship's unexplained disappearance (in spite of its metaphysical connotations) or, for that matter, the celebrated endings of *The French Lieutenant's Woman*. They may "challenge certainty" (48) and, like the four postscripts in Iris Murdoch's *The Black Prince*, they question the main text (Todd 114) and convey a sense of relativity but not the genuine ontological doubt supposed to be a major feature of post-modernist fiction.

These few and admittedly arbitrarily chosen examples suggest that post-modernism still functions within a tradition in which it is difficult to envisage genuinely new and different modes of perception.[3] The continuing impact of tradition as expression of established culture and outlook, and a return to it, were already evidenced five years ago in some of the negative responses to an inquiry by *PN Review* (1985) on the "New Orthodoxy" in critical theory. It is also interesting to note that a return to realistic narrative is being hailed from ideologically opposite quarters.[4]

Wilson Harris's conception of tradition was the subject of his first major essay and, just as *Palace of the Peacock* contains embryonically all further fictional developments in his work, so *Tradition, the Writer and Society* contains the quintessence of all further developments and conceptualizations of his thought. I do not think, incidentally, that Harris puts forward "theories," though *some* of his views have been theorized and used in criticism. His own critical essays are usually written after or, judging from their dating, in parallel with some of his fiction, and the premises in both are largely non-rational, as a close scrutiny of his writing shows (cf. *The Womb of Space*). Even though the general trend of his essays develops as a "logical" argument, there are, as it were, "gaps" in the logic filled by what are for Harris wholly intuitive insights. As often with original writers, his fiction and critical writings are most profitably read in the light of each other for a better understanding of his vision and thought as of their unique symbiosis. Harris's conception of tradition, inspired, as is well-known, by the West Indian experience of void and so-called "historylessness" (*Tradition*), is a good example of the resistance of his views to theorization. Its non-rational tenor has not been sufficiently emphasized though, as he said in an interview in which he connected post-colonial allegory and tradition, "the absent body is rooted in an understanding of presence which lies *beyond logical presence*" (Interview 1988: 49). To rationally minded critics (myself included) the full implications of the italicized words are not easy to grasp, yet they are the very essence (if one still dares use that word) of Harris's art. They account for his mode of writing as a visionary, predominantly "dream-like" yet transformative re-enactment of the past, for the "deconstruction" of the surface reality and the decentering of the narrative perspective in his fiction, not in playfulness or, at the other extreme, out of despair in a world become meaningless but, on the contrary, to make possible the quest for value and meaning which, as we saw, he clearly advocates. Though it does have ideological and political implications (if only in its rejection of any kind of imperialism and authoritarianism), decentering for Harris, while denying hierarchy, does not express his suspicion of "truth" or "reality" and implies more than Derrida's awareness that contamination by the metaphysical is impossible to escape (Lentricchia 174). But he too rejects the notion of all absolutes and the notion of a "transcendental signifier" through which "truth or reality . . . will act [and should act] as the foundation of all our thought, language and experience" (Eagleton 131). The foundation of truth is, for Harris, "unpinnable" and absolute truth can never be reached, not even through a "reconciliation of opposites," which, as the protagonist of *The Four Banks of the River of Space* realizes, is "too uncreative or mechanical" a formula (51).

I am in fact arguing that Harris's thought, like the linguistic fabric of his prose, defies categorization. His works of art, to reverse Lyotard's much quoted phrase (81), are not looking for rules and categories, and both his fiction and criticism seek "to translate/re-dress all *codes* into fractions and factors of truth" (*Womb of Space* 86, italics mine). The truth his characters are in quest of, "the inimitable ground of Being" (*Four Banks* 51), is never reached and its existence is only perceived intuitively through "a glimmering apprehension of the magic of creative nature, the life of sculpture, the genesis of art, the being of music" (*Four Banks* 39). The God Harris seems to believe in is not, if I understand rightly, a reality exclusively beyond man but essentially a creator, "a true Creator, whose unknowable limits are *our* creaturely infinity" (*Four Banks* 32, italics mine). I hope this will become clearer as we go along. The point I am making here is that Harris's God exists through men as much as they through Him, just as in his novels the creative process develops through an interaction between the author/sometimes "editor"/sometimes protagonist and his characters (see below). At one stage in his imaginative quest the protagonist in *Four Banks* thinks:

> I had missed the subtle linkages of a parent-Imagination *in, through and beyond* all creatures, all elements, a Parent beyond fixed comprehension until I began to retrace my steps. (125, italics mine)

Retracing one's steps is the process in which Harris's protagonists have been involved in from *The Guyana Quartet* onwards. Through their experiences and encounters with a vanished past, lost cultures or deprived individuals and groups (apparently non-existent yet agents of the sacred in his fiction), his protagonists confront "areas of tradition that have sunken away and apparently disappeared and vanished and yet that are still active at some level" (Interview 1988: 48). Harris continues that "one has to make a distinction between *activity* as a kind of mechanical process and *movement* as something which is rooted in . . . a combination of faculties in the imagination," thus clearly linking the creative process to the kind of tradition ("absent body" beyond logical presence) he has in mind. From whatever angle one approaches his fiction or essays, one comes up against this enigmatic "presence" which he himself says he apprehends through "intuitive clues" (see above) and which takes on innumerable shapes in his novels. The dreaming recreation of New World conquest in *Palace of the Peacock* is a surfacing of that lost tradition into consciousness, as are the runaway slaves Fenwick encounters in *The Secret Ladder* but also the mysterious presence which hovers over Catalena when they threaten to execute her. The Indians in *Tumatumari*, the pre-Columbian vestiges into which Idiot Nameless falls in *Companions*, the Nameless country in *Black Marsden*, the canvas Da Silva "revises" are so many faces (sometimes paradoxically faceless) or manifestations of tradition, which sometimes erupts with unpredictable force and can arouse terror as much as ecstasy.

> I am convinced that there is a tradition in depth *which returns, which nourishes us even though it appears to have vanished,* and that it creates a fiction in the ways in which the creative imagination comes into dialogue with clues of revisionary moment. The spectral burden of vanishing and re-appearing is at the heart of the writer's task. ("Literacy" 27)

It is this subterranean living tradition ("living fossil texts" is, as we shall see, another expression for it) which informs the notions of "reversal," "re-vision"[5] and "infinite rehearsal," *a-posteriori* conceptualizations of his fictional practice, now frequently applied in post-colonial criticism, though not always in the sense meant by Harris because the critic, perhaps inevitably, ignores the complex overlapping of layers of reality and the intuitive thrust in exploring them, the *faith* in the power of intuition by which Harris has radicalized fiction. In addition, his conception of a lost tradition and of texts coming alive, as it were, of their own volition, texts which he scans for frail clues he (or any other author) may not have been aware of planting there himself ("Comedy" 131), suggests that the text not only has a life of its own but an intention of its own. Harris convincingly substantiates this view in *The Womb of Space* by his wholly personal and original reading of novels which had previously received considerable attention of a more conventional kind.[6]

It should already be clear that the uncertain enigmatic reality which, for Harris, is the substance of tradition differs from what is usually called the post-modernist indeterminacy. That reality is not only rooted in a lost past but in the physical world and in man's psyche ("the womb of space"): "It is not a question of rootlessness but of the miracle of roots, the miracle of a dialogue with eclipsed selves" (*Explorations* 65–66). It naturally influences his conception and rendering of character. The "dissolution of ego boundaries," the fragmentation of the self, characteristic of much post-modernist fiction, entail in his novels neither mere uncertainty of identity nor, at the opposite pole, the assertion of one that is merely "other," as in some Black American writing and criticism or, for that matter, much post-colonial writing. Neither the author nor the characters are "sovereign" in his view, by which he means that they do not embody one given personality but rather a series of personalities born out of "one complex womb" (*Palace* 41): "personality is cognizant of many existences [who] become agents of personality" (*Kas-Kas* 53). Already in *Palace* Harris had presented the men who accompany Donne on his quest as "the eccentric emotional lives of the crew every man mans and lives in his inmost ship and theatre and mind" (48).

In this first novel also Harris anticipated what post-structuralist critics call "the disappearance of the author," though with a different effect and meaning. Barthes proclaimed the death of the author as the exclusive and original source of meaning concomitant with his authority as the unique producer of that meaning (see, among other writings, "The Death of the Author"). The act of creation becomes in Linda Hutcheon's words "performative inscription" produced *here and now*, whose significance largely depends on the receiver's role (*Poetics* 76–77), as we know from Iser's theories. Or, according to Hutcheon, the author can be, as in Coetzee's *Foe*, an "*agent provocateur/manipulateur*" (*Poetics* 78). The disappearance of the author in Harris's fiction implies more than a provoking stance, a challenging of received truths (though it does this as well) or an escape into parody. He becomes a vessel through whom other voices speak. As he or the narrator disappears, like the "I" narrator in *Palace* or the third person narrator in *The Tree of the Sun*, the serial personalities that speak through him become capable of provoking change (like Donne in his trial when the "I" narrator temporarily vanishes). The characters thus become "agents" creating fiction themselves and even fictionalizing their creator. This dialogical process is increasingly foregrounded in Harris's later novels such as *The Tree of the Sun* and *The Infinite Rehearsal*.[7] It recalls my interpretation above of God as both Creator and Created. It also explains why the author is "an agent of real change" (Interview 1986: 2) who can still influence humanity and civilization through the transformation of both art and life. There is no doubt an element of Shelleyan Romanticism in the belief that imagination can awaken mankind, though, to Harris, the "literacy of the imagination" is first and foremost a deep perception of the fallacies and false clarities which imprison man in a one-directional role. It is not the appendage of an elite, intellectual or other, as he shows in his discussion of Beti in *The Far Journey of Oudin* ("Literacy"). Though illiterate, she *reads* Oudin and because she is intuitively capable of grasping his need in his extremity, she creates him anew.

Harris's repeated emphasis on conversion, transformation and translation is also rooted in his vision of an apparently lost tradition which he sees as "the true source of the text" when it (the text) "comes profoundly alive" ("Literacy" 22). If one keeps in mind that the "soil of tradition" is also "the soil of the world's unconscious" ("Literacy" 22–23), the text coming alive clearly shows that the author is a mediator, as indeed Harris suggests when he writes that "[the author] is susceptible to an unpredictable movement of consciousness-in-unconsciousness" ("Literacy" 23). Although critics have repeatedly emphasized the importance of transformation in Harris's fiction, little attention has been paid so far to his vision of creation as a transfer or "translation" of the substance of fiction from unconsciousness into consciousness. Yet in a much quoted essay like "Comedy and Modern Allegory" Harris refers five times to "a bridge between the collective unconscious of the human race and the miracle of consciousness" (135), a bridge "from the limbo of the lost to the limbo of the saved" (132), not a static or finished bridge but one that grows out of a response to "intuitive clues."

The ceaseless elaboration and "unfinished genesis" of that bridge is what Harris means by cross-culturalism as distinct from multi-culturalism, which designates the co-existence and recognition of different cultures but not necessarily their interaction, distinct also from the post-modernist pluralism discussed above. His most frequent example of cross-culturalism in his essays (but also fictionalized in "The Sleepers of Roraima") is that of the Carib bone-flute which points to a nascent posthumous dialogue between two cultures, one conquering, the other defeated and lost but revived imaginatively. He has explained that the Caribs used to carve a flute out of the bones of their cannibalized Spanish enemies and eat a morsel of their flesh in order to enter their mind, sense their adversarial hate, and intuit the kind of attack they might wage against themselves. It would seem that the Caribs also saw in the bone-flute the very origins of music. The flute was therefore "the seed of an intimate revelation . . . of *mutual spaces* they shared with the enemy . . . within which to vizualize the *rhythm* of strategy, the *rhythm* of attack or defence the enemy would dream to employ against them" ("On the Beach" 339, italics mine).[8] I wish to emphasize here Harris's description of the flute as a "bridge of soul" ("Comedy" 9), "a fine, a spider's web, revolving bridge, upon which the ghost of music runs, moves between the living and the dead, the living and the living, the living and the unborn" ("On the Beach" 339). The revulsive impact of cannibalism has long hidden this "mutuality" but it (cannibalism) now "begins to give ground to a deeply hidden moral compulsion" to conquer the "inner rage, inner fire associated with cruel prejudice" ("On the Beach" 339). Harris insists on the need to probe "the links between moral being [the consumption of hideous bias] and profoundest creativity," as he also metaphorizes in the bone-flute his conviction that "adversarial contexts" such as the encounter between inimical cultures can generate creativity since both destruction (cannibalism) and creation (music) coalesce in the instrument, and that catastrophe can so destroy the monolithic outlook of a people as to offer an opportunity for spiritual recovery and new growth.

Understandably then, Harris's dynamic conception of creativeness as a bridge between the invisible and the visible, unconsciousness and consciousness, a "mutuality between perishing and surviving" ("Comedy" 132), is wholly incompatible with realism, even revised, and its post-modernist forms, which he most objects to on the ground that "the postmodernists have discarded depth, they have discarded the unconscious" ("Literacy" 27) and fail to probe the deeper psychological strata in individual psyche and culture. His own insistence on the surfacing and translation into consciousness of experience buried in the unconscious also accounts for his transformation of genres. When Linda Hutcheon writes of post-modernism as an art which interrogates and pushes limits (*Poetics* 8) and explains that literary genres have become fluid (9), she exemplifies this mainly by pointing to a blurring or mixing of categories as, for example, between various forms of elitist and popular art. Harris's questioning and re-definition of traditional forms of narrative entails in practice a complete reversal of conventional expectations in major genres. The "drama of consciousness" (*Tradition* 34; 55) in which his characters have been involved from his first novel, enacting an "infinite rehearsal" yet never total mutation of established patterns of existence in the past, his "re-visions" of allegory and epic into "modern" fictional modes, these are also informed by the convertibility of experience at once personal and historical[9] which I have discussed. However sublime, Homer's great epics and Dante's *Divine Comedy* express a vision of life and death in keeping with their time and inspired by man's longing for the infinite in a form which, if imitated, can be immobilized in its very sublimity. Harris replaces the "allegorical stasis of divine comedy" by an "evolving metaphysic" of the imagination ("Quest for Form" 27; 26) which he deems necessary to save humanity from the catastrophic death-wish it has given into in its very desire for the infinite. In many of his novels "convertible images" alter the formerly separate and distinct Inferno, Purgatorio and Paradiso into fluid, overlapping states. Commenting on Donne's perception of the hell he is responsible for, when he hangs from a cliff in an invisible noose, prior to his conversion and evanescent vision of what may be called "Paradise," Harris modifies Gertrude Stein's expression of continuity ("a rose is a rose is a rose") into "a noose is a noose is *not* a noose" and even "a rose is a noose is a particle is a wave" ("Comedy" 129):

> An alteration, however intuitive, in allegorical stasis of divine comedy of existence must affect Faustian hubris. The very cornerstones of European literature may alter and acquire different creative emphases within a world that has so long been

endangered and abused in the name of the virtues of the superman, virtues that are synonymous with a lust for infinity. ("Quest for Form" 27)

It is within this perspective that Harris has revised and altered the leading thread and issue of *The Divine Comedy*,[10] Goethe's *Faustus* and major aspects of Ulysses' quest in his latest trilogy, *Carnival*, *The Infinite Rehearsal* and *The Four Banks of the River of Space*. In this latest novel Harris transforms the character and fate of his Penelope and Ulysses as radically as he had "revised" his Guyanese divine comedy in *Carnival*, a revision of epic which is also "cross-cultural dialogue between imaginations" ("Comedy" 128).

A major feature of Harris's revision of allegory, which follows from the upsurge of reality from the unconscious is the apparition of "guides" in the narrative who belong to the buried past (as Virgil guided Dante through his quest) and are "substantial to the fiction" the novelist creates, helpers in the creative process ("Validation" 47–48). One thinks, for example, of the Caribs Cristo envisions in the forest in *The Whole Armour*, of the formerly vanished yet reappearing Da Silva in *Heartland*, Hosé in *Companions* (also a literal guide through Mexico), as well as of characters acting more obviously as spiritual guides through the labyrinth of memory, like Masters in *Carnival*, Faust in *The Infinite Rehearsal*, and the characters, "live absences," who help Anselm translate "epic fate into inimitable freedom" in *Four Banks* (xiii, 9). I am, of course, oversimplifying what is actually a complex process in Harris's novels. If I am not mistaken, the guides who, as he has explained, "arise from the collective unconscious encompassing the living and the dead" are linked with, and partly personify, an "inner objectivity" ("Comedy" 127) which underlies the manifold manifestations of the phenomenological world. They usually belong in his novels with the living and the dead (see Masters in *Carnival* or Ghost in *The Infinite Rehearsal*) and partake of both the human and the divine. I think that Harris sees in the "inner objectivity" a kind of unifying function (though it is obviously more than that) embracing both reason and imagination, the undivided faculties of man which still operated in unison in alchemy. In both fiction and essays he has shown a preoccupation with the need to reconcile art and science, which were tragically separated as a result of the excessive rationalism of the Enlightenment:[11]

The Enlightenment . . . began to turn its back on the life of the intuitive imagination. It negated the necessity to visualize in new ways, to . . . re-interpret in far-reaching ways, subtle links and bridges between the arts and the sciences, between poem and painting, between music and figurations of memory associated with architecture. ("Brodber" 2)

Finally, I would suggest that the substance of fiction which comes to life through "the complex arousal of imprisoned or eclipsed faculties and their genuine — in contradistinction to sublimated — contribution to a creative humanity" ("Oedipus" 5) is what Harris has called "living fossil strata" or "live fossil myth" ("Validation" 11,5).

Space is lacking to comment on the major role and transformative potential of myth in Harris's fiction,[12] which should be the subject of a separate essay. Suffice it to say that "myth becomes a basic corrective to tyrannous or despotic immediacy" ("Liberty" 5). Harris's emphasis on the livingness of a fossil reality can be associated to the "revisionary potential within imageries in texts of reality" ("Fabric" 176). That "texts of reality" or "texts of being" (180) should be capable of "revising themselves" because they are alive (yet another formulation of the living tradition) brings to light an identification between art and life, which at first sight may resemble the disappearance of "the familiar humanist separation of art and life" Linda Hutcheon presents as characteristic of post-modernism (*Poetics* 7). Again, her example shows that the fusion takes place at a fictional realistic level, even one of "journalistic facticity"(10), whereas Harris's characters re-live the torments of calamitous events as if experiencing them or their consequences. So that while post-modernist metafiction usually stresses the fictionality of narrative as a subjective human construct no better or worse than another (if, by post-structuralist standards, judgements of value are to be excluded), Harris boldly connects the transformation of images of a terrifying past through an act of imagination with a possible rebirth from catastrophe. And just as he thinks there is no short cut to solutions of the calamities of the world ("Validation" 40), so "there is no short cut into the evolution of new or original novel-form susceptible to, immersed in, the heterogeneity of the modern world" (*Explorations* 128). As he further explained, "without a profound alteration of fictional imagery in narrative bodies . . . catastrophe appears to endure and to eclipse the annunciation [change, rebirth] of humanity" ("Quest for Form" 26–27).

Nor is this correspondence between life and art a rendering of the Leavisite "unmediated reality" Homi Bhabha criticizes (85) since Harris's not only breaks the mould of realism specific to the "great tradition" but the artist himself is, as I have argued, a mediator. Another consequence of this is that Harris's conception of language differs from the "post-structuralist views of Postmodernism which declare all attempts to turn any language into an instrument of positive knowledge utterly futile" (Bertens 22). Language is not "*self-referential*" (Eagleton 8), though Harris would probably not deny Eagleton's description of it as a "web-like complexity of signs . . . the back and forth, present and absent, forward and sideways [Harris would say backward] movement of language in its actual processes" (132). Harris's conception of language is naturally in keeping with his belief in the correspondence between art and life. Commenting on the narrator's "living, closed eye" in *Palace*, he writes:

> The living, closed eye therefore *is* a verbal construct, but it is something sculpted as
> well. In the beginning was the Word, in the beginning was the language of sculpture,
> in the beginning was the intuitive/inner voice of the mask, in the beginning was the
> painted cosmos and its orchestra of light and darkness. ("Literacy" 26)

"Language is world" Harris also wrote ("Validation" 51), stressing a correspondence which he developed in a recent discussion of justice in *The Whole Armour*:

For what is at stake . . . is the flexible placement of associations *within a pregnant form, a living language, a pregnant Word*. Such pregnant form gives life to the hollow appearance of justice. That is my intuition of fiction and . . . its bearing on the scope and capacity of the Word to come into equation with inimitable truth. ("Liberty" 9)

"To come into equation with inimitable truth" will probably mark him out as an "essentialist," as he is in one sense when he writes "That goal [of his protagonist] or infinite domain is never reached or taken but it remains an essence that underpins, translates, transfigures the ground of all experience" (*Four Banks* xiii). One must emphasize that what Harris has in mind in terms of "essence" or "centre" remains, like wholeness as opposed to totality, forever "unnameable" or "unfathomable" (Interview 1979: 24) and cannot be encompassed in any "frame of dogma" ("Liberty" 3); it can never be the privileged source of authority of any given culture or civilization. I return to this aspect of his work because, if I understand rightly, this cohering, mediating but ungraspable force (*Womb of Space* xix, 56) is also the "untrappable source of language," which *because* it cannot be trapped (*The Eye* 96) is the instrument "which continuously transforms inner and outer formal categories of experience" (*Tradition* 32). This is the transformation illustrated through his work by "convertible imageries."

It is also this mysterious reality which makes of Harris a post-colonial writer and, perhaps paradoxically, has inspired some post-colonial criticism in recent years. To place my major argument in the post-colonial context, the victims of imperialism (vanished peoples and cultures), its psychological legacies, eclipsed "areas of sensibility," and their impact on landscape(s), the present-day deprived whom the powerful choose not to see, are all part of what Harris has called "an apparent non-existent ground of being" (expressed differently above) which nevertheless possesses a "regenerative force" (Interview 1979: 19; 25). For it is on that apparently non-existent ground that the frail transformative clues appear on the canvas of existence and art. This ground of loss (both inner and outer space) is also the driving moral force of his conception of fiction as "conversion of deprivations" (*Womb of Space* 63; 137. See also "On the Beach" 339), as constant re-vision, a fiction which, in the now much-quoted phrase "seeks to consume its own biases" (*Guyana Quartet* 9). I think this phrase means more than a negation of the authority of the text and an acknowledgement of the author's inevitable subjectivity. I would suggest that it applies mainly to Harris's working method, when he revises his drafts and concentrates on them with extreme attention, "scanning them for clues" ("Literacy" 19) and revising imageries which he will not accept as final, as their development throughout his fiction shows.

The point I have been driving at is that the immaterial/material perspectives and the unconsciousness/consciousness nexus which make Harris reject post-modernism as nihilistic are the very premises of his post-colonial outlook. Harris has expressed agreement with the post-colonial position provided one is aware of a hypnotic transference of influence from colonialism to post-colonialism and the fact that the latter is still partly bound up with the former (Interview 1986: 7). His objection to much post-colonial writing is that it has adopted the realism of imperial cultures in both form and content, as some former colonies have in political practice: "punitive logic [like that of the slave owners] continues as the philosophy of post-colonial regimes" ("Oedipus" 18). He has also commented in several essays on Caribbean philistinism and its "refusal to perceive its own dismembered psychical world" (*Womb of Space* 122) as well as on the one-sided militantism of the literature and criticism of the formerly oppressed, particularly when they present themselves as "the antithesis of the thesis of white supremacy" (Ashcroft et al. 21). I have argued that his own cross-culturalism is deeply rooted in a perception in depth of lost, "alien" experience, of vanished, supposedly "savage" cultures (e.g. the pre-Columbian) with which the "civilized" must enter into dialogue as they retrieve them from the abyss of oblivion. It is precisely the "abysmal otherness," the never wholly perceptible third nameless dimension which underlies all Harris's narratives and may "bring resources to alter . . . the fabric of imagination in the direction of a therapeutic ceaselessly unfinished genesis"[13] ("Fabric" 182) which is the mainspring of Harris's post-colonialism. As he recently pointed out,

> Extremity or marginality . . . lifts the medium of diverse experience to a new angle of possibility. Marginality is not so much a geographical situation . . . it is rather an angle of creative capacity as the turbulent twentieth century draws to a close. ("Liberty" 13)

This may appear as yet another formulation of the creative potential of the subterranean tradition. But it calls for an important reservation as to the applicability of Harris's thinking to post-colonial criticism. One of the tenets of that criticism, as indeed of post-structuralism, has been the rejection of the notion of universality as an expression of cultural imperialism. Harris's view of that imperialism and his response to "universal" Western masterpieces are much more *nuancé* and, to that extent, his adherence to the post-colonial approach in criticism is a qualified one. It is not just a question of the meaning one attributes to words (though it is partly that) but also of his vision of universality, which, as much as post-colonial criticism, precludes any easy assimilation of the universal to the Western. But in this as in other aspects of his thought and writing, he has conceived his own third way. He has recently expressed his deep attachment to the English language in several essays and when he describes it as "a changing, subtle medium" which has acquired "some of the rhythms and incantatory spirit of the alien tongues of [his] mixed ancestry" ("Liberty" 13), this is not just, I think, a passing reference to the hybridization of English but a "validation" of his dynamic view of cross-culturalism and its transformative potential. He has also asserted that

> Homer, Dante, Shakespeare, Goethe are as much the heritage of black men and women as of white men and women because the triggers of conflicting tradition . . . lie in, and need to be re-activated through, the cross-cultural psyche of humanity, a cross-cultural psyche that bristles with the tone and fabric of encounters between so-called savage cultures and so-called civilised cultures. ("Comedy" 137)

These words together with Harris's insistence on "diversity-within-universality" ("Brodber" 1) point once more to the bridge between a tradition rooted in a "universal unconscious" and the creative imagination:

> The universal imagination — if it has any value or meaning — has its roots in subconscious and unconscious strata that disclose themselves profoundly within re-visionary strategies through intuitive clues that appear in a text one creates. That text moves or works in concert with other texts to create a multi-textual dialogue. ("Validation" 44)

I am aware that, while insisting on the importance of Harris's intuitive method and the bridge between the unconscious and consciousness in his creative process, I have been "hypnotized" to a large extent by my cartesian training and have presented a rational argumentation that considerable reduces and tames the creative energy, the complex vision, the significance and the stunning beauty of his metaphorical language, which inform his fiction. I don't mean by this that Harris's writing resists critical analysis, only that it is in his novels that the reader will discover the "visionary counterpoint of resources" ("Oedipus" 18) he brings to light; "the hidden numinous proportions within the mechanisms of colonialism and post-colonialism" ("Fabric" 176).

NOTES

1. Since I have mentioned Harris's affinity with Modernism, I should say here that Harris's own view of tradition is very different from Eliot's and the reverse of authoritarian though there is similarity between the two in their viewing it as a living phenomenon, and, as is obvious from his many references to Eliot's criticism, Harris admires it. Also, as we shall see, Harris's aesthetic is not "an aesthetic of the sublime" though Lyotard's phrasing of "modern aesthetics" (81) needs to be qualified.

2. Stephen Slemon also comments on this aspect of her criticism in "Modernism's Last Post" on page two in this collection.

3. I am aware that I have only drawn attention to the kind of criticism which points to post-modernist features that most clearly contrast with Harris's writing and that my brief discussion must give an impression of unqualified generalization. I would argue, for example, that Swift's *Waterland* and even D.M. Thomas's *The White Hotel* are better examples of what post-modernism is usually said to be than Fowles's novels. Some of the more original aspects of post-modernism are discussed in D'Haen and Bertens.

4. See, for example, Wilde, review article on Larry McCaffery, ed., *Postmodern Fiction: A Bio-Bibliographical Guide,* in *Contemporary Literature* XXX.1 (1989), and its conclusion: "Welcome back, World !"

5. Harris's conception of "re-vision" was expressed many years before Adrienne Rich's, a predominantly feminist concept often considered as breaking new ground. See Rich.

6. Umberto Eco has just recently expressed a similar view when he wrote that "between the intention of the author . . . and the intention of the interpreter . . . there is an *intention of the text*." Another parallel with Harris's thought (see, among others, "Comedy," "Fabric," and Harris's latest novels) lies in his assertion that "modern quantitative science is born, *inter alia*, in a dialogue with the qualitative knowledge of Hermeticism." Eco, 666; 678.
7. There is some affinity between this dialogical process and Bakhtin's conception of dialogue as explained by Julia Kristeva in "Word, Dialogue and Novel," though there are also differences. For a discussion of Harris's affinities with Bakhtin, see McDougall.
8. The full implications of Harris's interpretation of the bone-flute cannot be discussed here and I refer the reader to his essays in *Explorations* and to "On the Beach," "Adversarial Contexts and Creativity," "Comedy and Modern Allegory."
9. On the transformation of history see Slemon.
10. It is interesting to compare Harris's interpretation and "transformation" of the structure of *The Divine Comedy* with Said's in *Orientalism*. Said sees it as typical of "the Orientalist attitude in general which shares with magic . . . and with mythology [a classification Harris would strongly object to] the self-containing, self-reinforcing character of a closed system" (70). His criticism stops at Dante's rejection of Islam.
11. When alluding to this division, Harris often refers to Frances Yates's analysis in *The Art of Memory* of lost apects of tradition and of the split between "arts of memory" since the Renaissance.
12. On the subject of myth see *Explorations* and most of Harris's recent essays.
13. Harris's latest image for this "unfinished genesis" is the "ravelling/unravelling" of "the coat of tradition that never quite seems to fit the globe" Penelope weaves in *Four Banks* (121, 54–55, 58–59).

WORKS CITED

Ashcroft, Bill, Griffiths, Gareth, and Tiffin, Helen. *The Empire Writes Back: Theory and Practice in Post-Colonial Literatures*. London and New York: Routledge, 1989.

Barthes, Roland. "The Death of the Author." *Modern Criticism and Theory: A Reader*. Ed. David Lodge. London and New York: Longman, 1988. 167–172.

Bertens, Hans. "The Postmodern *Weltanschauung* and its Relation with Modernism: An Introductory Survey." Fokkema and Bertens, 9–51.

Bhabha, Homi K. "Representation and the Colonial Text: A Critique of Some Forms of Mimeticism." *The Theory of Reading*. Ed. Frank Gloversmith. Brighton: Harvester, 1984. 93–112.

D'Haen, Theo and Hans Bertens, eds. *Postmodern Fiction in Europe and the Americas*. Postmodern Studies 1. Amsterdam: Rodopi & Antwerpen: Restant, 1988.

Eagleton, Terry. *Literary Theory: An Introduction*. Oxford: Basil Blackwell, 1983.

Eco, Umberto. "After Secret Knowledge." *The Times Literary Supplement* 22–28 June 1990. 666, 678.

Fokkema, Douwe & Hans Bertens, eds. *Approaching Postmodernism*. Papers Presented at a Workshop on Postmodernism, 21–23 September 1984, University of Utrecht. Amsterdam and Philadelphia: John Benjamins, 1986.

Graff, Gerald. "The Myth of the Postmodernist Breakthrough." *The Novel Today*. Ed. Malcolm Bradbury. Glasgow: Fontana/Collins. 217–249.

Harris, Wilson. *Palace of the Peacock*. London: Faber, 1960.

——. *The Far Journey of Oudin*. London: Faber, 1961.

——. *The Whole Armour*. London: Faber, 1962.

——. *The Secret Ladder*. London: Faber, 1963.

——. *Heartland*. London: Faber, 1964.

——. *The Eye of the Scarecrow*. London: Faber, 1965.

——. *Tradition, the Writer and Society*. London: New Beacon Books, 1967.

——. *Tumatumari*. London: Faber, 1968.

——. *The Sleepers of Roraima*, A Carib Trilogy. London: Faber, 1970.

——. *Black Marsden*, London: Faber, 1972.

——. Interview. By Ian Munro and Reinhard Sander. *Kas-Kas*. Austin: University of Texas at Austin, 1972. 43–55.

——. *Companions of the Day and Night*. London: Faber, 1975.

——. *The Tree of the Sun*. London: Faber, 1978.

——. Interview. By Helen Tiffin. *New Literature Review* 7 (1979). 18–19.

——. *Explorations*, A Selection of Talks and Articles, 1966–1981. Ed. with Introduction Hena Maes-Jelinek. Aarhus: Dangaroo Press, 1981.

——. *The Womb of Space, The Cross-Cultural Imagination*. Westport, Connecticut: Greenwood Press, 1983.

——. "The Quest for Form." *Kunapipi* V.1 (1983), 21–27.

——. "On the Beach." *Landfall* 39. 3 (September 1985): 335–341.

———. *Carnival*. London: Faber, 1985.

———. "Adversarial Contexts and Creativity." *New Left Review* 154 (Nov./Dec. 1985): 124–128.

———. "A Note on the Genesis of *The Guyana Quartet*." The Guyana Quartet. London: Faber, 1985. 7–14.

———. Unpublished interview. By Stephen Slemon and Helen Tiffin. 24 April 1986.

———. *The Infinite Rehearsal*. London: Faber, 1987.

———. Interview. By Stephen Slemon, *ARIEL* 19. 3 (July 1988): 47–56.

———. "Literacy and the Imagination." *The Literate Imagination: Essays on the Novels of Wilson Harris*. Ed. Michael Gilkes. London: Macmillan, 1989. 13–30.

———. "Validation of Fiction: A Personal View of Imaginative Truth." *Tibisiri*, Caribbean Writers and Critics. Ed. Maggie Butcher. Aarhus: Dangaroo Press, 1989. 40–51.

———. "Comedy and Modern Allegory: A Personal View." *A Shaping of Connections, Commonwealth Literature Studies — Then and Now*. Eds. Hena Maes-Jelinek, Kirsten Holst Petersen and Anna Rutherford. Aarhus: Dangaroo Press, 1989. 127–140. Text of a lecture given at the University of Turin in October 1985.

———. "Oedipus and the Middle Passage." *Crisis and Creativity in the New Literatures in English*. Eds. Geoffrey V. Davis and Hena Maes-Jelinek. Amsterdam-Atlanta: Rodopi, 1990. 9–21.

———. "The Fabric of the Imagination." *Third World Quarterly* 12. 1 (January 1990): 175–186.

———. *The Four Banks of the River of Space*. London: Faber, 1990.

———. "In the Name of Liberty." Forthcoming in *Third Text* (1990). 15 pp.

———. "The Life of Myth and its Possible Bearing on Erna Brodber's Fictions, *Jane and Louisa Will Soon Come Home* and *Myal*. Forthcoming in *Kunapipi*. 8 pp.

Hutcheon, Linda. *Narcissistic Narrative: the Metafictional Paradox*. New York and London: Methuen, 1980.

———. *A Theory of Parody: The Teaching of Twentieth-Century Art Forms*. New York and London: Methuen, 1985.

———. *A Poetics of Postmodernism: History, Theory, Fiction*. New York and London: Methuen, 1988.

Iser, Wolfgang: "The Reading Process: A Phenomenological Approach." *Modern Criticism and Theory: A Reader*. Ed. David Lodge. London and New York: Longman, 1988. 212–228.

Kristeva, Julia. "Word, Dialogue and Novel." *The Kristeva Reader*. Ed. Toril Moi. Oxford: Basil Blackwell, 1986. 34–61.

Lentricchia, Frank. *After the New Criticism*. London: Methuen, 1980.

Lyotard, Jean-François. *The Postmodern Condition: A Report on Knowledge*. Trans. Geoff. Bennington and Brian Massumi. 1979. Manchester University Press, 1987.

McDougall, Russell. "Native Capacity, Blocked Psyche: 'Carnival' and 'Capricornia.' " *The Literate Imagination: Essays on the Novels of Wilson Harris*. Ed. Michael Gilkes. London: MacMillan, 1989. 152–171.

PN Review 48 (1985).

Rich, Adrienne. "When We Dead Awaken: Writing as Re-Vision." *College English* XXXIV. 1 (October 1972): 18–25.

Said, Edward W. *Orientalism*. 1978. London: Penguin Books, 1985.

Slemon, Stephen. "Post-Colonial Allegory and the Transformation of History." *The Journal of Commonwealth Literature* XXIII. 1. (1988): 156–168.

Suleiman, Susan Rubin. "Naming and Difference: Reflections on 'Modernism versus Postmodernism in Literature.' " Fokkema and Bertens. 255–270.

Todd, Richard. "The Presence of Postmodernism in British Fiction: Aspects of Style and Selfhood." Fokkema and Bertens. 99–117.

Wilde, Alan. "Postmodernism from A to Z." *Contemporary Literature* XXX.1 (1989): 133–141.

Yates, Frances. *The Art of Memory*. 1966. Penguin Books, 1969.

"The Empire Writes Back":
Language and History in *Shame* and
Midnight's Children

ARUNA SRIVASTAVA

1. *Handcuffed to and Fathered by History as She is Writ*

> To make the preparation of any account a reasonable account [the historian] would
> have to adopt an attitude towards the available material. The action of such an attitude
> is rather like that of a sieve. Only what is relevant to such an attitude gets through.
> The rest gets thrown away. The real relevance and truth of what gets through the mess
> depends on the relevance and truth of the attitude.
>
> PAUL SCOTT, Robin White in *The Jewel in the Crown*

One of the most important aspects of Salman Rushdie's work is the almost excessively self-conscious and playful process by which Saleem Sinai in *Midnight's Children* and *Shame's* narrator, through its "protagonist," Omar Khayam, try to come to terms with their personal and national histories as colonized people. In *Midnight's Children*, Rushdie and Saleem explore notions of history, time, autobiography, and writing. In *Shame*, the narrator/writer is self-conscious about his position as an Indian writer in English, exploring throughout the novel (with reference to ideas of history and time) his tortured position as a disinherited writer with a double literary inheritance.

Saleem Sinai defines himself by his relation to India's history. By writing his autobiography he hopes not only to fend off his own inevitable decay and death, but also that of his country. As one of her midnight children (195), born at the stroke of midnight on Independence Day, Saleem *is* India: he is All-India radio, a map of India, the instigator of her fierce language riots. The trials and tribulations of his body and his family are inextricably entwined with those of his country — the various births, labours and deaths in the book correspond exactly to major events in Indian history: the Jallianwallah Bagh massacre, Independence Day itself, Indira Gandhi's rise to and tenacious hold on power, her Emergency Rule, her trial. But Saleem's relationship to history is not all that simple, despite his constant assertions that he (and the other children of midnight) are "fathered by history" (118), and "handcuffed" to it (9).

As he writes the novel, Saleem wrestles with a chronological view of history, passed on by the ruling British and now part of the Indian national consciousness, and (to him) a more ephemeral, (Mahatma) Gandhian, mythical view of history — properly and traditionally Indian, but suppressed by more "progressive" ideas about history and its relation to time. The first historical model (and "model" is a very apposite term) needs the linear narrative, the act of plotting, to describe its cause-and-effect basis. Far from being objective, this type of history-telling is an act of "remembering forward" in Barthesian terms (White, "Question" 13), of knowing the end result, and linking it retrospectively to its beginning. Historical events then have no immanent structure, but only one imposed by an ideologically conditioned historian. The act of creating histories, then, is an ideological act, designed to support political and moral systems.

An imperialist venture, like that of the British in India, depends on such a traditional view of history for its sustenance. Saleem therefore quite perceptively associates his enslavement to this view of history with his parentage. This idea of lineage is a patriarchal and paternalistic historical concept and Saleem needs to know who his father is: is he British or Indian? Throughout the novel he faces that dilemma and that choice. *Shame*'s narrator writes, of Omar Khayam's adoption of Rodrigues as his father (Khayam too doesn't know whether his father is British or Indian), "choose yourself a father and you also choose your inheritance" (49). Is Saleem indeed "fathered" by this chronological, British-born(e) manipulation of history? If he is, he must live with his feeling of impotence, which is also reflected physically, in the face of an oppressive sense of destiny or fate that this mode of history entails. The impotence of the Nietzschean historical man results from the desire of those in power to control history. According to *Shame*'s narrator, this kind of history is passive and "loves to be dominated" (124). Indeed, Saleem's handcuff image not only binds him to history, but equally binds history to Saleem. Joseph Esposito writes that capitalist societies have little need for a true historical sense; rather, they romanticize it in genres such as the historical novel, and are really concerned with "frozen essences and natures" (36). Such a view is vividly evoked in Saleem's description of Indian politicians, who, in their desire for immortality, are "clutching Time in their mummified fingers and refusing to let it move" (327). Only when the British want to leave India does time move again — the sound of clocks ticking reverberates as Independence draws near. A true sense of history, then, gets lost in politically ideological attempts at control. This burial of a real historical sense, according to Roland Barthes in "Myth Today," is necessary for an ideology — in Barthes's terms "myth" is a dominant ideology — to perpetuate itself and continue to exert power (142). Peter Kemp may be describing the early Saleem, and the impulse behind a traditional mode of history, as well as its relationship to existing systems of power:

> Thus, the "modern man" who believes in his own historicity is a being who, despite historical finitude, has given birth to the illusion that he can dominate both time and the past by the sheer omnipotence of his thinking, as if there were no radical difference between now and then, between here and there, between the same and other. (94)

By using the romantic literary/historical genre of the historical novel, then, Saleem is, at the beginning of the novel, apparently supporting this conventional or traditional view of history; however, he subverts this view more and more, not only in terms of a change in his thought, but by his trouble with his story's form and structure. He finds himself constantly resisting the urge to linearize, to narrativize in the sense of historians, at the same time as fervently wishing to fulfil his and his nation's "longing for form" (300), and to record for posterity, in writing, the history of this "nation of forgetters" (37), which — because of its domination by others — is, as a nation, "simply run[ning] out of steam" (327).

As Saleem writes, he rearranges events, misremembers dates, and creates causes and effects for "real" events that are utterly fictional (he is himself a fiction after all). *Midnight's Children* points to the fact that history is a method of fictionalizing experience, as is the telling of lives — biography and autobiography. For Saleem, reality and truth are not quantifiable and not ascertainable. They are constructs of imagination and experience, and of language. For him, the truth of a story lies in its telling and is a reflection of the idiosyncratic process of selecting events from memory:

> I say yet again, "Memory's truth, because memory has its own special kind. It selects, it eliminates, alters, exaggerates, minimizes, glorifies, and vilifies also; but in the end it creates its own reality, its heterogeneous but usually coherent version of events; and no sane human being ever trusts someone else's version more than his own." Yes: I said "sane". (211)

In fact, in *Shame*, the narrator finds the creation of history to be subject to memory as an almost living and independent entity, for he faces "the problem of history: what to retain, what to dump, how to hold on to what memory insists on relinquishing, how to deal with change" (87–8).

What the imposition of an imperialist view of India's history has done, of course, is to repress the Indians' version of their own history, based on their own language and culture. Using the language of patrilineage again, Saleem explains what this has done to himself and his country "he was the child of a father who was not his father; but also the child of a time which damaged reality so badly that nobody ever managed to put it together again" (420). What Saleem attempts by writing the novel is to avoid the confining selective process involved in chronological history-telling, and instead to follow the Indian urge to "encapsulate the whole of reality" (75), to understand lives and nations by "swallow[ing]" them. The gradual change in Saleem's view of history is signalled in the following passage, in which he reiterates his claim that history-making involves this "swallowing" of lives:

> I am the sum total of everything that went before me, of all I have been seen done, of everything done-to-me. I am everyone everything whose being-in-the world affected was affected by mine. I am anything that happens after I've gone which would not

have happened if I had not come. Nor am I particularly exceptional in this matter; each "I", every one of the now-six-hundred-million-plus of us, contains a similar multitude. I repeat for the last time: to understand me, you'll have to swallow a world. (383)

2. Transcending History and the Body: Gandhi, Foucault, Nietzsche, Sinai

The insight this had given him into the possibly important part played in Anglo-Indian history by an incipient, intermittent or chronic diarrhoea in the bowels of the raj was one of the few definite academic advantages he felt he had gained by coming to India.
                    PAUL SCOTT, on Guy Perron in *A Division of the Spoils*

Saleem thus begins to come to terms with the role of the first, traditional historical mode, as well as recognizing that beyond lies a much larger, almost mythical, view of history found in Indian philosophy and religion from which the Indian concept of *māyā*, or the illusoriness of life, derives, and only foreign sensibilities (or those of the colonized, completely estranged from their original cultures) find it alien, nihilistic, and frightening. For a man like Gandhi, this second mode of historical thinking is essential. For him " 'that which is permanent eludes the historian of events. Truth transcends history' " (quoted in Gokhale 217). What he termed "inner history" could not be seen in terms of dates, events, and quantifiable time, but rather in terms of time "quite different from those of conventional history for they have a larger rhythm and a larger interval; the word used is Yuga, an entire age or aeon" (Gokhale 224). Saleem also considers this concept when he argues for a sense of proportion in the telling of stories:

Think of this: history, in my version, entered a new phase on August 15th, 1947 — but in another version, that inescapable date is no more than one fleeting instant in the Age of Darkness, Kali-Yuga [which] . . . began on Friday, February 18th, 3102 B.C.; and will last a mere 432,000 years! Already feeling somewhat dwarfed, I should add nevertheless that the Age of Darkness is only the fourth phase of the present Maha-Yuga cycle which is, in total, ten times as long; and when you consider that it takes a thousand Maha-Yugas to make just one Day of Brahma, you'll see what I mean about proportion. (194)

In this passage, we can see Saleem's understanding of the transcendental view of history, alongside the mundane concern with accuracy in numbers and dates. In an excellent article on Gandhi's philosophy of history, Balkrishna Gokhale discusses Franklin Edgerton's analysis of two strands of Indian philosophy: the interpenetration of the "ordinary" and the "extraordinary" (224). This combination of two levels of thought is what is so disturbing to a Western mind resolutely entrenched in just one, the "ordinary." These double strands also account for the totally different concept of time which is also essential to a transcendental view of history. With some irritation, Saleem remarks that "no people whose word for 'yesterday' is the same as their word for 'tomorrow' can be said to have a firm grip on the time" (106), and the narrator in *Shame* also pinpoints this as the central problem in his attempt to narrate the story of Khayami, remarking that "it seems that the future cannot be restrained, and insists on seeping back into the past" (24).

And yet, this view of history, while potentially liberating, is extremely threatening. The impulse to narrate and to create stories is an impulse to order, to make sense of an apparently chaotic world, to create a coherent sense of self. *Midnight's Children* is about Saleem's struggle to make himself and his country into a unified subject, to assert his lineage, his family and national ties, and alliances. According to David Carroll, questioning conventional history threatens the very basis of subjectivity:

> The uncertainty of the representation of the past (of history and memory) when the origin and end of history are no longer assumed to be present, when the sense or direction of history is in question, cannot simply be dismissed as constituting a subjectivist view of history . . . for it is the subject itself, as an individual or collectivity (type) that depends on teleological views of history for its support. The derivation of the individual subject . . . the subject as unified presence . . . is problematical when history is not accepted in its "domesticated," rational, metaphysical form as the optimistic resolution of contradictions. (112)

Both Saleem Sinai's and Omar Khayam's obsession with place and, in particular, family (the search for lineage, the outlining of ancestry, the adoption if necessary of "foster" family) can also be seen, in Carroll's terms, as this desire for a unified and coherent subjectivity. The desire for origin is for Carroll a desire to immortalize and retain the past. The family and the family home are the foci of this desire:

> The context of this subject is the family, which defines a structure, an enclosure where the subject takes on an identity and becomes what it is, equal to itself. Memory within this enclosure protects the identity of the subject and is a means of recalling the sense of the subject to itself. . . . The family is one as the subject is one. The family seems to have overcome the problem of the reconstruction of the past by offering a substantial, natural context in which the reconstruction can take place. (149)

Clearly, both Khayam and Sinai share this desire to be able to place the family home, family name, and family context. And, just as clearly, their lack of knowledge about their fathers, their very origins, thwarts any such attempts to reconstruct — for themselves, India, or Pakistan — a unified, coherent, sense of self, nationality or ethnicity. Saleem says as much of the personality of Pakistan when he suggests that

> at the deep foundations of their unease lay the fear of schizophrenia, of splitting, that was buried like an umbilical cord in every Pakistani heart. In those days, the country's East and West wings were separated by the unbridgeable land-mass of India; but past and present, too, are divided by an unbridgeable gulf. Religion was the glue of

Pakistan, holding the halves together; just as consciousness, the awareness of oneself as a homogeneous entity in time, a blend of past and present, is the glue of personality, holding together our then and our now. (351)

It is this dilemma of history that the narrator/Rushdie laments of the Pakistanis in *Shame*. "All migrants leave their pasts behind, he writes; it is the fate of migrants to be stripped of history" (63). Given that their origins are obscure, and are for all practical purposes non-existent, both Sinai and Khayam have to confront squarely the problem of identity and history. After he has destroyed the objects associated with his childhood, Khayam gazes in dismay at what he describes as his "massacred history" (32). For Saleem Sinai, the impetus is external; when the bulldozer robs him of his silver spittoon, he comments: "[I was] deprived of the last object connecting me to my more tangible, historically verifiable past" (432). A few pages later, Saleem tiredly admits that he is indeed "no longer connected to history" (442).

Both Khayam and Saleem fear being annihilated from and by history altogether. Khayam is afraid of "never emerging from the disintegrating history of his race" (32), and the amnesiac buddha-Sinai talks of "seceding from history" (351). Both point up the place of and necessity for discontinuity in a historical way of thinking that does not oppress, confine, and rigidify. Both India/Saleem and Pakistan/Khayam are indeed in danger of disappearing entirely from a conventional historical approach. In strikingly Foucauldian terms, Rushdie reveals Khayam, just before his massacre of his history, to be exploring "beyond history into what seemed the positively archaeological antiquity of Nishapur" (31). In his essay "Nietzsche, Genealogy, History," Foucault opposes conventional history to the search for genealogy, or the analysis of descent, which he also shows to be a very disquieting alternative, for "it disturbs what was previously considered immobile; it fragments what was thought unified; it shows the heterogeneity of what was imagined consistent with itself" (147). Foucault adds that descent attaches itself to the body (147), a statement again striking in its applicability to *Midnight's Children*. Saleem suffers history through his body. He is concerned always with its decay, which grows more and more rapid as his novel progresses. The history of India, and his own, is dependent on his nose, depleting body parts, his transistor-like head. In *Midnight's Children* the body is, as Foucault describes it,

the pretext of . . . insurmountable conflict . . . the inscribed surface of events (traced by language and dissolved by ideas), the locus of a disassociated Self (adopting the illusion of a substantial unity), and a volume in perpetual disintegration. Genealogy, as an analysis of descent, is thus situated within the articulation of the body and history. Its task is to expose a body totally imprinted by history and the process of history's destruction of the body. (148)

Foucault thus derogates the impulse of traditional history to create a unified subject, its attempt to dominate the past. Using Nietzsche's terms, Foucault prefers an "effective" history, suggesting that "History becomes effective to the degree that it introduces discontinuity into our very being" (154). What is liberating, despite the threat of fragmentation and discontinuity, is the fact that such a view of history does not allow humans to hide behind ideas of destiny, or fate. Here (in spite of some important philosophical differences), Foucault comes closest in his view of history to Gandhi's. Indeed, Gandhi is one of Foucault's "successes of history" — someone who is able to subvert the rules of the dominant group to his own ends. Although Foucault's view of humanity is far more pessimistic than Gandhi's, their views on the history of the human race show remarkable similarities. Foucault writes that "humanity installs each of its violences in a system of rules and this proceeds from domination to domination" (151). In such a system of rules, like traditional history, Gandhi felt that "the spirit of man lay buried under such events as wars and revolutions, empires and domination of one race by another" (Gokhale 217). Yet, in Gandhi's "effective" history, there is room for optimism and relief. He too believes that a sense of fate is crippling. Individuals must recognize that they have, and must exercise, their freedom to make choices. With this freedom comes the ability to confront the self (and recognize its fragmentary nature) and thus to come to terms with a type of history in which "All conflicts will be finally resolved, and history will transcend its own timebound nature" (Gokhale 223).

To Gandhi, then, as to Nietzsche (Foucault seems to valorize only genealogy as a pursuit), all modes of historical thinking are necessary, although some are more limiting than others. In *The Use and Abuse of History*, Nietzsche argues for a combination of three modes of historical consciousness: the unhistorical, which comprises the power of "forgetting," of limiting one's horizon (43); the historical, which is what we understand by conventional history — the mode from which Nietzsche feels we suffer an excess (this is the paralyzing "burden of history" which is the source of Saleem's impotence [42]); and finally, the superhistorical — a sense that allows for a greater cultural vision, one which encompasses art and religion (43). In this way, Nietzsche hopes to combat the "disguised theology" that traditional history has become (49). In fact, the initial effects of his "remedy" to the ills of the "historical" mode are described by Nietzsche at the end of his short work in terms strikingly similar to Saleem's at the end of *Midnight's Children*. Nietzsche writes:

> The unhistorical and the superhistorical are the natural antidotes against the over-powering of life by history; they are the cures for the historical disease. We who are sick of the disease may suffer a little from the antidote. But this is no proof that the treatment we have chosen is wrong. (70)

And this is Saleem:

> One day, perhaps, the world may taste the pickles of history. They may be too strong for some palates, their smell may be overpowering, tears may rise to the eyes; I hope

nevertheless that it will be possible to say to them that they possess the authentic taste of truth . . . that they are, despite everything, acts of love. (461)

The Gandhian view of history is even more encompassing, however, than Nietzsche's three modes of history, although the impulse is the same: to free people from stultifying concepts of progress and time. What is striking about Gandhi's view is its biaxial nature; it is indeed a very similar conceptual model to the structuralist one of synchronic and diachronic historical axes; but in fact subsumes both those indices into one: in Gandhi's scheme, Foucault's and Nietzsche's effective history and three modes of historical consciousness are within the realm of conventional history. Both the synchronic and diachronic, archaeology and chronology, are placed on the vertical axis, while a transcendent concept of history must also encompass, along the horizontal axis, what Gandhi calls myths and mythologies, or fictions.

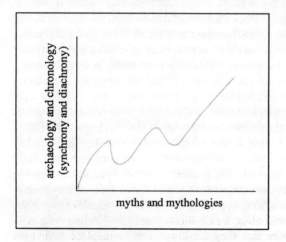

Gandhi's view of history: Foucault's and Nietzsche's 'effective' history are still in this scheme within the realm of conventional history, on the vertical axis. A true and transcendent history must encompass both axes, with each of their component parts.

This model clearly reveals the complexity of historical thinking with which Saleem is attempting to come to terms. By the end of the novel, he comes to accept the uncertainty of the forever-empty pickle jar, and acquiesces to the fact of his (and his country's) disintegration in conventional (bio)historical terms. He has, in fact, managed to see, for all its terror, a larger picture and context, and recognizes a different sense of proportion. Still, his is not the passive acceptance that outsiders see the doctrine of *māyā* leading to. Like any good son of the British Empire, he is terrified at the prospect of annihilation:

Yes, they will trample me underfoot, the numbers marching one two three, four hundred million five hundred six, reducing me to specks of voiceless dust, just as, all in good time, they will trample my son who is not my son, and his son who will not be his, and his who will not be his, until the thousand and first generation, until a thousand and one midnights have bestowed their terrible gifts and a thousand and one children have died, because it is the privilege and the curse of midnight's children to be both masters and victims of their times, to forsake privacy and be sucked into the annihilating whirlpool of the multitudes, and to be unable to live or die in peace. (463)

3. *"The Decolonizing of English"*

Hindi, you see, is spare and beautiful. In it we can think thoughts that have the merit of simplicity and truth. And between each other convey these thoughts in correspondingly spare, simple, truthful images. English is not spare. But it is beautiful. It cannot be called truthful because its subtleties are infinite. It is the language of a people who have probably earned their reputation for perfidy and hypocrisy because their language itself is so flexible . . . At least, this is so when it is written, and the English have usually confided their noblest aspirations to paper.

PAUL SCOTT, Duleep Kumar in *The Jewel in the Crown*

In an article on *Midnight's Children*, Uma Parameswaran employs the phrase "the decolonizing of English" in her assertion that the major mode of the "colonial" writer is irony. The previous section on history showed the intimate connection of writing and language to history. Indian concepts of time are reflected in their language ('yesterday' is the same as the word for 'tomorrow'), and this language determines their philosophical thinking. The English language, on the other hand, reinforces and determines the linear, chronological, narrative tendency of a more generally Western philosophy of history. As the language used by imperialists in India, English coloured, displaced, and obscured India's own languages (in part simply because English fulfilled an extremely practical function as a *lingua franca*). Such a pervasive influence could not fail to remain long after Britain granted India independence, and the confusion of the two cultures and their languages can perhaps be most clearly seen in the current state of Indo-Anglian writing (a problematic term for Indian writing in the English language). For, while inheriting a rich literary tradition, Indian writers in English must constantly be aware that they are continuing to displace their own tradition, that they are, to put it bluntly, not only working in, but also valorizing, the language of their (former) colonizers, to the detriment of others.

In *Shame* in particular Rushdie is acutely aware of this split, a sense of schizophrenia in himself as narrator. And, as in *Midnight's Children*, he correlates this to the uneasy political situation and confused historical sense of India and Pakistan. However, with respect to their sense of history, and their consequent construction of a national sense of "self," Rushdie sees Pakistan and India very differently. He has already commented in *Shame* that Pakistanis suffer from a lack of history as migrants (63). But the creation of their new national history is also problematic:

It is well known that the term "Pakistan," an acronym, was originally thought up in England by a group of Muslim intellectuals. P for the Punjabis, A for the Afghans, K for the Kashmiris, S for Sind and the "tan," they say, for Baluchistan. . . . So it was a word born in exile which then went East, was borne-across or translated, and imposed itself on history; a returning migrant, settling down on partitioned land, forming a palimpsest on the past. A palimpsest obscures what lies beneath. To build Pakistan it was necessary to cover up Indian history, to deny that Indian centuries lay just beneath the surface of Pakistani Standard Time. The past was rewritten; there was nothing else to be done.

Who commandeered the job of rewriting history? — The immigrants, the *mohajirs*. In what languages? — Urdu and English, both imported tongues. (87)

This artificial construction of history, in foreign languages, creates for Pakistan even more confusion than that already encountered by India. In *Midnight's Children*, Saleem points out what he perceives to be the fundamental differences in the two countries. India, despite her subjugation, has managed to hold on to a little of her philosophical tradition:

> In a country where truth is what it is instructed to be, reality quite literally ceases to exist, so that everything becomes possible except what we are told is the case; and maybe this was the difference between my Indian childhood and Pakistani adolescence — that in the first I was beset by an infinity of alternative realities, while in the second I was adrift, disoriented, amid an equally infinite number of falsenesses, unrealities and lies. (326)

What Rushdie is demonstrating is the necessity for a sense of tradition and continuity in language, history, and politics. Nevertheless, writing is itself doubleedged. Saleem Sinai's bodily decay is correlated with the progress of his written novel. The faster, and the more, he writes, the more rapid his decay. Clearly, when the writing is completed, the end of this process can no longer be deferred. By writing his history for posterity, then, Saleem has also ensured his complete disintegration, the prospect with which he leaves us at the end of the novel.

As if recognizing the paradoxical failure of his transcription of history, and his attempt at inscribing himself as subject as well, Saleem also narrates his story to the illiterate Padma. For Rushdie the oral tradition is strong, and is life-affirming. Saleem's attempt to escape linearity in writing cannot be completely successful, and his denigration of Padma's "what-happened-nextism" (39) is both mis- and dis-placed. Padma's discomfort as a listener is not so much at Saleem's failure to provide a linear narrative, but at his evident lack of success in *not* doing so. As a listener, within oral storytelling conventions, she needs a greater sense of continuity than does the reader with the luxury of the printed page. Nevertheless her pleasure at how fast he *can* tell a story doubtless results from its expansive and mythic quality — its evocation of a holistic historical view — rather than its linearity. Implicitly in *Midnight's Children* and much more openly in *Shame*, Rushdie seems to point to a male (and imperialist) weakness — his penchant for valuing the written word above all. It is by telling his story orally that buddha-Sinai reclaims his forgotten history, and Bilquìs Hyder's storytelling in the novel *Shame* is, like other oral histories, "a rite of blood" (77).

The act of writing does, however, have its value. Carroll finds that its very paradoxical nature is valuable in that it points to its own limitations: "writing . . . is a repeated process of reordering and reinscription from the traces of history and at the same time an assertion of the limitations of any one order or inscription" (137). Later on, he singles out the value of the novel as written form, describing quite accurately what *Midnight's Children* actually is, an attempt to reach beyond its own circumscribed genre, the historical novel: "The novel must transcend its own language, its own linearity, and constitute a space in which linearity is simply an element" (145). In a form of language which is by its physical nature linear, any written work which tries to thwart its linearity is not going to succeed, but the virtue, it seems, lies in the attempt.

Rushdie always returns, though, to his own dilemma as an Indo-Anglian writer. Some readers have commented that his work is becoming more and more British in idiom and style. In *Shame*, the narrator admits that this may be the case, but concludes that he will never be able to sever his connections with the East:

> I tell myself this will be a novel of leavetaking, my last words on the East, from which, many years ago, I began to come loose. I do not always believe myself when I say this. It is part of the world to which, whether I like it or not, I am still joined, if only by elastic bands. (28)

But, although continued writing in another language may indeed divorce a writer even further from the Indian part of her or his literary heritage, Rushdie counters the following objection: "*we know you, with your foreign language wrapped around you like a flag; speaking about us in your forked tongue, what can you tell but lies?*" (28), with this observation: "I, too, am a translated man. I have been *borne across*. It is generally believed that something is always lost in translation; I cling to the notion . . . that something can also be gained" (29).

Certainly, Rushdie's work constantly and consistently jolts its readers into an awareness of their ethno- and linguo-centrism. As a passing remark, Saleem mentions that none of the dialogue in this novel is in English; he specifically mentions that at one point he is speaking Urdu. Similarly, our assumptions of written linearity as a given are challenged in *Shame*. The Shakil sisters dismiss Khayam's desire to read English out of hand. " 'Angrez doubledutch,' said Chhunni-ma, and the three mothers shrugged as one. 'Who is to understand the brains of those crazy types?' asked Munnee-in-the-middle, in tones of final dismissal. 'They read books from left to right' " (36). These recurring acts of reader estrangements serve a political end; they force the reader to question her own ideological assumptions about literature, language, and culture, and they are a way of redressing a balance. Although the Indo-Anglian writer is treading a fine line, she can very effectively thumb her nose at the colonizer by using his system and "controlling this complex mechanism [in this case, literature] . . . so as to overcome the rulers through their own rules" (Foucault 151).

This is the sentiment behind Rushdie's delightful title in an article called "The Empire Writes Back with a Vengeance." The so-called colonial writers he writes about are determined to subvert the "myth" (in Barthes's terminology) of literary tradition and canon, to revolutionize the language through (among others) metafictive techniques. What they point to by using the dominant language is Barthes's view that the myth-language of an oppressive group is "rich, multiform, supple" — it eternalizes the world, by relying on intransitive language (149). If "myth" is essentially right wing, then writing is revolutionary and left wing and, to the consternation of the dominant group of mythmakers, extremely committed literature (Barthes 148, 156). To those who are still sceptical about the value of using writing as a political tool, Catherine Belsey cautions that any political struggle has to be verbalized in order to escape being forever marginalized (21). Rushdie echoes this view in *Shame*: "Silence: the ancient language of defeat" (89) serves as a maxim for all of Rushdie's novels. Moreover, Rushdie is not blind to the fact of his own role as political propagandist:

> Few mythologies survive close examination, however. And they can become very unpopular indeed if they're rammed down people's throats. . . . But the ramming-down-the-throat point stands. In the end you get sick of it, you lose faith in the faith, if not *qua* faith then certainly as the basis for a state. And then the dictator falls, and it is discovered that he has brought God down with him, that the justifying myth of the nation has been unmade. This leaves only two options: disintegration, or a new dictatorship . . . no, there is a third, and I shall not be so pessimistic as to deny its possibility. The third option is the substitution of a new myth for the old one. Here are three such myths, all available from stock at short notice: liberty; equality; fraternity.
> I recommend them highly. (*Shame* 251)

Rushdie's novels are intensely political. Like Saleem's, his "Anglepoised" writing is a way of co-opting political and literary power. One of the disturbing things about conflicting historical narratives, according to Louis Mink, is that they displace each other in the reader's mind — they cannot co-exist as literary narratives can. By bringing in the historical, and by forcing readers to confront their notions of both history and fiction, and of the place of commitment in literature, Rushdie is seeing to it that his stories, too, displace more politically acceptable ones. Echoing Mink, *Shame*'s narrator says that "every story one chooses to tell is a kind of censorship, it prevents the telling of other tales" (71). The narrator thus puts himself in a position of power — he has the ability to silence, rather than simply remaining silent, and admitting defeat. Rushdie's brand of metafiction is not vainly narcissistic, nor does it fall into the nihilism of linguistic determinism that much "post-modern" fiction does. He recognizes, as Saleem does at the end of *Midnight's Children*, that "life unlike syntax allows one more than three, and at last somewhere the striking of a clock, twelve chimes, release" (463). Having been released from the syntax of the novel, the reader nevertheless is left with the unmistakable taste of pickles and the assurance that Rushdie's novels, for all their complexity and playfulness, are deeply committed "acts of love."

WORKS CITED OR CONSULTED

Barthes, Roland. "Myth Today." *Mythologies*. London: Granada, 1982.

Belsey, Catherine. "Literature, History, Politics." *Literature and History* 9.1 (1983): 17–27.

Braudel, Fernand. *On History*. Trans. Sarah Matthews. Chicago: U of Chicago P, 1980.

Carroll, David. *The Subject in Question: The Languages of Theory and the Strategies of Fiction*. Chicago: U of Chicago P, 1982.

Chesneaux, Jean. *Pasts and Futures or What is History for?* London: Thaines and Hudson, 1978.

Esposito, Joseph L. *The Transcendence of History: Essays on the Evolution of Historical Consciousness*. Athens: Ohio UP, 1984.

Foucault, Michel. "Nietzsche, Genealogy, History." *Language, Counter-Memory, Practice*. Ithaca: Cornell UP, 1977.

Gokhale, Balkrishna Govind. "Gandhi and History." *History and Theory* 11 (1972): 214–25.

Gossman, Lionel. "History and Literature: Reproduction or Signification." *The Writing of History: Literary Form and Social Understanding*. Ed. Robert H. Canary and Henry Kozicki. Madison: U of Wisconsin P, 1978. 3–40.

Kemp, Peter. Review of *Beyond Structuralism and Hermeneutics* by Hubert L. Dreyfus and Paul Rabinow. *History and Theory* 23.1 (1984): 84–104.

Mink, Louis O. "Narrative Form as Cognitive Instrument." Canary and Kozicki 129–50.

Munz, Peter. *The Shapes of Time: A New Look at the Philosophy of History*. Middletown: Wesleyan UP, 1977.

Nietzsche, Friedrich. *The Use and Abuse of History*. New York: Liberal Arts, 1957.

Parameswaran, Uma. "Handcuffed to History: Salmon Rushdie's Art." *ARIEL* 14.4 (1983): 34–45.

Rushdie, Salman. *Midnight's Children*. London: Pan, 1982.

———. *Shame*. London: Jonathan Cape, 1983.

Scott, Paul. *A Division of the Spoils*. London: Granada, 1977.

————. *The Jewel in the Crown*. London: Granada, 1973.

White, Hayden. "The Question of Narrative in Contemporary Historical Theory." *History and Theory* 23.1 (1984): 1–33.

————. " The Value of Narrativity in the Representation of Reality." *Critical Inquiry* 7.1 (1980): 5–28.

Breaking the Chain:
Anti-Saussurean Resistance in
Birney, Carey and C.S. Peirce

IAN ADAM

she knew theyd gone off
the deep end got off on the wrong
foot they had been stepping out
of line losing rime for some
time or reason they could not keep
time the way they limped or walked
they were one royal pain in the ass

DENNIS COOLEY, "poet laureate"

1. *Introductory*

The post-colonial and the post-modern: how they converge, merge, diverge. They converge in appearing as prominent literary practices in post-colonial cultures, equally committed to a subversion of authoritative and monocultural forms of genre, history and discourse. They merge in such overlapping formal practices as discontinuity, polyphony, and derealization, so that writers such as India's Rushdie or Canada's Kroetsch may be analyzed under either label. But they also diverge. They diverge in historical reach, so that the post-colonial may be detected, in some cases, in the heyday of colonialism and in works of some of its most articulate defenders (e.g. Kipling) while the post-modern stays resolutely contemporary; they diverge in generic variety, with revolutionary realist writers such as Ngugi still under the mantle of one while seen as perpetuating "illusionism" by the other; and they diverge in their sites of production, the one emerging from social and political self-assertion, the other from a resolute skepticism about such possibilities of identity. That they diverge in theoretical base is also becoming increasingly evident. Though post-colonialism owes much to the stunning developments of structuralist and post-structuralist literary theory which also form the base for post-modernism, there are many indications that departures from their programmatic formalism are in process of building. This essay is intended as a provisional, tentative contribution to such construction.

The discussion in this essay will rest on a foundation firmly established, the concept of counter-discourse. Drawn, through Terdiman, from such concepts of discourse as those of Althusser and Foucault, counter-discourse introduces a notion of generalized agency which sits uneasily with the determinism of its European counterparts. Disseminated largely through the work of Helen Tiffin and Stephen Slemon (see especially Tiffin, "Post-Colonial"; Slemon, "Monuments,"), it has become phenomenally generative for both theory and critical practice. Counter-discursive modes are *necessarily* inscribed in post-colonial writing, though with different degrees of conscious articulation and prominence from work to work, artist to artist, perhaps culture to culture. The variation goes from unconscious adjustment of European models to particulars of place and local culture, to active subversion of modalities seen as imperialistically aggressive and possessive. One mode of counter-discursivity not stressed by Slemon and Tiffin can be seen as successive to the range of practices suggested above, that of indigenization. The artist, that is, becomes increasingly conscious of and chooses to work within modalities particular to his or her culture which have very little in the way of European counterparts. One thinks of Mazisi Kunene's English-language version of his Zulu epic, *Emperor Shaka the Great*, of the "nation-language" of Edward Kamau Brathwaite (Brathwaite), or of the anecdotal poem so prominently established by Canadian Al Purdy. Counter-discourse at this point moves *towards* a discourse of utter difference.[1]

All of these modes have, of course, their theoretical counterparts. In a recent essay, for example, Stephen Slemon outlines the counter-discursive development of Commonwealth critical perspectives from within a hegemonic New Critical practice (Slemon, "Reading" 108–111), and, as mentioned above, counter-discourse is itself a concept growing out of (but also critically replacing) European theories of discourse. My double project will be to trace counter-discursive practices in two texts by post-colonial writers, and to outline a non-Saussurean linguistics which points towards an "indigenized" base for post-colonial theory as well as providing a coherent account of the works considered. Inevitably, the paper will work towards a critique of the foundations of Euro-American deconstruction in Saussurean linguistics.

2. *Fathers*

I choose to work with two texts in which counter-discourse is embodied in Oedipal relations, Canadian Earle Birney's classic narrative poem "David" and Australian Peter Carey's short story "Do You Love Me?" Both concern themselves with paternal figures of authority, Carey's short story with a literal father, and Birney's poem with the eponymic David, friend and mentor to the narrator. In both the father-figures suffer classic Oedipal fates. David teaches the narrator the lore of the mountains, and is viewed with affection, not to say passion by him, but nonetheless it is through the narrator's careless error that he is crippled in a fall, forcing his disciple, in an euthanasiaistic gesture, to comply with his request to push him over a cliff. In "Do You Love Me" the father is one of the cartographers — the "archetypal cartographer"

(46) we are told — making up the elite of a nation with a passion for exactitude about itself. But the elite has problems. Despite its knowledge, or rather because of the kind of knowledge it has, things start inexplicably disappearing: first, areas of the nation (in the "nether regions"), then buildings, finally people. When his son can't tell him that he loves him the father becomes one of those who vanish. This isn't even death, it's meaner.

3. *Cartographers*

I take Carey's trope for both works. Both fathers are cartographers. They deal in codes which allow for mapping, possession. But how? Birney's David is the namer. It is important to note that he not only names — or defines — verbally, but also ostensively. He dubs a menacing mountain "the Finger," but he also shows the narrator how to vault from shale, how to climb a "chimney." He gives the knowledge which, so to speak, is "innered" to allow the poet to write of the mountains with extraordinary vividness. In Carey's father the authority is less that of namer than as coder, in his case as a professional and scientific one. His activity is epitomized in the cartogrophers' annual census, "a total inventory of the contents of the nation . . ." (Carey 44). While in Birney we get a strong intimation of the father's full *presence*, in Carey the father is sketched, an outline, a function as cartographer, subsumed into the broader category of authority ("as proud and cruel as Ghengis Khan" [46]). He doesn't teach, he instructs. His is the voice of power: "if they didn't have Cartographers the fools . . . wouldn't know if they were up themselves. . . . The world needs Cartographers . . . it fucking well needs Cartographers" (53). Nevertheless he is not confident in his power, but anxious. He knows there is something wrong.

4. *Aesthesias*

The son in Birney accepts the gift of mountain-knowledge, but is finally terrified by its power. No matter how much he seems to master it, it exceeds his possession. Beyond that possession is time and death: narrative, really. So, at the poem's conclusion, he flees down the mountain.

> I remember
> Only the pounding fear I would stumble on It [2]
> When I came to the grave-cold maw of the bergschrund . . .
>   reeling
> Over the sun-cankered snowbridge, shying the caves
> In the névé, the fear, the need to make sure It was there
> On the ice, the running and falling and running, leaping
> Of gaping greenthroated crevasses, alone and pursued
> By the Finger's lengthening shadow.
>   (Birney, *Collected* 1: 112–13)

Hyperaesthesia is too much for him.

The son in Carey is suspicious, rejects the gift of professional authority. The gift, for its purposes, possesses totally, yet outside those purposes is love, lyric, rapture. His father scares him. Here he addresses the son.

"We had no use for these areas, these deserts, swamps and coastlines which is why, of course, they disappeared. They were merely possessions of ours and if they had any use at all it was merely as symbols for our poets, writers and film-makers. They were used as symbols of alienation, lovelessness, loneliness, uselessness and so on. Do you get what I mean?"

"Yes," I said, "I get what you mean." (51)

Anaesthesia is too little for him.

5. *Forms of Cartography*

The father for Birney is associated with his literary father, "international" modernism. That is, he represents for the narrator the kind of authority in the real world that the modernists did in language. But he is, unlike the modernists, indigene, non-literary, experiential in his knowledge. The son will transform his teaching, fuse it with that of the modernists to create that paradoxical and subversive hybrid, Canadian modernism, a nationalist transformation of an international mode (Adam), of which the poem "David" is a classic example. He will share the modernist skepticism about extraterrestial absolutes embodied in religions, political parties, manifest destinies, and educational institutions, but will also share a lack of skepticism in one area, language itself. There will be a teleological certainty about the possibilities of writing. The artist can attain something like total referentiality; there will be no surplus of signified sliding away from the signifier. This confidence may be seen in "David's" dense texturing of image and sound patterns. The map is a three-dimensional relief. It is contoured to scale.

For Carey, the father is post-modernism. The story is out of the group making up his first two collections, *War Crimes* and *The Fat Man in History*, whose brilliant mixture of modes of fantasy, science fiction, and contemporary satire established his reputation. The skepticism of absolutes that in Birney stops with language is here extended to all codes: those governing maps, government campaigns, and romantic love, for example. Behind them all lie designs of master-coders, ideological controllers. Birney's goal of absolute linguistic apprehension is exposed as illusion. Language is seen as *always* occlusive and misrepresentative as it *constitutes* reality for some relative and functional end. But the father, representative of such doctrines, is, unlike Birney's David, the subject of suspicion, suspicion paradoxically raised by his own doctrines. If nothing exists but the constituting language, the objects we perceive, the selves we introspect, are illusory — indeed, should disappear. And do. Carey's prose and formal structures reflect this skepticism: the former is spare and flat, deliberately avoiding the resonances which suggest recovery and deep meaning, while his story is organized under "Notebook" headings (e.g. "Some Theories Which Arose At the Time") which underline both skepticism and cool precision. The map is stylized, a schema of lines and angles. There would be numbers.

6. *Of Blanks*

Birney's faith in absolute referentiality may seem arrogant, but it is actually deferential. Language is the servant of the real world, which, with strenuous effort, it may justly embody. The father's skepticism in Carey may be interpreted as deferential, but it is actually arrogant. It denies any ultimate meaning anterior to that assigned by that human construct, language.

At this time it is pertinent to cite J. M. Coetzee, who has stated:

> One knows of the explorer's position in front of a waste-land: his response is covering it [sic] with words. This is not different from what one does in front of a blank page. (Mayoux 8–9)

The comment applies to both Birney and Carey.

Birney filled a blank. He named the mountains in poetry, replicating the pedagogical exercise of David for readers across Canada. "David" became, and probably remains, the best-known poem in the country, appearing in numerous anthologies and in school texts for over half a century after its first publication in *Canadian Forum* in 1940. (Birney gives an entertaining account of its history in *The Cow Jumped Over the Moon*). "David" was to become, for thousands of readers, the poem that showed them that Canada (or at least part of it) was a real place, with an identity as strong as that of Wordsworth's Lake Country or Hardy's Wessex, and that it could be written about in a way that did not sound like Tennyson.

To apply Coetzee's remark to Carey, we have to re-read it, and a re-reading puts it in a more sinister light. What is this wasteland faced by the explorer? P.K. Page wrote of Cook's naming of the Glass Mountains near present-day Brisbane: "It was his gaze/that glazed each one." Cook covered an area with words, he conquered it. But there were people there, and an eco-system, of which the people were not only a part, but aware of themselves as such. It was a wasteland only to Cook, and to his language-system. His was an Imperial exercise, the venture of Carey's cartographers (cf. Carter).

7. *Interrogations*

In both Birney and Carey language concerns are paramount and expressed, as I have indicated, in the formal stylistic features, resonant and austere, of modernism and post-modernism.[3] But in both these formal features are also interrogated and sub-verted. They are interrogated and subverted by narrative. Narrative is about the failure of form, or rather about the failure of what form asserts. The language usages parallel the differing ontologies of modernism and post-modernism, but the stories undermine those ontologies. The stories are epistemological. In Birney's narrative an ostensible subject, Nature, is initially seen as a marvel but ultimately reveals itself as deceiving and treacherous, just as the real theme, language, is full of marvels but ultimately betrays those seeking the absolute — or absolution — through it. It is a kind of reversal of Yeats's "Sailing to Byzantium." Birney sails from timeless art — the transcendental signified — into time. It is a crisis of the symbol.

Carey's story is based on more cautious assumptions. The ostensible subject, again Nature, is not the object of a transcendental quest, but rather the *subject* in another sense, since it is subjugated. It is subjugated not by the view that language may be absolutely referential, as in Birney, but that it is absolute in its self-reference. The inner hum of the cartographic system determines all. But this view of language also creates a nemesis. The object of the language-code resists hypostatic definition, establishes itself as other by denial — in this case by disappearance. It is a kind of extension of linguistic skepticism, skepticism such as we see, say, in Murray Bail's *Homesickness*. Applied to that work all the remnants in the Museums would disappear, as would the author, his works, and, most painfully of all, his royalty cheques. It is a crisis of the sign.

8. *Counter-Discursivity*

Both narratives are counter-discursive of the conditions of their formation. The structure of one trembles at its point of highest apparent stability; that of the other is in process of visible erosion from its inception. The post-modern, with its gaps, indeterminacies, and abysses, is the flip side, the shadow or anima of Birney's poem, while the post-colonial, with its recuperative and tentative reconstruction of referentiality and meaning, is that of Carey's story. The post-modern inevitably threatens with succession the modern of Birney's poem, inevitably because its European terms are deeply implicated in those of the modernism it denies (Graff). Birney is later to evade those seductions of post-modernism before which he recoils in "David." His abandonment of modernism (or, more precisely, Canadian moder-nism) moves instead into more definitive post-colonial modes grounded in idiom and place and play, perhaps most clearly defined in his "In Purdy's Ameliasburg/(*first visit*, 1965)" and in his experiments in sound poetry (Adam). In moving from modernism directly into the post-colonial, avoiding the post-modern, he is not alone among the

Canadian modernists: the poetry of Dorothy Livesay or F.R. Scott provide other outstanding examples.

Carey immerses himself in post-modernism, but within its play he improvises a new game which denies it. In post-modernism's inversion of modernism, as absolute in its denial of construction as modernism was in its affirmation, the aesthetic categories of paradox and symbol are negatively reinscribed, and become those of slippage and *mise en abyme* (which sometimes does double duty as a new form of closure). It is no accident that an *hypostasized* irony is a favorite trope of both. In Carey irony is turned on the ironist. The father scorns those who deny the cartographic system — the "fools" — but the system, language without subject, words without object — is the ultimate denial. The counter-discourse calls for their re-insertion. This is not post-modern play with the textuality of self and world, but an assertion of their distinction from text, and a call for action. All the stories in Carey's collections are charged with the imperatives of anger: anger at conditions of being which poison rather than feed, which deceive rather than illuminate, which destroy rather than nourish, though it is not until the novel *Bliss* that Carey will imagine a future beyond anger, with love and honey replacing chemicals and cancer.

Carey and the later Birney deny linguistic absolutism. The son in Carey's story seeks language suggestive of what lies beyond it, *not* as transcendent, *but* as unsignified, unrepresented, just as Birney's later procedures emphasize restless variety and tentativeness. Both would be aware of a third possible reading of Coetzee's comments, their own critical reading. The landscape is neither totally apprehensible nor empty. It is not analogous to a blank piece of paper, on which anything can be written.[4] When Cook claimed the mountains with language he erred, but he would equally err to say they were not there as resistances to some forms of naming over others (as valleys, for example). Post-colonial experience is particularly sensitive to this fact. Some of the early agrarian settlers of Australia tried to write Arthur Hugh Clough's ". . . westward, look, the land is bright" onto the interior, but it didn't help them one bit. Both Birney's poem and Carey's story point to this difficulty. Their narratives point to a reality pre-existent to language, resisting arrogance about its appropriability in Birney, and arrogance about its deniability in Carey.

9. *Logocentricity*

The key for both works studied here is partiality. The awareness is of the multiple significance of "partial"; it implies both incompleteness and bias, exclusion and commitment. The awareness is of the impossibility of "presence" through language, and equally of the impossibility of "absence" as an alternative. They are aware that to use the word "absent" is to make something less than absent. In formal linguistic terms, the escape is from lexis to icon and index. Both modernism and post-modernism take the lexis as the model for language. Modernism sees the lexis — Flaubert's "le mot juste" — as the means of total apprehension; post-modernism the lexis — "le mot injuste" — as the arbitrary to which reality is the denied Other. For both, in the beginning is the word, and they never get past the beginning to process, the sentence. They stay with the great "I am" of Cartesianism, which splits subject from object, knower from known.

The attack on modernism's assumption of referentiality is, of course, post-Saussurean, but post-Saussurean thought is trapped in the same lexical fixation as the object of its critique. It is, once more, not an alternative view, but a negative re-inscription. No more than modernism does it apprehend those partially accessing signs embedded in language use that are so underlined in the writings of the post-colonial semiotician, the American philosopher Charles Sanders Peirce (1839–1914), the foundation of whose project is an assault on the skepticism of that European Cartesianism whose legacy is still manifest in post-structuralist theory (Michaels). ("I lingue, therefore I am" [Lacan], or, transvalued, "I am thought, therefore I am not" [Althusser]). As his dates indicate, the neglect of Peirce's analysis of signs, much less his place in histories of philosophy, cannot be attributed to his recent arrival on the scene. Perhaps other, more political reasons have to be sought.

10. The Terrorism of the Saussureans

I now cite the opening paragraphs of a story by Peter Carey, or rather by one of his Canadian disciples.

> They dropped from the Imperium, the flying Saussures, flying Saussures descending to conferences all over the world. They were saying that the world fucking well needs Saussureans because otherwise the fools wouldn't know if they were up themselves.[5] Soon people were saying there is only language. There are no people using it and it is about nothing. Then they and their places started to disappear.
>
> This period coincided with that in which the inhabitants of marginal territories were becoming most conscious of their history and place and what they really were.

11. Peirce

Peirce's linguistic model differs from that of the formalist and signifier-centred Saussure in placing greater emphasis on the language receiver (a rough term for what Peirce calls "interpretant") and on the referent, which he calls the "object." His semiotics restores to language theory what Saussure removed, organic subjects, who are agents in meaning, and the world, through which they both find and create it.[6] He also, while affirming Saussure's notion of arbitrariness for many signs, classifies many others as less than arbitrary. His equivalent for the Saussurean "signifier" is "symbol," but he discriminates such further concepts as "icon" and "index." An icon represents the referent, sometimes mimetically (as in a portrait), sometimes in stylized fashion (as in sign language), and sometimes analogically (as in metaphor). An index seems to correspond, in a rough way, to the Derridean "trace": it points to origins. A poem by Birney or a story by Carey, insofar as the poem/story is stylistically attributable to the authors, is, for example, an index of Birney and Carey.[7] Finally, for Peirce, as for Birney and Carey, "resistance" is an important word. For him, sign-making and the perception with which it is intertwined are inevitably partial, but it does not follow that they are doomed to the illusory status that for many is entailed by "arbitrariness." Rather concepts embedded in signs are made conditional by resistances in objects apprehended, which expose their *insufficiency*. So the objects apprehended by Birney and the father in Carey's story expose the insufficiency of the language attempting to contain them. So Birney and Carey resist the cultural signing systems imposed on them, and inscribe the insufficiency of these onto their work.

12. *Perception and Realism*

In his essay in this volume Stephen Slemon cites Craig Tapping in speaking of a "perhaps 'theoretically' contradictory" dual agenda in post-colonial criticism, that of simultaneously deconstructing the realist project of Empire and deconstructing its deconstructive project in the interests of a post-colonial "realism" (6). As pointed out by Slemon and others (notably Maes-Jelenik) elsewhere, it is in Wilson Harris that one resolution of this contradiction is found, for Harris situates that new mimetic practice precisely in the triply layered records of the shattered experience of the colonized, the overwriting documents of imperialism, and his imaginative constructs. To inscribe on and through the archive of imperialism of that whose inscription was buried: that is a "realist" project. It would meet with the approval of Peirce, who similarly multilayers signing systems, say a "common sense" realist, factual account of everyday reality, an artist's sensuous and impressionistic rendering, and a physicist's analysis of it according to abstract laws, and any given account of all three, all enmeshed in his ontological categories of Firstness, Secondness and Thirdness.

The question which remains, of course, is that of the *source* of those systems: if they are of signing, of what do they signify? One obvious answer (at least, or at last, obvious today) is that they signify each other, and that is fundamentally Peirce's position not only in relation to them but to signs generally. "All thought . . . must necessarily be in signs" (5.251); "life is a train of thought" (5.314).[8] This seems to be entirely consistent with both Saussurean and post-Saussurean thought, but there are major and qualitative differences. For my purposes I will focus on one. Peirce gives an account of why alternative signing systems are sought. There is no reason, after all, if signing is arbitrary, why we should seek alternatives to any one explanatory mode for such propositional systems as Imperial history, Derridean deconstruction, or the common sense view that the sun rises and sets. Alternative systems are sought because signs are incomplete, and perceived as such. Though the mimetic project, whereby signing system complements signing system, is virtually limitless, it is controlled by certain constants in its exercise — Peirce's "resistances" (1.431; Buchler 308–09). For this reason, what would at first appear identical with deconstructive slippage is in fact its "différance": accumulated insights rather than crushing undersights. Whether we can finally achieve any invariant foundation for knowledge through such practice is something Peirce apparently never finally settled; two major commentators disagree on the consistency with which he holds this view (Goudge 32–35; Buchler "Empiricism" 58ff.). What does seem certain is that he believed that something like perceptual access is possible and determining (cf. Derrida, who states emphatically in his most widely disseminated essay that "I don't believe that anything like perception exists" [272]), and that we could achieve highly sophisticated, albeit provisional, modes of knowledge.[9]

Among post-colonial critics, W.D. Ashcroft is perhaps the first to direct our attention to the inadequacies of the Saussurean response to such questions of context and referentiality. In his "Constitutive Graphonomy: A Post-Colonial Theory of Literary Writing," he underlines the hegemonic implications of the Saussurean subordination of *parole* to *langue* (Ashcroft 62–64). The language *form* of the works of Birney and Carey under consideration here is scarcely *langue* — a Platonic concept, an Ideal Language never uttered — but it is, like *langue*, the creation of exclusions of the varied signifying practices by which the everyday business of living is actually carried out. Peirce's semiotic is much more attuned to these practices, emphasizing not only the inevitability of multiple *paroles*, but also the desirability of awareness of them, and not only such inevitability and desirability in relation to language, but also in relation to other signing systems used in human communication. (And in non-human organisms as well — say bees [Gallie 118–19], or sunflowers [2.274]. That Peirce is not merely concerned with our species is another aspect of his assault on Cartesianism.)[10]

13. *The Story Once More*

Birney's anxiety that representation can never be more than partial, and Carey's concern that representation is unattainable and that the illusion of it is only a mask for power, which find expression in their *narratives*, are, as I have argued, also answered through those narratives. In continuing that argument I have to define more closely the role of David. I have referred to his gift to the narrator of knowledge which allows him to "create" the mountains. But the narrator does not fully understand that knowledge. As I have suggested, in an obvious way he does not understand the lessons about death. In a less obvious way he does not understand the larger lesson about time, when David shows him fossil remains of trilobites which indicate that the Rocky Mountains were once part of a sea-bed. For the language of the poem, freezing the mountains as mountains, symbols of permanence, modernist monuments, does not convey that. The fossil remains are, of course, in Peircean terms, indexes, just as the ostensive language of climbing training referred to earlier is Peircean icon, or sign language, if you like. David's language represents a plurality of signing systems, and is in sharp contrast to that of the narrator, moving uniformly in the freighted symbolic discourse of high modernism. The contrast embodies the major lesson that the narrator does not understand, that no one signing mode is privileged in access to knowledge, but rather it is through their plurality that we may arrive at knowledge, or, perhaps more precisely, the approximation of knowledge.

When I consider the analogue in Carey's story I have to break down the residual symmetry of this paper, a symmetry which in some ways echoes the binary structures of presence/absence, either/or, like/unlike, Self/Other it has suggested these narratives attack. For the paper, as for the narratives, the reality is awkward, ungainly, and asymmetrical, because the father-son opposition with which I began cannot be sustained. The filial narrator of "David," in his quest for the poetic absolute, is closer to the father of Carey's story than to the son. He strives for the high symbolic mode just as the father recognizes only one privileged discourse in the symbols of a science. To return to Captain Cook, we have to remember that P.K. Page's poem is in praise of him as an *artist*: "his tongue/silvered with paradox and metaphor." If Cook is an artist, is Birney a conquerer? Certainly in relation to the native peoples of Canada he can be seen as such, though it would be absurd to see as identical to Cook's purpose the other dimension of his *context*, one of appropriating a universalist modernism in order to patriate it. But the absolutism of the attempt at control is tellingly similar.

The signifier-fixation of the father in Carey is an impossible denial. Signifiers (or "symbols") cannot function alone for communication; not only do they grow etymologically out of referentially oriented iconic practices (2.280; Hamilton), iconic and indexical practices accompany them in all linguistic use (2.280; 2.293–95; Goudge 146–47). Recent work in attempts at computer (Artificial Intelligence) simulation of human use of language is confirming Peirce's insight (Colomb), reinforcing the claim frequently made that he was the greatest nineteenth-century philosopher. The father's insight into his lack and the lack itself are expressed in "A Contradiction": "We only exist through the love of others," he says, but he cannot give love himself: "Look at those fools . . . they wouldn't know if they were up themselves" (50). "Love" for the father is literally an empty symbol; it has no referent; only contempt and fear — the solipsistic feelings — have reality. It is the son in Carey's story, in his feeling for the something more than "single vision," who becomes linked to the paternal David, with his awareness of multiple discourse, conscious that a mountain may be a poetic "Finger," a geological blink, a site for a shale springboard, or a source of death. Beyond fathers and sons lie the post-colonial artist, the post-colonial venture.[11]

NOTES

1. See Pratt 249–50 and During 373–74 on the virtual impossibility of *total* indigenization.
2. The body of David.
3. Of two dominant modes of post-modernism, the austere and the exuberant, and, the minimalist and the maximist forms of the denial of realism, Carey's story falls into the minimalist category.

4. Though one could engage the subtleties of writing "I am not writing this on a blank piece of paper."

5. Cf. Michael Awkward's comment in "Appropriative Gestures" that post-colonial critics simply have to "master the discourse of contemporary literary theory" (cited Slemon and Tiffin, "Introduction" xiii) and, for a contrast along the lines of this "story," see Christian's essay.

6. My focus in this paper is on the sign's relation to the object. For a detailed discussion of its relation to the interpretant, and of the inadequacies of the Saussurean dyadic sign system, see Sheriff's important book.

7. Peirce is not, generally, an easy philosopher to read, but he has a flair for a telling phrase ("Anything which startles us is an index . . ." [2.285]), or for a concrete example, viz.: ". . . a constituent of a Symbol may be an Index, and a constituent may be an Icon. A man walking with a child points his arm up into the air and says, 'There is a balloon.' The pointing arm is an essential part of the symbol without which the latter would convey no information. But if the child asks, 'What is a balloon,' and the man replies, 'It is something like a great big soap bubble,' he makes the image a part of the symbol" (2.293). See note 8, below.

8. References are first to volume, then to paragraph number in the *Collected Papers*.

9. Another indication of Peirce's departure (*avant la lettre*) from post-structuralism may be seen in his rejection (*avant la lettre*) of the post-structuralist metaphor of the signifying "chain." A chain is no stronger than its weakest link; Peirce prefers the figure of "a cable whose fibers may be ever so slender, provided they are sufficiently numerous and intimately connected" (5.265).

10. Feibleman explains this best: " 'Every thought is a sign' (1.538; 5.253) but not every sign is a thought. Subjectivism or psychologism is easily avoided in Peirce's logic in that the category of signs is greatly wider than that of thoughts. Of a legisign Peirce says, 'This law is usually established by men.' (2.246) Usually — but not always or necessarily. Again, the interpretant is a second 'and more developed' sign created by the representamen in the the mind of 'somebody.' (2.228) It is clear that Peirces's emphasis is on the arousal of sign by a sign, and that 'somebody' means anybody, or anything, capable of receiving a sign. Where the semiotic relation becomes a series, the 'interpretant becoming in turn a sign,' (2.203) 'no doubt, intelligent consciousness must enter into the series,' since nothing else, as far as we have been able to discover, is capable of receiving such developed signs as the hierarchy of representation produces; yet even here participation by intelligent consciousness is only an element in the relation and not its determining factor" (95, n.18). Post-structuralist thought, in restricting sign theory to human language, remains anthropocentric.

11. A version of this article was originally delivered at the fourth biennial conference of ACSANZ (Association of Canadian Studies in Australia and New Zealand), Canberra, 22 June 1988. My thanks to my colleague Lee McLeod for his insights on Birney, and to University of Calgary graduate students Rick Patterson and Donna Batycki for their insights on Australian post-modernism and allegory respectively.

WORKS CITED

Adam, Ian. "Marginality and the Tradition: Earle Birney and Wilson Harris." *Journal of Commonwealth Literature* 24.1 (1989): 88–102.

Ashcroft, W.D. "Constitutive Graphonomy: A Post-Colonial Theory of Literary Writing." Slemon and Tiffin, 58–73.

Awkward, Michael. "Appropriative Gestures: Theory and Afro-American Literary Criticism." *Gender and Theory: Dialogues on Feminist Criticism*. Ed. Linda Kauffman. London: Blackwell, 1989. 238–48.

Bail, Murray. *Homesickness*. London: Faber, 1980.

Birney, Earle. *The Collected Poems of Earle Birney*. 2 vols. Toronto: McClelland and Stewart, 1975.

———. *The Cow Jumped Over the Moon*. Toronto: Holt-Rinehart, 1972.

Brathwaite, Edward Kamau. "English in the Caribbean: Notes on Nation-Language and Poetry An Electronic Lecture." *Opening Up the Canon*. Selected Papers from the English Institute, 1979. New Series, no. 4. Ed. Leslie A. Fiedler and Houston A. Baker, Jr. Baltimore: Johns Hopkins UP, 1981. 15–53.

Buchler, Justus, ed. *Philosophical Writings of Peirce*. 1940. New York: Dover, 1955.

———. *Charles Peirce's Empiricism*. New York and London: Kegan Paul, Trench, Trubner & Co. Ltd., 1939.

Carey, Peter. *Bliss*. London: Picador, 1981.

———. *Exotic Pleasures*. London: Picador, 1980. Made up of selections from *The Fat Man in History* and *War Crimes*. St. Lucia: U of Queensland P: 1974; 1979.

Carter, Paul. *The Road to Botany Bay : An Exploration of Landscape and History*. Knopf: New York, 1988.

Christian, Barbara. "The Race for Theory." *Cultural Critique* 6 (1987): 51–63.

Colomb, Gregory G. and Mark Turner. "Computers, Literary Theory and Theory of Meaning." *Future Literary Theory*. Ed. Ralph Cohen. London: Routledge, 1989. 386–410.

Cooley, Dennis. "poet laureate." Forthcoming in *ARIEL*.

Derrida, Jacques. "Structure, Sign and Play in the Discourse of the Human Sciences." *The Languages of Criticism and the Sciences of Man: The Structuralist Controversy*. Ed.

Richard Macksey and Eugenio Donato. Baltimore and London: Johns Hopkins UP, 1970. 247–72.

During, Simon. "Postmodernism or Postcolonialism?" *Landfall* 39.3 (1985): 366–80.

Feibleman, James K. *An Introduction to Peirce's Philosophy*. London: Allen & Unwin, 1960.

Gallie, W.B. *Peirce and Pragmatism*. Harmondsworth: Penguin, 1952.

Goudge, Thomas A. *The Thought of C.S. Peirce*. 1950. New York: Dover, 1969.

Graff, Gerald. "The Myth of the Post-Modernist Breakthrough." *The Novel Today*. Ed. Malcolm Bradbury. London: Fontana, 1977. 217–49.

Hamilton, Gordon. "Alphabet." Unpublished paper.

Kunene, Mazisi. *Emperor Shaka the Great*. London: Heinemann, 1979.

Maes-Jelenik, Hena. *Wilson Harris*. Boston: Twayne, 1982.

Mayoux, Sophie. "J.M. Coetzee and Language: A Translator's View." *Commonwealth* 9.1 (1986): 8–10.

Michaels, Walter Benn. "The Interpreter's Self: Peirce on the Cartesian 'Subject'." *Georgia Review* 31 (1977): 383–402.

Page, P.K. "Cook's Mountains." *A 20th Century Anthology: Essays, Stories, and Poems*. Ed. William New and W.E. Messenger. Scarborough, Ont.: Prentice-Hall, 1984. 246–47.

Peirce, Charles Sanders, *Collected Papers* (8 vols.). Ed. Charles Hartshorne, Paul Weiss and Arthur W. Burks. Cambridge, Mass.: Harvard UP, 1931–58.

Pratt, Mary Louise. "Margin Release: Canadian and Latin American Literature in the Context of Dependency." *Proceedings of the Xth Congress of the International Comparative Literature Association, 1982*. Vol. 2. New York: Garland, 1985. 247–256.

Sheriff, John K. *The Fate of Meaning: Charles Peirce, Structuralism, and Literature*. Princeton N.J.: Princeton UP, 1989.

Slemon, Stephen. "Reading for Resistance in the Post-Colonial Literatures." *A Shaping of Connections: Commonwealth Literature Studies—Then and Now*. Ed. Hena Maes-Jelinek, Kirsten Holst Petersen and Anna Rutherford. Mundelstrup: Dangaroo Press, 1989. 100–115.

———. "Monuments of Empire: Allegory/Counter-Discourse/Post-Colonial Writing." *KUNAPIPI* 9.3 (1987): 1–16.

Slemon, Stephen and Helen Tiffin, eds. *After Europe: Critical Theory and Post-Colonial Writing*. Mundelstrup: Dangaroo Press, 1989.

———. "Introduction." *After Europe* ix-xxiii.

Tapping, Craig. "Literary Reflections of Orality: Colin Johnson's *Dr. Wooreddy's Prescription for Enduring the Ending of the World.*" Paper delivered MLA Convention, New Orleans, December 1988.

Terdiman, Richard. *Discourse/Counter-Discourse: The Theory and Practice of Symbolic Resistance in Nineteenth-Century France.* Ithaca: Cornell UP, 1985.

Tiffin, Helen. "Post-Colonial Literatures and Counter-Discourse." *KUNAPIPI* 9.3 (1987): 17–34.

Post, Post and Post. Or, Where is South African Literature in All This?

ANNAMARIA CARUSI

There is a rupture in South African literary discourse between the practices of literature and of literary criticism on the one hand, and the type of discourse about literature produced by post-structuralist theory and by post-modernism generally on the other. This rupture marks not only an incommunicability, but a mutual mistrust. In a sense, it is the result of South Africa's "post-colonial status" — or rather, of the fact that this status is in itself questionable.

The relation between post-structuralism and post-modernism and South African literary discourse will form the bulk of this article. More specifically, I will be restricting myself to a particular type of discourse within South African literary production, that of criticism and prescription produced under the rubric of liberation and resistance literature. I wish to place this discourse firmly on an institutional basis, as I will those of post-structuralism and post-modernism, particularly in relation to the university department teaching literature or literary theory. These institutions are one of the sites in which claims to culture and "cultural heritage" are being staked, usually along nationalistic lines. (See During, "Cultural Values," and Kistner for critiques of the discourses of nationalism and national philology.) Academics are being challenged here in a way that puts on the line not only the type of material included in the teaching curriculum but the manner in which this is being taught.[1] To some extent, this can be traced back to the different perspectives on colonialism and post-colonialism in South Africa.

I wish to argue then that South African literary production is being tossed about amongst these three "posts," without finding a particularly comfortable position in any one of them. At the crux of this is the question of the applicability or non-applicability of the post-colonial label. The type of things that are said about South African literary production, what it is, what it should be, stem from the uneasy hold of the post-colonial label on the South African context generally, and in a very specific way, on any form of its cultural production. Attitudes towards the label are differentiated according to linguistic and racial position, and more directly, in terms of political standpoint. If one thinks along the lines of the importance of the consolidation of national language (in South Africa, national languages — Afrikaans and English), and through this of a national culture, including racial, social and religious practices, there is a large part of the (white) population, for whom the label "post-colonialism" is not an issue at all. Post-colonialism, as a desirable state of affairs, has been accomplished, de facto, and in a most successful manner. The South African nation exists because of the success of the construction of Afrikanerdom. The only problem now is to defend it.

This is no small problem when one considers the numbers for whom post-colonialism is not an issue, not because it is a fait accompli, but because it never happened. For the black majority, whose literature however has a minority status in terms of the South African and international canon, to speak of post-colonialism is pre-emptive; in terms of political desirability, it is anyhow more useful and more practical to speak of "post-apartheid": the colonizer will not be got rid of, precisely because he does not see himself as such. What then is the use of the term "post-colonial" in a context where it is not seen as applicable by either one in the customary colonizer/colonized opposition, and where the terms themselves are in question?

Whether or not post-colonialism is a term which could describe an existing state of affairs in South Africa does not exclude the usefulness of post-colonial discourse for liberation and resistance literature. Firstly, in its recognition of the desire of a colonized or subjugated people for an identity and for self-determination (During, "Postmodernism" 44), it focuses attention on the central position of cultural production in the attainment of those goals in real terms. This is of particular importance in South Africa where almost every other path of resistance and of reconstruction is criminalized. Although there are evidently a number of similarities between South African cultural productions and those of the rest of Africa and of much of the previously colonized Third World, there is one crucial point of difference: in South Africa there is still a liberation struggle in the true sense of the word. For that reason, and because of the outlawing of other grassroots political activity, there is much at stake in the cultural arena.

Secondly, the discourse of post-colonialism has placed itself in a position to counter, with varying degrees of success, imperialistic strategies be they in the political, economic or cultural sphere. Whereas colonialism may not be an appropriately descriptive term for the way in which subjugation is carried out in this country, neo-imperialism certainly is.

Somewhere between the imperialist in South Africa who effectively says: "we are already there; see our Opperman, see our Van Wyk Louw, see even our Brink, our Gordimer" (and where it is a question only of throwing off the stigma of provinciality), and the resister who says "but we are not — see *your* Opperman, *your* Van Wyk Louw, yes, even *your* Brink and Gordimer," there are bodies and skins, the *visible* signifiers of either statement, whose identities are being specified, constructed, via a cultural discourse where the pluralism of post-modernism has no place at all, where, above all, it is a question of ultimate hegemony.

*   *   *

In my discussion of South African literary discourse, I wish to emphasize its three main thrusts: militancy or the battle-cry for freedom, where the writer reflects and gives voice to an oppressed people; the revaluation of humanism and especially African humanism; and the position of Marxist discourse, especially the notion of consciousness. It will be seen that each of these goes hand-in-hand with the discourse of liberal democracy. In view of the attempt to institute a post-apartheid society in South Africa in terms of a new (but original) national identity, a pre-colonial "innocence," and the urgent need for political intervention in writing, it would seem that post-structuralist and post-modernist discourses on the one hand, and liberation literature on the other, have nothing to say to one another. Therefore the relation between these would appear rather to be a non-relation: the emphasis on "identity" and unequivocal political standpoint eliminates it — or its very possibility — and would appear to set the one against the other from the outset. Post-structuralism and post-modernism, informed by such theories as the deconstructive and the psychoanalytic, permit neither self-determination nor identity. The trajectories of these discourses would appear then to be profoundly inimical to one another. However, this need not necessarily be the case: indeed dialogue between the two could not only be useful, but could be strategically necessary for the continuation and development of both projects. Post-structuralism and post-modernism are presently locked in a logical aporia as theoretical constructs. Post-colonialism, in its continued subjection to cultural and epistemic imperialism finds itself in the impossible situation of attempting to define itself on its own terms, while an examination of the terms and categories shows that there has been an internalization of Western discursive formations. That is, whereas there may be a difference in content, such categories as poetry and the novel, as well as a whole rhetorical armature, still persist.

In a recent article, the poet Don Mattera, in an outburst of liberation rhetoric, describes what he sees as the political status of the writer:

> And through the flow of our blood and our ink in the trenches of struggle, many of us have emerged to cultivate our honour and dignity and so forge keener blades of resistance through a literature of liberation, and by our practical sacrifice in the battlefield. Marching side-by-side with the black working class, and recording their refusal to be bruised down, black writers and other artists have etched for themselves a place of honour. (4)

The attitude towards literary production which underlies statements such as these is one which sees a structural similarity between what writers do in their poetry and stories, and what political or trade union activists do in the political and economic fields. As hyperbolic as it may sound, militant writers, who have often been affiliated with the Black Consciousness movement, have suffered exactly the same harassment as other activists. The authorities must therefore feel threatened by this type of discourse, although in Euro-American circles the direct political significance of writing is negligible. The reason for its power is precisely that it is at the furthest remove from post-modernism. Nevertheless, the rhetoric which is used to heighten the consciousness of the oppressed, and which should, and usually does purport to, reflect an essentially black experience, is very English and white in character. Its terms could be easily seen as those of a patriot shouting "Rule Britannia!"

The persistence of such discursive strategies is evident in much of black nationalism. One of its forms is the assertion that the "best" of Western liberal-humanism has always been a part of black tradition, which has however disintegrated under pressure from apartheid structures. Thus Eskia Mphahlele, in *Poetry and Humanism: Oral Beginnings*, makes a case for the compatibility and interchangeability of Western and African humanism, using, in particular, the work of Heidegger as a bridging point. This bid to reaffirm the equality of African culture with Western culture is not limited to literature: Nelson Mandela, in his writings against apartheid, states that the basic democratic thrust of liberal humanism is something which he learnt not in law school, but at the knees of his elders.

> The structure and organization of early African societies in this country fascinated me very much and greatly influenced the evolution of my political outlook.... There was much in such a society that was primitive and insecure and it certainly could never measure up to the demands of the present epoch. But in such a society are contained the seeds of revolutionary democracy in which none will be held in slavery or servitude, and in which poverty, want, and insecurity shall be no more.... (quoted in Meer 12)

Side-by-side with a discourse which affirms equality via sameness, there is that which revalorizes the difference of Africa. At times, what is to be found here is a positing of oppositionality, such that the binary oppositions of Western systems are affirmed by their very difference from African systems of thought. Thus we often find descriptions of the collective and communal nature of African art and oral literature, as opposed to the highly individualistic Western author-position; communal ownership in African societies as opposed to the materialistic greed of capitalism; African sexual expression, free of guilt-producing oedipalizing mechanisms, as opposed to Western sexual pathologies. This type of oppositionality can occur only where Western epistemic systems have become so powerful that they achieve universal value, to the extent that the colonized body identifies its difference in terms of the imperialist's binaries.

The discourse which would most likely seem to approximate that of black nationalism, and which has proved itself as strategically most useful, is that of Marxism. The emphasis on the working class has already been seen in Mattera's statement above, but it is also evident in the flourishing trade union theatre. At times South African and especially black literature is indicted for an over-emphasis on racial oppression to the downplaying of class and economic oppression. In a criticism of the stories of Mtutuzeli Matshoba, Michael Vaughan finds Matshoba's work to be limited because "There is no emphasis upon the positive potentiality of specifically working class consciousness, or working class forms of solidarity" (317).

The assimilation of racially oppressed people to the proletariat is, however, in itself limiting. While the fact that the masses do indeed function as a labour pool for neo-imperialism seems to support such a potential characterization (as does trade-union solidarity), this effectiveness is disputable in the cultural arena, and since an important part of opposition is precisely being played out in the bid for cultural dominance and the part it plays in the forging of national identity, a basis for cultural activity in working class culture is a limitation and foreclosure of other possibilities which may set in motion the more significant effectiveness of radical difference.

While the usefulness of Marxist strategies for opposition movements should not be minimized, their terms need to be looked at more closely. This very usefulness hinges on the notion of consciousness, the possibility of conscientizing and therefore mobilizing. With this emphasis on consciousness, post-colonialism lays itself open to a re-colonization by its very dependence on the notion of the subject as a *humanist* subject, and therefore inherits the limitations of the *imperialist* subject: in this case it would simply be a matter of replacing one ideology with another, with no difference in underlying structural relations occurring. Spivak states that "It is the force of a crisis that operates functional displacements in discursive fields" (202). This "falling back" on positivist essentialism would then appear to cause post-colonialism to attenuate the full effect of the crises of post-colonial contexts.

Calls for a return to pre-colonial identity based on just such a view of conscious-ness are evidently self-contradictory, since they construct identity precisely in the same terms as the bourgeois imperialist subject, cloaked however in a discourse of return and recovery. The conscientizing programme of literary discourse is apparent in prescriptions of what black or opposition literature and criticism *should* look like. Mphahlele has formulated his programme for black writing as follows:

> [Black people] need to be told now who they are, and where they come from, and what they should be doing about these things that we're talking about. That's where the scholar comes in; he must exploit that consciousness, the black consciousness, so as to probe deeper into the personality and move forward. (quoted in Manganyi 44)

Such statements, together with calls for a greater realism and reflection of "real conditions" in literature would seem to imply that what the black man *is* (let alone the black woman) is something which is simply recoverable — something essential as yet hidden by the decades of apartheid rule, but which can be recuperated in a pure form, and mobilized against the dominant culture. But original African culture, which would include perhaps a mode of subject-specification different from Western culture, has been eradicated and hybridized to a virtually irrecoverable degree. Furthermore, a discourse which includes in an un-ironic and un-parodic way terms such as "identity," "consciousness," "origin" appears both regressive and reactionary from a post-structuralist point of view. But a validation of the one discourse as against the other does not necessarily follow. In the next section, I will argue that it is precisely at the point where post-structuralist theory cannot account for post-colonial discourse, and where post-modernist literary strategies are shown to simply not be up to the post-colonial project, that they themselves collapse as viable discourses aimed at transformation.

*   *   *

Post-structuralism is often identified almost completely with Derridean deconstruction; the simultaneous development of a critique of humanism in the works of late semioticians such as Barthes and Kristeva is often ignored. In this way, the original thrust of post-structuralism as a contestation of bourgeois structures is attenuated. It is particularly in the project outlined by Kristeva in her reworking of semiotics into semanalysis that the desire for transformation and for a form of political "responsibility" is most evident. That this project finally gave way to an almost neo-romantic emphasis on the subject in her work as well as in that of Barthes is symptomatic of the post-structuralist project when it is confronted with the question of the political. Overcome by the multiple and insidious ways in which subjects are determined in a history, and in which modes of action are constrained and constantly compromised, or simply contradictory in terms of underlying theoretical presuppositions, it is the "individual experience" of *a* subject — albeit split, decentred and fragmented — which comes to be focused on. The culmination of this may in some ways be seen in Barthes's assertion in *The Pleasure of the Text* that "The text is (should be) that uninhibited person who shows his behind to the *Political Father*" (53). Herein lies the entire trajectory of post-structuralist political concerns.

The underlying reason for the difficulty that much of post-structuralism has in dealing with the political, or modes of political intervention, lies in the form which its critique of humanism, intertwined with the critique of Western metaphysics and of rationality, has taken. Post-modernism, as a cultural phenomenon, is generally theorized from a post-structuralist perspective. For this reason, and also because it shares the epistemic conditions of post-structuralism, it ultimately finds itself in the same position with regard to the political as does post-structuralism.

The metaphysical tenets of transcendence, closure and rationality are subverted in various ways by post-structuralism. The closure of dialectical negation, of binary oppositions in which the terms have always already been marked as positive or negative, the finitude of the Logos and of Rationality, the unity and transcendence of the subject of a teleological History: none of these has escaped the attacks of post-structuralism. Lacan's fragmented and split subject, constituted not in fullness but as a lack, Kristeva's significance, which constantly overflows and subverts the limits of the Logos, Derrida's différance, which reduces Meaning to a trace of absence/presence, Deleuze's desiring machines which attack the underpinnings of any Rational action, these are just some of the forms in which the foundations of a metaphysical Truth and the humanist subject which is concomitant with it have been radically undermined.

The post-structuralist project can in many ways be seen as the affirmation of difference as pure negativity, giving way to an infinite pluralism or dispersion: the index of its failure is the point at which it erupts into a positivity. With projects of overt political commitment, such as that of Kristeva, it is this very commitment, this desire for transformation which marks the point of the eruption into positivity. This is the point at which the theory becomes incoherent and self-contradictory. This is also the reason why every attempt to engage deconstruction in the service of a political agenda is immediately doomed to failure. This failure is at the same time the very proof of deconstruction.

If difference is to be followed through to its most radical conclusion, there is no possibility of marking a point in a signifying chain as just or unjust, no possibility of judging at all or even of deciding which is the "better" of two alternatives: in the terms of différance alternatives are textual traces endlessly open to deconstruction; no finality is possible. The subversion of Truth then brings with it a complete instability of rationality, with the consequence of the untenability of any political position. Western post-structuralism, despite its anti-humanist and transformative stance, offers neither a foundation for political action, nor any type of rationalization for a particular type of transformation.

The same conditions can be seen to hold true when one carries this argument into the realm of post-modernism. If post-modernism is characterized by a crisis of legitimation — which has also been shown to be a crisis of rationality[2] — in which social and cultural narratives co-exist in a utopia of equality and in which no narrative hegemonizes another, the political effectiveness and even desirability of any intervention is called into question. Undecidability, multiple and endless possibilities of meaning, the parody of the past which Linda Hutcheon places at the crux of the political effectiveness of post-modernism ("Beginning," "Politics") have no place in a context of real political urgency, where there is a need not for endless self-reflexivity, but for definite decisions to be made: in post-colonial literature the past is called upon, not as a parody, but in deadly earnest.[3]

If one takes only these aspects of post-structuralism and post-modernism into account, it is small wonder that Habermas has relegated them to the realms of neo-conservatism. Post-structuralist difference in this sense makes no difference at all.

However, to stop here and simply dismiss the project as irrelevant and politically ineffectual is over-hasty: its critique of humanism cannot simply be brushed away; one cannot continue as though it had never been. Something has changed in the discourse of the human sciences, and this change must be acknowledged and dealt with. Post-structuralism has made it impossible to continue simply on the road of self-present Rationality and Enlightenment; however, it is at the same time impossible for post-structuralism to continue in an indefinite affirmation of difference.

From a desire to overturn and transform the metaphysical tenets which underlie structuralism as a theory, as well as bourgeois institutions, post-structuralist thought has arrived at a point where it is incapable of transforming itself. Its radicalization of the tenets of structuralism, with its implicit transcendental subject and belief in the possibility of developing descriptive models for any system of signification pitted post-structuralist thinkers against the last avatar of metaphysical humanism. While its critique proved effective at each point at which it inserted itself, it has also consistently come up with the same limit to thought in each of its forms: the endless duality of the subject-object relation, an effect of the empirico-transcendental doublet posited by Foucault as being the condition for the modern concept of Man. That is, with the modern episteme and the collapse of classical categories of representation, man becomes at once the object of knowledge and the knowing subject (Foucault 323).[4] At the moment of this redoubling, finitude becomes the condition, as well as the limit of knowledge. The negative relation of the infinite — ultimately another figure of finitude — presents itself as anterior to the empiricity of man, as well as to the knowledge he could gain thereof. The result is "the interminable play of a redoubled reference: if knowledge of man is finite, it is because he is caught, within possible liberation, in the positive contents of language, of labour and of life; and inversely, if life, labour and language present themselves in their positivity, it is because knowledge has finite forms" (327). The result of this redoubling, in turn, is the introduction of the unthought, and the unthinkable, in modern forms of knowledge. "A form of reflection is installed ... where for the first time the being of man is in question, in this dimension wherein thought addresses itself to the unthought which articulates itself within man" (336).

The closure of the subject-object relation may be the goal of post-structuralist critique, but the attempts to account for this relation, and more specifically to posit something which is neither subject nor object (but which allows for the underlying process of infinite difference, for example) results in the postulation of something which resembles a zero-degree but which comes dangerously close to a repository for the ineffable, the transcendent. The forms which it takes are many: the unnameable, the unpresentable, the abject, the unknowable; in the language of psychoanalysis, the lack; in the language of deconstruction, the blank space; in the language of the early Foucault, death. Each of these terms can also be used to describe what for post-structuralism and all modern thought, is unthinkable: the otherness of the Other, which is by definition nothing in itself, but simply all that we project onto it, the repository of our desires (337). The Other remains entirely refractory to intelligibility; it becomes and remains the specular image of the Same (345). The naming of the Other *as Other* can be seen as a thetic and logocentric gesture on the part of post-structuralism whereby otherness is foreclosed. The fact that I continue to use the term here is a result of the embedding of my discourse in that tradition, and the impossibility of finding another term which is not simply a euphemism. The implications of this are the impossibility of breaking with Western systems of thought, of doing something different, of operating a radical transformation. This is the point beyond which post-structuralism as critique of humanism, cannot go. It is the one closure which it cannot undo.

This is at the same time the reason why when faced by the post-colonial or forms of neo-imperialism, while post-structuralism can account for the mechanism of imperialism, it cannot account for that which counters it. While Lyotard's notion of the *différend* at first appears as a tempting model to account for "injustice" in post-colonial discourse, where the victim is forced to express him/herself in the terms and the discourse of the oppressor, During has shown that the theory collapses when faced with something which is untranslatable, a residue which remains because of the particularity of natural languages: "In its flight from categories of totality, Lyotard's linguistic turn evades the one totality — so-called 'natural' language which it cannot reduce or ignore *on its own terms*. It is precisely to this totality that post-colonialism today appeals" ("Postmodernism" 44).[5]

A radical transformation is unthinkable in post-structuralist terms, because the site of "otherness" is a hole in its discourse. It would thus give ample reason for the suspicion and hostility it arouses in those who would set in motion a discourse which moves away from imperialism and seeks to replace it. Enter the post-colonial: what can be more irreducibly "other" to Western thought, and to those developments which problematize it, than the colonized body?

*   *   *

My discussion of post-colonial liberation literary discourse above underscores the irretrievability of "otherness" and pure difference even to the victim of imperialism; this does not, however, mean that there is no "otherness." What it does mean is that historicism must be repositioned; it needs to be brought in relation to present and future conditions rather than to the search for origins, and it needs to be brought in relation to a *re*constructive programme. In his address at the Writers' Forum Conference, Njabulo Ndebele outlines such a programme:

> They [the oppressed of South Africa] will want nothing less than the writing of their own texts.

> The path towards the new text should begin with the understanding that it is precisely where the official culture of South African oppression runs aground and becomes decadent and manipulative that the oppressed must come up with a reconstitutive

political and intellectual culture that will recreate and re-energize civilization in this country. (10)[6]

In statements such as these, there are the glimmerings of a sense in which the strategies deployed by what can be called "cultural workers" are not as far removed from the post-structuralist critique of humanism as they would at first seem. Spivak has begun to show the way to just such a rapprochement: speaking of the subaltern, she states that such cultural activity as that carried out by the Subaltern Studies Group is in a position to reveal the limits of the critique of humanism as produced in the West by a commitment to the subaltern as the *subject of his history* (209) and therefore, by implication, to develop this notion further.

What does this commitment to the subaltern as the subject of his/her history imply? Firstly, it forces us to re-evaluate the historicism of post-structuralist thought, an important element in the work of Althusser, Barthes, Kristeva and Foucault. The accusers of post-structuralism have claimed that this historicism is yet another mechanism of relativization, which leaves no space for eternal and universal Truths. This is all the more reason to take it into account. This historicism allows for the conceptualization of subject-effects *embedded* in a socio-historical configuration rather than simply of a *subject*. The concept of subject-effects, as opposed to that of subject, allows for an understanding of the materiality of a "body," traversed by plural and sometimes contradictory lines of determination, which constitute it as a subject capable of action in those socio-historical configurations. The subject-effect thus provides for the positioning of a subject as a discursive instance which is the effect of a variety of structures or discursive practices. The subject-effect is also a material instance, where the materiality has shifted from its localization in the unconscious and its language (as in Kristeva), to discourse (as in Foucault). Radical heterogeneity need not therefore be limited to unconscious processes or the semiotic disposition; its full effect can be felt instead in discursive clashes.

Therefore a subject-effect traversed by a line of conscientization and politicization does not find a unity in this line, but can use it — or be used — strategically. This does not diminish the heterogeneity of this (colonized) body to this line (the discourse of conscientization with its roots in humanism). At the same time it does not imply a compartmentalized view of a "subject" in which one line of determination is separable from the other — these would necessarily inflect one another in their effects.

This heterogeneity would thus be a difference that *does* make a difference, but it is not, for all that, a difference that can or should be named. The Other, theorized from a post-structuralist perspective (and at present we have no viable alternative), is irretrievable, unlocatable, refractory and by definition unnameable; it is there not as a positivity, but as an *effect*. And its effects are deeply felt in a society such as South African society. One of its effects, for example, is the very possibility of constructing a consciousness able to withstand Western homogenization. The traces of this are everywhere in black literature written in the language of the imperialist, where that language finds itself distorted, violated and transformed. Another of its effects is the very discomfiture of white writers and critics faced with the task of writing in South Africa. Yet another is the very fact that in this country I am forced to define myself as a white person: this very Whiteness constitutes me in this country as it would not do in another. And yet another effect is the group neurosis of the AWB[7] and its supporters.

The heterogeneous, as Kristeva has shown,[8] is in terms of the Logos a negativity; transformation is possible only where there is an unassimilable heterogeneity, and its concomitant negativity. Where that heterogeneity is not located in unconscious processes set in place by the exigencies of the Symbolic, but rather in other discursive possibilities, the potential of transformation becomes something real, with real effects. In this way, post-structuralist anti-humanism may find its only possible path of development with a view to transformative effect in post-colonial context, where the colonized body becomes the subject of its own history and turns the table on the imperialism of that humanism by *appropriating* its positivism from the position of its own negativity and heterogeneity. This is what we see at work in the appropriation of, for example, the categories of Western literature (realism, responsibility, etc.) by a "subject-effect" which is at once both within and without that tradition and that culture. There is here the possibility of transforming the sameness of the duality between same and other by the radical heterogeneity negatively inscribed in a subject-effect straddling a plurality of discursive positions. Consciousness is here only an effect, with *strategic* usefulness, of a plural and hybrid subject in a position eminently suited to appropriation of different discursive strategies, and therefore to turning each one against itself. Thus it is possible to foresee an appropriation of post-modernist strategies, in addition to and perhaps in the same place as various forms of realism, in black literature, which could be strategically useful to this literature and also mobilize post-modernism as a politically effective tool.

* * *

This article has been an attempt to set post-structuralist and post-modernist discourses in motion in a context of urgent cultural contestation, and to restore to them their political significance. At the same time, post-colonial liberation literary discourse stands to gain from such an inter-articulation in order to counter the reactionary tendencies implicit in any type of nationalism, while continuing to use certain notions for strategic effect. It must be reiterated, however, that the discourse I am using has its place in a particular institution. There are many who will point out that what I have said, and what anything that theory may say to the struggle against apartheid, has nothing to do with people living in the squatter camps, or under detention without trial. This argument, arising from the political urgency of opposition, is, however, a specious argument. Foucault provides us with the tools to understand strategies and counter-strategies of power. Although power may be everywhere and therefore inescapable, he has also shown that no one is completely without power. Grassroots activists in the townships do not need Foucault, or any theorist to tell them this, but academics working in university institutions perhaps do. There is a rupture between what we do in universities and what activists are doing, but this is not necessarily unhealthy. Speaking of the "ancient quarrel" between history and philosophy, Spivak points out that "it is incumbent upon us to realize that as *disciplines* they must both remain heterogeneous to, and discontinuous with subaltern social practice" (208). The usefulness of a discipline lies in its knowledge of the institution in which it works, and in its willingness to assume the power that goes with it. Commenting on the impossibility for modern thought to propose a morality, Foucault goes on to say that the reason for this is not that it is purely speculative, but rather that modern thought is "from the outset, and in its very thickness, a certain mode of action . . . for since the 19th century, thought has already 'exited' from itself and from its own being, it is no longer theory; from the moment it thinks, it wounds or reconciles, it draws closer or distances, it breaks, disassociates, ties or unties; it cannot stop itself from liberating or oppressing" (339). Those involved with the teaching of literature need to bear this in mind when they choose what is to be included in the curriculum, and the type of discourse that will accompany it.[9]

NOTES

1. It should not be forgotten that educational grievances were the central issue of the 1976 Soweto riots, and they remain potentially explosive.

2. See Watson. Love locates a similar notion of crisis in modernity and not in post-modernity, the latter not being perceived as a radical shift from the former.

3. This does not of course mean that there is no use at all of post-modern strategies. When used, however, the standpoint remains decisive. See, for example, Nadine Gordimer's *A Sport of Nature* where post-modern effects are evident, but do not ultimately interfere with the political standpoint of the novel, which therefore, from an epistemic point of view, overrides the post-modernism. J.M. Coetzee's *Foe*, on the other hand, is blatantly post-modernist, and achieves an ironic critique of colonialism thereby. The result, however, is much more ambivalent, for which he, as well as his post-structuralist commentators, has been heavily criticized. See Dovey as well as Chapman's review thereof for an example of the virulent attack to which post-structuralist critiques and post-modern literature are subjected.

4. All translations from *Les mots et les choses* are my own.

5. However, the return to a national natural language is foreclosed in South Africa, where there are a multiplicity of languages. This makes the problem of the choice of official and literary language extremely complex. This problem has not been tackled here, but obviously requires attention.

6. In this paper Ndebele also addresses the question of the written word, which Mphahlele, in his paper on oral literature, does not include. Evidently, when an oral culture is transcribed into print, a very definite transformation occurs, and a new problematic sets in. See also During, "Postmodernism."

7. AWB is Afrikaner Weerstandsbeweging, a far-right group advocating the return of the Afrikaner to supreme control in the two previous Afrikaner republics, i.e., the provinces of the Transvaal and the Orange Free State.
8. See, amongst others, *révolution*.
9. This article is a revised version of a paper read at the SAVAL Conference, Potchefstroom, South Africa (14–15 April 1989). I would like to thank Marianne de Jong, Simon During and Teresa Dovey for their critical readings.

WORKS CITED

Barthes, R. *The Pleasure of the Text*. New York: Hill & Wang, 1975.

Chapman, M. "The writing of politics and the politics of writing. On reading Dovey on reading Lacan on reading Coetzee on reading . . . (?)" *Journal of Literary Studies* 4.3 (1988): 327–41.

Coetzee, J.M. *Foe*. Johannesburg: Ravan Press, 1987.

Dovey, T. *The Novels of J.M. Coetzee*. Johannesburg: Ad Donker, 1988.

During, S. "On Cultural Values and Fascism." *Southern Review* 17 (1984): 167–81.

———. "Postmodernism or Post-Colonialism Today." *Textual Practice* 1.1 (1987): 32–47.

Foucault, M. *Les Mots et les choses: Une archéologie des sciences humaines*. Paris: Gallimard, 1966.

Gordimer, N. *A Sport of Nature*. Johannesburg: David Philip, 1987.

Habermas, J. "Modernity versus Postmodernity." *New German Critique* 22 (1981): 3–14.

Hutcheon, L. "The Politics of Postmodernism: Parody and History." *Cultural Critique* 5 (1986/7): 179–207.

———. "Beginning to Theorize Postmodernism." *Textual Practice* 1.1 (1987): 10–32.

Kistner, U. "Literature and the National Question." *Saval Kongresreferate* IX. Potchefstroom, 1989.

Kristeva, J. *La Révolution du langage poétique*. Paris: Editions du Seuil, 1974.

Love, N.S. *Marx, Nietzsche and Modernity*. New York: Columbia UP, 1986.

Manganyi, N. "Looking in: In Search of Ezekial Mphahlele. Interview." *Looking through the keyhole*. Johannesburg: Ravan Press, 1981.

Mattera, D. "At the Feet of the Nomad Gods." *Weekly Mail Literary Supplement*. 28 April–4 May 1989: 4.

Meer, F. *Higher than Hope*. Durban: Madiba, 1990.

Mphahlele, E. *Poetry and Humanism; Oral Beginnings*. Johannesburg: Witwatersrand UP for
   The Institute for the Study of Man, 1986.

Ndebele, N. "Against Pamphleteering the Future." *Stet* 5.1 (1987): 8–11.

Spivak, G. "Subaltern Studies: Deconstructing Historiography." *In Other Worlds: Essays in
   Cultural Politics*. New York and London: Methuen, 1987. 197–221.

Vaughan, M. "Can the Writer Become the Storyteller?" *Ten Years of Staffrider 1978–1988*. Ed.
   A.W. Oliphant and I. Vladislavic. Johannesburg: Ravan Press, 1988. 310–17.

Watson, S. "Jürgen Habermas and Jean-François Lyotard: Postmodernism and the Crisis of
   Rationality." *Philosophy and Social Criticism* 10 (1984): 1–24.

SLIP PAGE: Angela Carter, In/Out/In the Post-Modern Nexus

ROBERT RAWDON WILSON

Man is a practical even a penurious animal, and as such he has little patience with multiple labels. Some say "furze" and some say "gorse," but none, in a state of nature, will say both. Faced with two terms for the same thing, one tends to cast about for a distinction. W.V. QUINE, *Quiddities*

The preoccupations of literary theory are inseparable from their characteristic metaphors. The way one talks about the ways in which others talk may take its intellectual shape, its disciplined conceptual management, from phenomena as stark, and as occult, as models, but its expressive content, the actual placing of others' talk (in categories, in displays, in whatever discursive museum), flies the colours of metaphor.[1] Romantic criticism and its numerous inheritors, such as biographical criticism, speak in organic metaphors of growth, development, maturation, flowering, wholeness and perfection. New Criticism, another distant inheritor, preserves the array of organic metaphors, but adds distinctive turns of its own. The integrated wholes that New Criticism discovers comprise paradoxical double strands: aesthetic certitude flowers out of ambiguous incertitude, often held in mature perfection by nothing more substantial than a fluttering tone. Formalist criticism projects both mechanical (function, structure, concinnity) and isolating (motif, device, code) metaphors. Marxist criticism metaphorizes literature as systematic exchange between distinct levels: mirrors, reflection, production, consumption, commodification and class as ground, consciousness, identity, or mere disparity. These metaphors, immensely fruitful in focusing complex textual detail, discover only what they project.

Metaphors, however characteristic, are seldom the objects of examination and self-consciousness. They are more likely to wear the masks of translucency and fact, as being simply "things as they are." Christopher Norris has shown the extent to which philosophy attempts to "ignore or repress the figural dimension of language" (5). (It has never been clear whether New Critics were aware of the metaphoricity of their own language even while they pursued it in the language of others.) One of the joyful lessons of post-structuralism has been the insistence upon candid self-awareness: put metaphors up front, inscribe them (where they have come from, their passports, visas, all their slippery twists and turns) into the problematic. Post-structuralism's metaphors embrace puns, riddles, puzzles, paradoxes and aporia to show that literary texts can be held neither to single manifestations of (ideological) principles nor to reductive claims concerning conventions and genres. Genuinely heuristic metaphors, it is implied, stress the co-availability of contradictory terms. Excluded middles are retrieved and (re)placed squarely within textual foregrounds. Post-structuralism speaks, characteristically, in other metaphors of openness and fields: networks, threads (tangled, perplexed, wound and un-wound, followed and lost), wefts, weavings, de-weavings, ruptures, chiasmic zigzags, labyrinths. Unlike New Criticism's images of multiplexity, discovering always aesthetically integrated and closed text, post-structuralism's metaphors project an unstable and open text. If one begins to read according to the splintered mosaics of post-structuralist theory, then certainties will become uncertainties, boundaries will tremble and collapse, enclosures will split open and explicit ideological location will turn into the illusive play of random position. Serious terms, their conceptual enclosures ruptured, metamorphose into playthings, keeping a serious use only under erasure. As Derrida argues, the problem of textual classification, genre, can never look the same. A genre must be seen to exemplify the delusion of boundaries (so congenial to normal interpretive models) as either a transient rigidification of the textual field or as a momentary lapse of the reader's attention.

Is "post-modernism" a genre? Is it only a label for an historical period? What kind of boundaries does it possess? Are there entities either within or without its boundaries that might be, preposterously, (re)placed? In this paper, I shall argue that post-modernism is peculiarly the nexus of boundaries that traverse each other. The problem of boundaries has become central issue in many theoretical writings about literature. It is not merely that post-structuralism's metaphors evoke images of boundaries in various stages of disrepair and dissolution, but nearly all current theory does so as well. Bakhtin, for instance, might be said to have developed a literary theory that exclusively inhabits boundaries. For Bakhtin everything depends upon the kinds of transactions that are possible across boundaries: that divide languages, cultures, historical periods, speakers as well as the private, axiological worlds that their utterances entail. Narratology and semiotics concern themselves with the drawing of boundaries between signifying systems, codes, types of speech acts, levels of discourse, metonymic segments, shifts in voice or focalization. The pervasive emphasis upon boundaries (either the capacity, in theory, to draw them or the incapacity to do so) makes every cultural entity strange. The conceptual machinery exists to allow anyone to transgress all boundaries and, strapping on a propulsion system of mysterious benefit, to deduce oneself into a notional world of insubsistencies and insipidities. Once stable period-terms, such as "Renaissance," do not stand up well against either suspicion or proliferation with regard to boundaries. The Renaissance, which once fixed the demarcations for a period in European cultural history that ranged from Petrarch (or Giotto) to Milton, its boundaries essentially temporal if also cultural and national, now seems to designate a loosely intra-threaded cluster, like uncombable elf-knots, of discursive practices, ways of writing and otherwise employing symbols. (The true "Renaissance" person, hence, is the one whose symbology replicates, say, Spenser or Cervantes.) Post-modernism's utility and charm lies in focusing with dazzling exuberance the problem of boundaries. Whatever wanders within its nexus (and everything, anything at all, might) reflects, *nota notae*, the gargantuan incertitude of the whole.

Even graduate students at the University of Ultima Thule will have heard that "post-modernism" is a slipshod term. It does too much work, and thus no single task well. It lends itself, as E.A. Grosz remarks, to "evasion and ambiguity" (8). It has proved depressingly not to be "straightforwardly chronological" (Arac x–xi), but always displaying itself in remote times, embarrassingly out of synch with its period-founded definition(s). Furthermore, despite its evasiveness, post-modernism has never admitted simple solutions, and no writer who uses the term may expect to be let off easily. (If there were academic prisons, where everyone's candidate for Worst Offender against the norms of clarity and good sense could be penned, the cells would rankle with theorists of the post-modern.) To "have a position" on post-modernism seems to entail "not just to offer an analysis of its genesis and contours but to let the world know whether you are for it or against it, and in fairly bald terms" (Arac xii). One is likely to be held to standards higher, both for clarity and for theoretical acuity, than the topic itself will allow. What the graduate students at Ultima Thule may not know is that post-modernism bears within itself a nebulous frontier, an unmapped zone of bogs and tangled brush, between its uses as a period, and as an analytic-descriptive, term. It is a secret boundary that lies between radically disparate dimensions of experience, or between ways of perceiving that experience, that effectively blank out each other's vision. What (to invert Quine's dictum in this paper's epigraph) should one do faced with one label and diverse experiences? One may conflate, of course, and thus follow the normal course of writers on post-modernism when, or if, they admit this multiplicity. One may also, borrowing yet another phrase from Quine, play with the "fiction of sharp distinctions" (57).

More than any other insight into post-modernism, the students at Ultima Thule need to know that the disparate uses of the term drag along with them two separate, and differently organized, baggage-trains. As a concept, post-modernism (if it *is* a concept) unpacks in more than one manner. In effect, there are two distinct archives, two sets of relevant primary and secondary texts, behind the usage of "post-modern." As a period-term, it possesses a vast baggage of analysis that turns directly towards the state of Western culture either to describe the contours of popular and mass media expression or to highlight the cultural manifestations ("commodifications") of the most recent stage in the history of its industrial-economic infrastructure. The period, of course, is always NOW, this "post-age" (Ulmer), and many kinds of evidence are available to its cartographers. (An intelligent student now asks, "What evidence would be irrelevant?" The brightest rejoins, "How could any evidence be irrelevant?") The essays collected in the recent *Postmodernism and Continental Philosophy* illustrate the voraciousness of the enterprise: all thinking about the present, the issues, the difficulties, all advertised solutions, coheres within the umbrella schema. This archive inspires analyses that slip towards reification, granting to "post-modern" a unitary hanging-togetherness that one would no longer cheerfully accord to, say, "Renaissance."

The first archive constructs post-modernism as this period-term, esurient in its consumption of evidence, exiguous in its production of interpretation, to name NOW. All culture reflects the economic forces that have created the conditions of its possibility: it shows, in the torsions of commodification, its acned etiology. "That the logic of commodification has come to structure every aspect of contemporary life, not least the culture-aesthetic," David Bennett writes, "is now a commonplace of periodizing theories of post-modernism" (17). What has happened, Fredric Jameson mordantly observes, is that "aesthetic production today has become integrated into commodity production generally: the frantic economic urgency of producing fresh waves of ever more novel-seeming goods (from clothing to airplanes), at ever greater rates of turnover, now assigns an increasingly essential structural function and position to aesthetic innovation and experimentation" ("Postmodernism" 56). Fresh, novel-seeming commodities flood contemporary marketplaces driven forward by economic forecasts, the calibration of trends, the capitalist ferocity with regard to market-expansion. Jameson's analysis displayed, the graduate students at Ultima Thule can easily see that post-modernism is only a stage, a mere period, in the history of late capital ("Postmodernism" 60, 78). (It is not a purpose of this paper to argue that Jameson, or anyone, is *wrong*. No terrier-questions about, say, airplanes, for which commodity the technology of production is said to lag thirty or so years behind that of the drawing board, shall be allowed to slip in.) There are many echoes: post-modernist culture, Terry Eagleton writes, will "dissolve its own boundaries and become coextensive with ordinary commodified life itself, whose ceaseless exchanges and mutations in any case recognize no formal frontiers which are not constantly transgressed" (141). Its boundaries slipping irreversibly into dissolution, post-modernism as an historical period shows, throughout its commodified culture, a number of bleak, downcasting characteristics. Jameson notes its depthlessness, its weakening of historicity, its "deep constitutive relationships" to new technologies, among other features and, in general, a pervasive "waning of affect" ("Postmodernism" 58, 61). Writers within the first archive seldom evince much enthusiasm for post-modernism. It is difficult to esteem artifacts that seem endlessly to repeat similar patterns and rules for combination, like bright little *Lego* blocks, always remote, keeping their distance even while urging consumption. There is too much fragmentation, too much bittiness, all wan and inauthentic, and dark, implacable forces make things tick.

Neo-Marxism is not the only course run within the first archive. Jean-François Lyotard, whom Eagleton identifies as making "ageing-hippie points" (93), sees post-modernism as a descriptive term to designate the state of culture in the wake of all the "transformations which, since the end of the nineteenth century, have altered the game rules for science, literature, and the arts" (xxiii), a culture for which all master narratives have decayed and ceased to grip. Though difficult to separate post-modernism from modernism in these terms, a sweeping overview of the NOW emerges with great clarity: many small narratives replace the large ones of the past, distinct language games, a kind of micro-ludism, crowd the playfield. Only a slight lateral shift reveals the bizarre playfield of the NOW that Jean Baudrillard has discovered: a discursive space wholly filled, jampacked indeed, with images, simulations, displacements of "reality." Simulation, he writes, is the "generation of models of a real without origin or reality: a hyperreal" ("Simulacra" 166). A "precession of simulacra" maps and, in so doing, engenders the territory of the present. The age of simulations is also, it seems, the age of the disappearance of history which, like dead trees in certain societies, now commands only "symbolic necessity," killed by stupefaction and the mithridatization in the face of too many images and too much information, though still capable of supporting the weight of a few victims ("The Year 2000" 27, 20–21). These are not all the same thing, the most perceptive students will point out, and they make quite different claims upon one's powers for cognitive synthesis. Yet they do agree upon the fragmentary discreteness of the post-modern NOW, its tentacular technologies and mind-numbing replications. They agree that it is something new (though anticipated, always already, from the industrial revolution and the origins of international capitalism), even if "fresh" might not be *quite* the term. Theories of post-modernism as an historical period, Bennett writes, "rather than as aesthetic genre or style typically entail a notion of cultural *coupure*" in which the present is updated in, and by, defamiliarization (30). If post-modernism is considered as a period, and not as "aesthetic genre or style," then it will have to be mapped in fairly stark colours with large, heavily marked (though perhaps wholly illusive) boundaries.

The second archive constructs post-modernism as a highly flexible analytic-descriptive term capable of isolating conventions, devices and techniques across the range of all the cultural products (though architecture, painting and fiction seem privileged) that can be caught in a widely flung transnational net. Post-modern, in the writings of the second archive, is very much an "aesthetic genre or style" and very little a period term. Both Ihab Hassan and Linda Hutcheon, in their many discussions of post-modernism, have used the term in this sense. Post-modernism, Hassan writes, is (in contrast to modernism) "playful, paratactical and deconstructionist . . . it recalls the spirit of the avant-garde, and so carries sometimes the label of neo-avant garde" (91). Its playfulness is "the vice and joy of post-modernism" (105). Post-modernist art forms, thrusting their play into the foreground, constituting it as a dominant, are normally seen as "fundamentally self-reflexive . . . self-consciously art (or artifice)" in that there is no mistaking them (Hutcheon, *The Canadian Postmodern* 1). There is no illusion of translucency, no pretence of windowness, to delude the reader/viewer, but only the hard intellectual work of playing intricate formal games. The sense that post-modernism involves play, or is perhaps *essentially* play, seems widespread within the second archive as a positive, even laudatory, judgement upon style and mannerisms. (Writers in the first archive may also discern a playfulness in post-modernism, but they are more likely to judge this negatively, as trivial or misdirected.) Allen Thiher, discussing the "play of language within language" that characterizes post-modernism, argues that the "postmodern lives in a world in which play has become a generalized and shared therapeutic metaphor to describe the ontology of both language and fiction" (160). As a stylistic or generic term, post-modernism does more or less the same conceptual work that another term, "metafiction," performs ("*see also* metafiction," advises the entry on post-modernism in the index to Linda Hutcheon's *A Theory of Parody*) and thus invites one, in Quine's phrase, to "cast about for a distinction."

The distinction, even for those with a gift for that special fiction, has not been easy to locate. At the University of Ultima Thule, the graduate students, an ordinarily well-intentioned group, manifest signs of irritation at the task. They understand metafiction well enough, and can recognize that Renaissance texts, such as *Hamlet* or *Don Quijote*, while full of *it*, are paradoxically lacking in post-modernism.[2] As an epithet to label style(s), post-modern, applying to architecture or zoögraphics as well as to fiction, encompasses more than metafiction. However, as the inventor of the term, William H. Gass, remarks, it is easy to join "meta" to words, creating, as desire prompts, any number of "lingos to converse about lingos" (24) The "meta" terms creep up on post-modernism ("metadrama," of course, "metacinema," "metafilm" or, as you like it, "metavideo"), swamping its greater utility and scope. The most viable distinction appears to be, after all, the appeal to culture. Writers in the second archive do refer to post-modernism as a cultural phenomenon, though not consistently or with any precise model of culture in mind. "We live," Hassan writes, "in a time of political terrorism, moral improvisation, spiritual *bricolage*" (196). There is no mechanism behind this appeal to culture, no bogey of international capitalism, neither a myth of History's inevitable on-goingness nor of its unlamented end, but merely the bare postulate of a determining "culture." (Why is our age one of political terrorism? Are the spiritual *bricoleurs* to be found everywhere? Only in New Age religions? In Islam or the Roman Catholic Church as well? Hassan does not ask these questions.) Brian McHale's *Postmodernist Fiction*, a concise encyclopedia of the second archive, formulates an hypothesis of cultural oscillation in which historical periods shift between epistemological and ontological ages. In an ontological age, writers become preoccupied with the creation of fictional worlds (and care less how worlds come to be known, or about the cognitive difficulties they raise) and fashion complex, bevelled texts that incorporate plural worldhoods. Modernism reflects an epistemological dominance; post-modernism, an ontological dominance. "In post-modernist texts . . . epistemology is *backgrounded*, as the price for foregrounding ontology" (*Postmodernist* 11). There is no mechanism behind McHale's model any more than behind Hassan's. All fictions project "worlds," but some, in an age when an ontological dominant operates, such as this post-modern one, do so "in full view and in slow motion" only, it may be, abruptly to suspend the world-making process (McHale, "Telling Postmodernist Stories" 563), but *why* this should be so remains unfocused. The shifts, it must appear, simply occur, known *post hoc* through the formal, stylistic properties of the texts that they make possible.

One possesses, thus, in "post-modern," a term that both conflates disparate ways of talking and discongruent bodies of evidence, but also promotes superfluous distinctions. No one who shaves with Ockham's razor would invest a penny's worth of energy in its uncertain rewards. Yet recent literary and cultural theory has returned obsessively to its lure. Taming post-modernism, making it assume subservient, domestic positions, often seems to be, if not the only, the best game in town. Jameson claims that his pluralistic approach to post-modernism has been an attempt to "outflank" it ("Regarding Postmodernism" 54), though his fierce charge through all the thickets might rather seem to be an attempt to capture it definitively. (The famous *New Left Review* essay is more a cage, an almost-sealed yet leaky pen, than an ambush.) I want now to propose an altogether different approach to post-modernism: confront it (that is, the diverse kinds of evidence that "it" constellates) as an educational challenge. Post-modernism is a paradigm-case of the problem of boundaries and slipping categories: collapsing borders, fuzzy sets and unmappable zones. For the inveterate collector of literary nomenclature, it is the true Disney World.

The two archives overlap and coincide. They form this nexus not only because they appeal to some of the same evidence, but also because whatever becomes evidence (for either archive) can be analyzed in both ways. (After all, the world does not naturally brim with evidence. Jameson does leave his Californian home each morning to wade knee-deep in evidence. What becomes evidence is always argument's kidnapped child.) I shall look at a short tale in Angela Carter's 1979 collection, *The Bloody Chamber*. All the narratives in this collection retell traditional European folktales from a feminist perspective imbued with psychoanalytic insights. All the tales in *The Bloody Chamber* are artful, resonant with the allusive interplay of other texts, perhaps "wan" in their affects; all, powerful in their historicity, in their awareness of human temporality within its socio-cultural chains. I shall argue that the tale I have chosen to discuss, "Lady of The House of Love," exemplifies the nexus of intersecting archives. On its surface, the tale seems to possess only those properties that writers of the second archive esteem. It is heavily overcoded and calls upon a number of intertextual frames. It is a piece of fiction "about" fiction in which, without explicitly citing a specific antecedent fiction, a large number of motifs associated with vampire tales are playfully reprised. The actual title is itself overcoded. It calls to mind the houses in Medieval literature (e.g., "The House of Fame") or the allegorical houses in works such as *The Faerie Queene* but also such common frames as manor houses, family properties that descend through generations, and brothels. The "lady" of the title suggests the aristocratic associations inherent in the notion of a "house" such as the doomed Lady of Shallot. The title turns out to be ironic and that, too, is the kind of textualist duplicity that appeals to the second archive. Surely, it would seem that this is the kind of fiction that makes writers of the first archive despondent and grimly judgemental, that flaunts its depthlessness, that shows the "certain flatness" that Jameson finds in the art of this late capitalist period ("Regarding Postmodernism" 30), that promotes pastiche at the expense of parody and that actively displaces historicity by the "play of random stylistic allusion," by (in some sense) intertextuality ("Postmodernism" 64–66). "Lady of The House of Love" displays, surely, the "waning of affect" that Jameson laments. Yet, for all that it is formally decontextualized and transnational in its orientation, the tale clamorously proclaims its recognition of context, its historicity.

I shall begin by giving the "story" in a series of basic narrative macropropositions in order to show the *fabula* as clearly as possible. It is early in this century. A beautiful young woman lives in an old castle. She is a vampire. She is the daughter of Nosferatu. She feeds on young men. An old woman helps her find young men to devour. She is always ravenous. She does not like to kill young men. She would like to be human. A young, beautiful Englishman arrives. He is an officer in the British army. He rides a bicycle. He is invited into the castle and given a meal. The vampire turns up the card of the Lover in her Tarot deck. She falls in love with the Englishman. He is innocent and heroic. He wishes to help the young woman whom he perceives as a sickly, underfed child. She invites him to bed. He follows because he fears for her health. He would like only to protect her. She breaks her glasses. She cuts her finger on a shard of glass. He kisses the wound as, he believes, her mother would have done. He puts her to bed and sleeps on the floor with his jacket for a pillow. In the morning she is dead. He returns to Bucharest. In Bucharest he receives a telegram ordering him to rejoin his regiment. He discovers that, unknowingly, he has carried with him a black rose that he had found on the young woman's dead body. It is still fragrant. His regiment embarks for France.

Carter makes full use of literary resonances. One could say, using an older terminology, that she plays with literary allusions, or, using the analytic lexicon of semiotics, that she requires the reader to bring numerous "intertextual" frames to bear. At one point, the beautiful daughter of Nosferatu is actually called "the tenebrous belle." The archaic phrase, in its very archaism, does the job of calling for a frame drawn from the previous reading of literature. (It should call to mind Romance writing in general, a very specific poem by John Keats, "La Belle Dame Sans Merci," or even the strong associations in French literature with the word from which derives "tenebrous" — *tenebre, tenebreux* — a word much loved by French poets of the latter nineteenth century.) Consider the way Carter begins her narrative. The number of stylistically self-conscious words with literary associations, the heavy overcoding, is evidentially explicit:

> At last the revenants become so troublesome the peasants abandoned the village and it fell solely into the possession of subtle and vindictive inhabitants who manifest their presences by shadows that fall almost imperceptibly awry, too many shadows, even at midday, shadows that have no source in anything visible; by the sound, sometimes, of sobbing in a derelict bedroom where a cracked mirror suspended from a wall does not reflect a presence; by a sense of unease that will afflict the traveller unwise enough to pause to drink from the fountain in the square that still gushes spring water from a faucet stuck in the lion's mouth. A cat prowls in a weedy garden; he grins and spits, arches his back, bounces away from an intangible on four fear-stiffened legs. Now all

shun the village below the chateau in which the beautiful somnabulist helplessly perpetuates her ancestral crimes.

Wearing an antique bridal gown, the beautiful queen of the vampires sits all alone in her dark, high house under the eyes of the portraits of her demented and atrocious ancestors, each one of whom, through her, projects a baleful posthumous existence; she counts out the Tarot cards, ceaselessly construing a constellation of possibilities as if the random fall of the cards on the red plush tablecloth before her could precipitate her from her chill, shuttered room into a country of perpetual summer and obliterate the perennial sadness of a girl who is both death and a maiden.

Her voice is filled with distant sonorities, like reverberations in a cave. . . . Her hair falls down like tears. (93)

The "distant sonorities" that fill her voice also fill the narrative. I shall cite only one example. Cats seem to have, perhaps quite unfairly, a bad reputation in popular literature, but Carter makes this cat perform a double role: it both fits into the pattern of supernatural allusions as a vehicle or agent and also registers the environment by showing fear. Later in the narrative, Carter re-employs the cat image to define the English officer. As he follows "Nosferatu's sanguinary rosebud" into her bedroom, "He was struck, once again, by the birdlike, predatory claws which tipped her marvellous hands; the sense of strangeness that had been growing on him since he buried his head under the streaming water in the village, since he entered the dark portals of the fatal castle, now fully overcame him. Had he been a cat, he would have bounced backwards from her hands on four fear-stiffened legs, but he is not a cat: he is a hero" (103). Such heavy allusiveness marks a *literary* narrative, a manifestation of High Art as pastiche, an intelligent, self-conscious instance of the literary effects writers of the second archive admire. Even the young English officer is, it seems, an overcoded character from other stories. He is innocent and several times Carter emphasizes his "virginity." She does not call attention to the virginity of Nosferatu's daughter, though that epithet would describe her as well: as they enter the bedroom together, ". . . she keeps up a front of inconsequential chatter in French while her ancestors leer and grimace on the walls; however hard she tries to think of any other, she only knows one kind of consummation" (103). The English officer is as innocent as a hero in a child's romance ("he does not yet know what there is to be afraid of"), or, indeed, like many of the great heroes of older romance forms, like, say, Perceval, Galahad or Red Cross Knight. He is, thus, a special kind of hero, one who can encounter Evil and, having no secret evil hidden in his mind, remain untouched.

Carter's English hero is so pure that he cannot recognize the evil that Nosferatu's daughter represents. He does not even seem to realize that the invitation into her bedroom is, superficially at least, an invitation to sexual pleasure. Carter describes his state of mind as he enters her bedroom: "Then he padded into the boudoir, his mind busy with plans. We shall take her to Zürich, to a clinic; she will be treated for nervous hysteria. Then to an eye specialist, for her photophobia, and to a dentist to put her teeth into better shape. Any competent manicurist will deal with her claws. We shall turn her into the lovely girl she is; I shall cure her of all these nightmares" (107). When he kisses her bleeding finger, he does so thinking of himself as doing only what her mother would have done, and the ironic reversal of roles is lost on him, though not upon the reader who has brought the correct intertextual frames to the task.

One might very well wonder how such an artful narrative — so bursting with its self-conscious craftiness, its elaborate literariness, its allusions, its coded phrases in French ("suivez moi," "vous serez ma proi") — could do anything but fulfil the post-modernist criteria of literature as, among so many other things, the "play of language within language." Carter's tale is transnational, decontextualized, formal in all respects. Or is it? Consider some of the questions that anyone might ask whose literary interests were contextual.

First, consider the narrative's explicit setting. Carter sets the action in the Transylvania of traditional vampire legends. However, she also specifies it as a part of Romania and Bucharest, the national capital, is cited. Is there significance to this part of Europe other than as the traditional locale of vampires? Should one remember, or forget, the history of Eastern Europe prior to the First World War? Second, Carter both obliquely and then precisely indicates the time of the narrative. The young English officer is introduced in this manner: "One hot, ripe summer in the pubescent years of the present century, a young officer in the British army, blond, blue-eyed, heavy-muscled, visiting friends in Vienna, decided to spend the remainder of his furlough exploring the little-known uplands of Romania" (97). In the conclusion, it is stated exactly that "his regiment embarked for France" (108). Should one pursue, or neglect, the apparent suggestion that this was the summer of 1914, the final calm before the Great War began? Should one note, as good readers, that the soldier leaves from Vienna for his trip? Is it important that Vienna was the capital of the Austro-Hungarian Empire, of which Romania was a part? Third, should one make anything of the bicycle? It is, to be sure, a mode of transportation that a young Englishman in 1914 *might have* chosen. Still, it is forcefully, unmistakably even, encoded into the text. It is mentioned repeatedly and more than once described as "rational." Should one infer, or neglect, the apparent allusion to England's advanced technology and industrial power? Perhaps one should infer that the narrative, in part anyway, seems to deal with the contrast between English "rationality" and Eastern European superstition? It is important to remember that the First World War pitted industrial nations against one another and that, in the up-shot, Europe was transformed. The future was shown to have been on the side of technology and industrialization, not superstition, not tradition. The dilapidation and decay of the village and the vampire's castle suggests something further. When the young Englishman is escorted to meet Nosferatu's daughter, he is surprised "to find how ruinous the interior of the house was — cobwebs, worm-eaten beams, crumbling plaster" (100) and later, bending to pick up the Tarot cards that she has let slip in her surprise at seeing him, he is once more surprised to see that the carpet "was part rotted away, partly encroached upon by all kinds of virulent-looking fungi" (101). The reader, having (in this case) the right extratextual frames, would find it difficult to read the tale's physical descriptions and *not* think about European civilization prior to the War — that "old bitch gone in the teeth" as Ezra Pound's Hugh Selwyn Mauberley remarks. Fourth, the reader may also try to look into the extratextual future of the narrative. One may infer that the narrative is about death in a wider sense than seems evident at first. The vampire kills passing shepherds and lustful, but careless, young men who wander through the deserted village, and she herself dies, but the narrative also implies the more massive, and the more significant, deaths that occurred in the War. The very class to which the young Englishman belongs was wiped nearly out. His own death in the war, implicit in the conclusion, may represent the much larger national catastrophe, or, at least, the reader may draw this inference. The fruit of that War, for England as well as for the Continent, was the decimation of an entire generation and a social class.

What should the reader make of the black rose? If one reads the narrative only as a "formalist" (pejorative epithet of uncertain range) analyzing motifs, discovering patterns, one might see it as a sexual symbol. Nosferatu's daughter actually imagines that she will hand it to him with just that significance: "And I leave you as a souvenir the dark, fanged rose I plucked from between my thighs, like a flower laid on a grave. On a grave" (107). Strikingly overcoded (overdetermined, in the specifically psychoanalytic sense), the black rose is also a symbol of difference, of isolation and loneliness. Thus Patrick White, in his *The Aunt's Story*, uses the symbol of the black rose to express Theodora Goodman's isolation, her radical set-apartness. She bears it with her into madness and captivity. A black rose may also be, as the liturgical colour for grief, mourning, and penitence, a symbol of death. The Englishman, one remembers, carries it with him as he embarks for France. The symbol of the black rose, so explicitly sexual, asserts the tale's historicity, its recognition of the bleak forwardness of human temporality.

There are many more contextual questions that a reader might either ignore or neglect. The castle of vampires itself, one might observe, contains not merely decay, but relationships of subordination and subservience. Carter's narrative concerns power. It is marginally about the power of a feudal class over peasants and servants. It is made quite clear that the relationship of the castle to the village is a feudal one. The servant within the castle seems unmistakably bound feudally to the House of Nosferatu. If one reads more closely, it is possible to perceive an even more important hierarchy of subordinations. The beautiful vampire does not like to kill, she would like, somehow, to be human. (It is the sheer impossibility of being human, of responding to kindness with kindness, or of exchanging love for love, that seems to kill her.) Here is how Carter describes her state of mind:

All day, she lies in her coffin in her négligé of blood-stained lace. When the sun drops behind the mountain, she yawns and stirs and puts on the only dress she has, her mother's wedding dress, to sit and read her cards until she grows hungry. She loathes the food she eats; she would have liked to take the rabbits home with her, feed them on lettuce, pet them and make them a nest in her red-and-black chinoiserie escritoire, but hunger always overcomes her. She sinks her teeth into the neck where an artery throbs with fear; she will drop the deflated skin from which she has extracted all the nourishment with a small cry of both pain and disgust. And it is the same with the shepherd boys and gipsy lads. . . . (96)

What power makes her do what she loathes? The answer seems to be symbolized by the leering, grinning ancestral portraits that are mentioned more than once. The weight of tradition chains her to her loathed fate. However, this tradition does not seem to be identical with the decaying tradition of European political power, concentrated in the Vienna that was the capital of the Austro-Hungarian Empire. The narrative explicitly identifies the beautiful vampire's male line of descent: ". . . her claws and teeth have been sharpened on centuries of corpses, she is the last bud of the poison tree that sprang from the loins of Vlad the Impaler who picnicked on corpses in the forests of Transylvania" (94). When her father was killed, staked out at a crossroads by an Orthodox priest while she was still a baby, he cried: "Nosferatu is dead; long live Nosferatu" (95). A tradition has fallen upon her, and the narrative is quite unmistakable that it is a male tradition. She is subordinated, within her decaying castle ("[d]epredations of rot and fungus everywhere" [94]), dressed in her antique wedding gown, to a tradition established, and maintained, by men. The leering, ancestral portraits forcefully incorporate this male tradition into the narrative.

Carter's "Lady of The House of Love" demonstrates that, even when the text appears crystalline in its artfulness, evidently hostile to "real" human issues, such as history and temporality, there will be conclusions for the contextualist to draw. Once the right questions have been posed, the narrative shows that it is about more than the sad fate of vampires, more even than the sad fate of empires and armies. It is also about the fate of women in a patriarchal world. It is about power, and who, in such a world, normally possesses power. The wedding dress, seen from a contextualist perspective, becomes more than a pathetic element in the theatrical setting of rot and decay, more even than a crafty allusion (salient in the intertextual welter, Miss Havisham mysteriously smiles) to other texts. Once the narrative's feminist preoccupations and concerns have been identified, the wedding dress emerges abruptly as the most poignant motif of all: the symbol of women's voicelessness, subordination and narrowly limited expectations, their unelected social roles handed down, in a patriarchal society. One may certainly argue that Carter uses history in a "destabilizing" manner, problematizing without interpreting, as Hutcheon writes of *The Infernal Desire Machines of Doctor Hoffman* ("Postmodern Problematizing" 380), equally a positive or a negative textual property (depending upon the archive), but it is also the case that a genuine concern for human deprivation, what has not found fulfilment in history, pervades the text.

Post-modernism designates a nexus of intersecting discourses, constituting separate archives, each largely blind to opposed discursive formations. It exemplifies the fruitfulness of post-structuralist metaphors that project splintered, unstable textual mosaics in which all categories, both genres and periods, will display the decay of boundaries and, inevitably, their degenerescence. It also shows the relevance of those other metaphors about boundaries that characteristically play important roles in Bakhtin's thinking: metaphors in which alien languages confront each other in public fora, in which different speakers, bearing with them dissimilar axiological worlds, exchange utterances, seeking meanings that will never reside exclusively in either's speech. Mocking the duplicitous "fiction of sharp distinctions" (behind, or beyond, the ineluctably fuzzy borders of which stuff falls, and then falls again), post-modernism offers the opportunity to read both texts and culture with "parted eye" in which, as Hermia exclaims in *A Midsummer Night's Dream*, everything "seems double" (Shakespeare 241). It is an opportunity, and neither a catastrophe nor a punishment for the fallen *gerede* that one must speak, since the possibilities for reflexivity, for self-consciously inscribing the problematic of one's own explorations, are always exciting. For the time being, it may be the most provocative, splendidly liminal specimen of what Howard Felperin calls the "slippery grounds of discourse" (123) available. And, as a discursive nexus, it continues to open towards multiplex investigations.

NOTES

1. This is not the place to analyze the paradoxicality inherent to the classificatory procedures of museums. In "The Discourse of Museums," I discuss some aspects of the duplicity of collections and the appeal of this double-sidedness for two post-modern writers, Murray Bail and Robert Kroetsch. Precisely because they unselfconsciously encode the aporia of sets, categories and boundaries, museums (or the idea of a museum) have become a topos of post-structuralist thinking and (some) post-modernist writing. See Donato; Stewart.

2. A cursory examination of *DAI* for the years 1983 to 1986 (vols. 43–46) reveals that there were nine Ph.D. theses written on "post-modernism" during those years. For the most part they deal with individual writers, such as Richard Brautigan, Iris Murdoch, Robert Creeley and Lord Byron (!), but there are also theses devoted to post-modernist fantasy, drama, dramatic theory and Paraguayan poetry. All these theses appear to have been written from within the second archive, using "post-modern" as a totalizing term for the sum of metafictional techniques and focusing upon "innovative literature." Only Jerry Andrew Varsava's thesis shows, in its abstract, a recognition of the first archive, and then only to refute it.

WORKS CITED

Arac, Jonathan, ed. *Postmodernism and Politics*. Minneapolis: Minnesota UP, 1986.

Baudrillard, Jean. "The Year 2000 Will Not Take Place." *Futur*Fall: Excursions into Post-Modernity*. 18–28.

———. "Simulacra and Simulations." *Jean Baudrillard: Selected Writings*. Ed. Mark Poster. Cambridge: Polity Press-Basil Blackwell, 1988. 166–84.

Bennett, David. "Wrapping Up Postmodernism: The Subject of Consumption versus the Subject of Cognition." *Postmodern Conditions*. Ed. Andrew Milner et al. Melbourne: Centre for General and Comparative Literature, Monash U, 1988. 15–36.

Carter, Angela. *The Bloody Chamber*. London: Penguin, 1981.

Derrida, Jacques. "The Law of Genre." *Critical Inquiry* 7.1 (1980): 55–81.

Donato, Eugenio. "The Museum's Furnace: Notes Toward a Contextual Reading of *Bouvard and Pécuchet*." *Textual Strategies: Perspectives in Post-Structuralist Criticism*. Ed. Josué V. Harari. Ithaca: Cornell UP, 1979. 213–38.

Eagleton, Terry. *Against the Grain: Essays 1975–1985*. London: Verso, 1986.

Felperin, Howard. *Beyond Deconstruction: The Uses and Abuses of Literary Theory*. Oxford: Clarendon, 1985.

Gass, William H. *Fiction and the Figures of Life*. New York: Knopf, 1970.

Grosz, E.A. et al., eds. *Futur*Fall: Excursions into Post-Modernity*. Sydney: Power Institute of Fine Arts, U of Sydney, 1986.

Hassan, Ihab. *The Postmodern Turn: Essays in Postmodern Theory and Culture*. Columbus: Ohio State UP, 1987.

Hutcheon, Linda. *A Theory of Parody: The Teachings of Twentieth-Century Art Forms*. New York: Methuen, 1985.

———. *The Canadian Postmodern: A Study of Contemporary English-Canadian Fiction*. Toronto: Oxford UP, 1988.

———. "The Postmodern Problematizing of History." *English Studies in Canada* 14 (1988): 365–82.

Jameson, Fredric. "Postmodernism, or the Cultural Logic of Late Capitalism." *New Left Review* 146 (1984): 53–92.

———. "Regarding Postmodernism A Conversation with Fredric Jameson." Ed. Anders Stephanson. *Social Text: Theory/Culture/Ideology* 17 [6.2] (1987): 29–54.

McHale, Brian. *Postmodernist Fiction*. New York: Methuen, 1987.

———. "Telling Postmodernist Stories." *Poetics Today* 9 (1988): 545–71.

Norris, Christopher. *The Deconstructive Turn: Essays in the Rhetoric of Philosophy.* London: Methuen, 1983.

Quine, W.V. *Quiddities: An Intermittently Philosophical Dictionary.* Cambridge: Harvard UP, 1987.

Silverman, Hugh J., and Donn Welton, eds. *Postmodernism and Continental Philosophy.* Albany: SU of New York P, 1988.

Shakespeare, William. *A Midsummer Night's Dream. The Riverside Shakespeare.* Ed. G. Blakemore Evans. Boston: Houghton Mifflin, 1974. 217–49.

Stewart, Susan. *On Language: Narrative of the Miniature, the Gigantic, the Souvenir, the Collection.* Baltimore: The Johns Hopkins UP, 1984.

Thiher, Allen. *Words in Reflection: Modern Language Theory and Post-modern Fiction.* Chicago: U of Chicago P, 1984.

Ulmer, Gregory. "The Post-Age." *Diacritics* 11 (1981): 39–56.

Varsava, Jerry Andrew. "The Mimetic Function of Postmodernist Literature." Diss. Vanderbilt U, 1984.

White, Patrick. *The Aunt's Story.* New York: Viking, 1948.

Wilson, Robert R. "The Discourse of Museums: Exhibiting Postmodernism." *Open Letter* 7th ser. 1 (1988): 93–110.

Decolonizing the Map: Post-Colonialism, Post-Structuralism and the Cartographic Connection

GRAHAM HUGGAN

We're not going to get away from structures. But we could do with some lithe, open, agile, portable structures, some articulating structures . . . we can't all go to the same place . . . we have to go together in different directions.
ROBERT BRINGHURST, *Pieces of Map, Pieces of Music*

The problem with maps is they take imagination.
Our need for contour invents the curve,
our demand for straight lines will have
measurement laid out in bones. Direction
rips the creel out of our hand. To let go now
is to become air-borne, a kite, map, journey . . . .
THOMAS SHAPCOTT, "Maps"

The fascination of Canadian, Australian and other post-colonial writers with the figure of the map has resulted in a wide range of literary responses both to physical (geographical) maps, which are shown to have operated effectively, but often restrictively or coercively, in the implementation of colonial policy, and to conceptual (metaphorical) maps which are perceived to operate as exemplars of, and therefore to provide a framework for the critique of, colonial disclosure.[1] The exemplary role of cartography in the demonstration of colonial discursive practices can be identified in a series of key rhetorical strategies implemented in the production of the map, such as the reinscription, enclosure and hierarchization of space, which provide an analogue for the acquisition, management and reinforcement of colonial power.[2] My initial focus in this paper, however, will be on a further point of contact between cartography and colonialism, namely the procedures, and implications, of mimetic representation.

Mimesis, besides providing a theoretical basis for cartographic practice, based now as throughout much of the history of cartography on the possibility of producing a plausible reconstruction of a specific geographical environment, has proved through the ages to be a cornerstone of Western culture. Although the viability of mimetic representation has been repeatedly contested at least since the time of Plato, mimesis has consistently provided a means of promoting and reinforcing the stability of Western culture.[3] Yet, as theorists of colonialism such as Homi Bhabha and Edward Said (among others) have shown, mimesis has also historically served the colonial discourse which justifies the dispossession and subjugation of so-called "non-Western" peoples; for the representation of reality endorsed by mimesis is, after all, the representation of a particular kind or view of reality: that of the West. In this context, the imitative operations of mimesis can be seen to have stabilized (or attempted to stabilize) a falsely essentialist view of the world which negates or suppresses alternative views which might endanger the privileged position of its Western perceiver. Edward Said has related this view to the "synchronic essentialism" which he envisages as characteristic of Orientalist and other forms of colonial discourse. Said emphasizes, however, that the apparent stability of colonial discursive formations has been placed under continual threat both by historical forces which disrupt or at least challenge the discursive system adopted and applied by the dominant culture (or cultural group), and by internal inconsistencies within the system itself. These inconsistencies, claims Said, are brought to light when the system is imposed on cultures perceptibly different from that of the dominant.

Supporting Said's claim, Homi Bhabha identifies colonial discourse as an agonistic rather than an antagonistic mode whose effect is not to reinforce colonial authority but rather to produce a form of hybridization which mimics that authority. Bhabha correspondingly distinguishes between mimesis as an apparently homogeneous system of representation and mimicry as the articulation of a desire for a "reformed, recognized other . . . as the subject of a difference that is almost the same, but not quite" ("Mimicry" 126). Colonial discourse, Bhabha goes on to suggest, is the site of a clash between the Western desire for a uniform self and the need to define that self against reformed "others" which, although produced in the self's likeness, are never quite the same; the result is a double articulation in which "the representation of a difference . . . is itself a process of disavowal" ("Mimicry" 126). The destabilizing process set in motion by colonial mimicry produces a set of deceptive, even derisive, "resemblances" which implicitly question the homogenizing practices of colonial discourse. Mimicry also invokes a wider challenge to the authority of colonial representation by redefining the desire of the colonial powers to "fix" its own position as a form of "fixation," an obsession which, manifested in the fetishization of the other (through the workings of stereotype, discriminatory classification, etc.), confirms the fear that the supposedly normative values of the colonizer will come to be challenged, and eventually displaced, by the colonized. Thus, argues Bhabha, there is an ambivalence written into colonial discourse through which the informing colonial presence is "split between its appearance as original and authoritative and its articulation as repetition and difference" ("Signs" 93).

I have dwelt on this — inevitably oversimplified — paraphrase of Bhabha's theory because it seems to me that the shortcomings of the discursive system he describes are strikingly similar to those of the map, itself split between its appearance as a "coherent," controlling structure and its articulation as a series of differential analogies. In this context, cartographic discourse can be considered to resemble colonial discourse as a "narrative in which the productivity and circulation of subjects and signs are bound in a reformed and recognized totality" (DC 156). Yet cartographic discourse, I would argue, is also characterized by the discrepancy between its authoritative status and its approximative function, a discrepancy which marks out the "recognizable totality" of the map as a manifestation of the desire for control rather than as an authenticating seal of coherence. The "uniformity" of the map therefore becomes the subject of a proposition rather than a statement of fact; moreover, this proposition comes to be identified with the "mimetic fallacy" through which an approximate, subjectively reconstituted and historically contingent model of the "real" world is passed off as an accurate, objectively presented and universally applicable copy.[4] I stated before that the "reality" represented mimetically by the map not only conforms to a particular version of the world but to a version which is specifically designed to empower its makers. José Rabasa's critical reading of Mercator's seventeenth-century *Atlas*, for example, reveals historical links between the "reality" represented by Western world-maps and a privileged Eurocentric organization of geographic space which "institute[s] a systematic forgetfulness of antecedent spatial configurations" (6). Corroborating Rabasa's thesis, Gayatri Spivak uses the more recent example of the cartographic reinscription of India by the British raj to illustrate the colonizer's "necessary yet contradictory assumption of an uninscribed earth" (133). This assumption, claims Spivak, "generates the force to make the [colonized] native see himself as other" (133); but as she implies in her use of the word "contradictory," the desire to appropriate, secure and perpetuate the position of an other or others manifested in the regulatory operations of cartographic discourse and, by analogy, in the stabilizing rhetoric of colonial discourse, neither guarantees the effectiveness of colonial rule nor ensures the coherence of the discursive system which underwrites it. To return to Rabasa's reading of Mercator, the apparent coherence of cartographic discourse is historically associated with the desire to stabilize the foundations of a self-privileging Western culture. But this coherence is then contradicted by what Rabasa calls "blind spots" in the map which, brought to light in a rigorous deconstructive reading, identify the map's supposedly "universal" mode of representation as a set of rhetorical strategies which reinforce the prelocated authority of its European makers. Furthermore, these blind spots reveal flaws in the overall presentation of the map which allow it to be read in alternative, "non-European" modes; what passes for "universal" history therefore remains undecidable "not on account of a theoretical deconstruction of teleology and eschatology, but due to an everpresent deconstruction of Eurocentric world views by the rest of the world" (12).

Rabasa's application of a deconstructive methodology to the critique of European colonialism suggests that a working alliance may be formed between deconstruction as a process of displacement which registers an attempted dissociation from a dominant discursive system and decolonization as a process of cultural transformation which involves the ongoing critique of colonial discourse. To explore more fully the implications of this alliance, I shall devote the next section of the paper to a brief commentary on three concepts which suggest the applicability of post-structuralist "positions" (Jacques Derrida's term) to the critique of colonial discourse: these terms are, respectively, structure, simulacrum, and displacement.

The most succinct discussion of the first of these concepts is in Derrida's seminal essay "Structure, Sign and Play in the Discourse of the Human Sciences." His claim is as follows:

> Structure, or rather the structurality of structure . . . has always been neutralized or reduced [in Western science and philosophy] by a process of giving it a centre or referring to a point of presence, a fixed origin. The function of this centre was not only to orient, balance and organize the structure, but above all to make sure that the organizing principle of the structure would limit what we might call the play of the structure. By orienting and organizing the coherence of the system, the centre of a structure permits the play of its elements within the total form . . . [but] the concept of a centred structure, although it represents coherence itself, the condition of the episteme as philosophy or science, is contradictorily coherent. ("Structure" 279)

Derrida's postulation of the "contradictory coherence" of a discursive system reliant on the concept of a "centred structure" recalls Bhabha's reading of the ambivalence of colonial discourse; it also undermines the claim to coherence of cartographic discourse by revealing that the exemplary structuralist activity involved in the production of the map (the demarcation of boundaries, allocation of points and connection of lines within an enclosed, self-sufficient unit) traces back to a point of presence whose stability cannot be guaranteed. The "rules" of cartography, both those which function overtly in the systematic organization of the map and those which are implied in the empowering methods of its production, are duly discovered to pertain to a desire for control expressed by the power-group or groups responsible for the articulation of the map. This desire, however, is controverted by insufficiencies both within the assembled structure and, by implication, within its controlling agency, which is discovered to have laid false claim to the fixity of its own origins and to the coherence of the system it orients and organizes. In this way, cartographic discourse can be seen to play an exemplary role not only in the demonstration of the empowering strategies of colonialist rhetoric but in the unwitting exposure of the deficiencies of these strategies. The "contradictory coherence" implied by the map's systematic inscription on a supposedly "uninscribed" earth reveals it, moreover, as a palimpsest covering over alternative spatial configurations which, once brought to light, indicate both the plurality of possible perspectives on, and the inadequacy of any single model of, the world. Thus, Swift's famous derision of those seventeenth-century European cartographers who "in their Afric-maps with savage-pictures fill[ed] their gaps" neatly complements Rabasa's deconstructive analysis of Mercator's (contemporary) *Atlas*, which highlights conspicuous gaps, absences and inconsistencies in the presented text as a means of exposing flaws in the wider discursive system it exemplifies. A similar argument can be brought to bear on conceptual maps; as Kevin Hart observes in his gloss on Derrida, "all maps seek to be both complete and consistent but . . . in each case there are hidden gaps of one kind or another . . . [which] occur because each thinker takes either the material world or the conceptual world to be an instance of full presence; and, as Derrida argues, there can be no such thing: what seems to be a plenitude of presence is always already divided against self" (110). The issue is thus not whether deconstruction can somehow provide a "better" map but the eventual problematization of "any discourse which proposes itself as an exact map of reality" (113).

Derrida's implied critique of cartographic exactitude involves a reassessment of the relation between structure and simulacrum. The goal of structuralist activity, explains Roland Barthes, is to

> reconstruct an object in such a way as to manifest the rules of its functioning . . .
> structure is therefore a simulacrum of the object, but a direct interested simulacrum,
> since the imitated object makes something appear which remained invisible or . . .
> unintelligible in the natural object . . . the simulacrum is intellect added to object, and
> this addition has an anthropological value, in that it is man himself, his history, his
> situation, his freedom, and the very resistance which nature offers to his mind.
> (214–15)

Here again, cartography can be seen to exemplify structuralist procedure. A simulacrum of the world (or part of it) is produced through the participation of the intellect in the abstract reorganization of its "natural object": the external environment. But this participation is never neutral; thus, turning Barthes's terms against himself in a characteristically deconstructive ploy, we can identify the "anthropological content" of the map not just in the history, but in the interested history of man. So in Eurocentric maps such as Mercator's, to retain the working example, what the "imitated object" (the map) "makes appear" in the "natural object" it reconstructs (the world) is the anterior presence of the West, which is consequently revealed as the common denominator for the exemplary structuralist activity involved in the production of, and vouchsafing the "coherence" of, the map. A deconstructive reading of the Western map, on the other hand, is one which, focusing on the inevitable discrepancy between the "natural" and the "imitated" object, displaces the "original" presence of the West in such a way as to undermine the ideology which justifies its relations of power. This operation of displacement is tantamount to a "decolonization" of the map, where decolonization entails an identification of and perceived dissociation from the empowering strategies of colonial discourse (including, for example, a rejection of its false claim to a "universal" history). The result is a dismantling of the self-privileging authority of the West which also suggests that the relations between the "natural" and the "imitated" object which inform the procedures of cartographic representation are motivated by the will to power and, further, that these relations ultimately pertain neither to an "objective" representation nor even to a "subjective" reconstruction of the "real" world but rather to a play between alternative simulacra which problematizes the easy distinction between object and subject. In this sense, Barthes's distinction between the "natural" and the "imitated" object is jeopardized from the outset because the metaphorical activity involved in the imitation of an object presupposes a stability and, to use Derrida's term, a "fullness of presence," which that "original" object does not possess. Thus, the process of displacement engendered by deconstruction can be seen as one which disrupts the neat distinction between oppositional terms by emphasizing the instability of both the terms themselves and the structural relation between them.[5] The relevance of this disruptive process to the practice of cartography is considerable; for not only is the metaphorical resemblance between the map and the reality it purports to represent invalidated, or at least called into question, by the displacement of the ontologically stable relation between the "original" and its "copy," but this proposed resemblance is discovered to be the product of an ideological imposition which traces back to an identifiable rhetorical bias. This bias is related by Derrida to the metaphysics of presence which he associates with Western logocentrism, but as Bhabha, Said and Spivak, among others, have illustrated in their analysis of the figures of colonial discourse, it must always be situated within its specific cultural and historical context.

Thus, as Jonathan Culler has observed, the disruptive manoeuvres involved in deconstructionist activity shift emphasis from a conceptual opposition based on binary logic to an ideological imposition where that logic is used to justify, maintain and reinforce a specific socio-political system based on rigidly defined relations of power (150). The usefulness of deconstruction in exposing and undermining systems of this kind suggests that, rather than being perceived as a decontextualized theory which leads to a form of political quietism through its deferral of the decisions which might engender social change, a form of philosophical anarchism through its insistent refutation of "standard" wisdoms (Hulme; Felperin), or a paradoxical reinforcement of Western authoritarianism through its disguised relocation of, rather than its alleged dislocation of, Western ontological and epistemological biases, deconstruction can, by contrast, be considered as a contextualized praxis which enables the exercise of cultural critique and, in particular, the exposure of and resistance to forms of cultural domination.[6] The rest of this paper concerns itself with a particular aspect of this praxis, namely the ironic and/or parodic treatment of maps as metaphors in post-colonial literary texts, the role played by these maps in the geographical and conceptual de/reterritorialization of post-colonial cultures, and the relevance of this process to the wider issue of cultural decolonization.

The prevalence of the map topos in contemporary post-colonial literary texts, and the frequency of its ironic and/or parodic usage in these texts, suggests a link between a de/reconstructive reading of maps and a revisioning of the history of European colonialism. This revisionary process is most obvious, perhaps, in the fiction of the Caribbean writer Wilson Harris, where the map features as a metaphor of perceptual transformation which allows for the revisioning of Caribbean cultural history in terms other than those of catastrophe or complex. Throughout his work, Harris stresses the relativity of modes of cultural perception; thus, although he recognizes that a deconstruction of the social text of European colonialism is the prerequisite for a reconstruction of post-colonial Caribbean culture, he emphasizes that this and other post-colonial cultures neither be perceived in essentialist terms, nor divested of its/their implication in the European colonial enterprise. The hybrid forms of Caribbean and other post-colonial cultures merely accentuate the transitional status of all cultures; so while the map is ironized on the one hand in Harris's work as a visual analogue for the inflexibility of colonial attitudes and for the "synchronic essentialism" of colonial discourse, it is celebrated on the other as an agent of cultural transformation and as a medium for the imaginative revisioning of cultural history.[7]

More recent developments in post-colonial writing and, in particular, in the Canadian and Australian literatures, suggest a shift of emphasis from the interrogation of European colonial history to the overt or implied critique of unquestioned nationalist attitudes which are viewed as "synchronic" formations particular not to post-colonial but, ironically, to colonial discourse. A characteristic of contemporary Canadian and Australian writing is a multiplication of spatial references which has resulted not only in an increased range of national and international locations but also in a series of "territorial disputes" which pose a challenge to the self-acknowledging "mainstreams" of metropolitan culture, to the hegemonic tendencies of patriarchal and ethnocentric discourses, and implicitly, I would argue, to the homogeneity assumed and/or imposed by colonialist rhetoric. These revised forms of cultural decolonization have brought with them a paradoxical alliance between internationalist and regionalist camps where the spaces occupied by the "international," like those by the "regional," do not so much forge new definitions as denote the semantic slippage between prescribed definitions of place.[8] The attempt by writers such as Hodgins and Malouf to project spaces other than, or by writers such as Van Herk and Atwood, to articulate the spaces between,[9] those prescribed by dominant cultures or cultural groups, indicates a resistance to the notion of cartographic enclosure and to the imposed cultural limits that notion implies. Yet the range of geographical locations and diversity of functions served by the map metaphor in the contemporary Canadian and Australian literatures suggests a desire on the part of their respective writers not merely to deterritorialize, but also to reterritorialize, their increasingly multiform cultures. The dual tendencies towards geographical dispersal (as, for example, in the "Asian" fictions of Koch and Rivard) and cultural decentralization (as, for example, in the hyperbolically fragmented texts of Bail and Kroetsch) can therefore be seen within the context of a resiting of the traditional "mimetic fallacy" of cartographic representation. The map no longer features as a visual paradigm for the ontological anxiety arising from frustrated attempts to define a national culture, but rather as a locus of productive dissimilarity where the provisional connections of cartography suggest an ongoing perceptual transformation which in turn stresses the transitional nature of post-colonial discourse. This transformation has been placed within the context of a shift from an earlier "colonial" fiction obsessed with the problems of writing in a "colonial space" to a later, "post-colonial" fiction which emphasizes the provisionality of all cultures and which celebrates the particular diversity of formerly colonized cultures whose ethnic mix can no longer be considered in terms of the colonial stigmas associated with mixed blood or cultural schizophrenia.[10] Thus, while it would be unwise to suggest that the traditional Canadian and Australian concerns with cultural identity have become outmoded, the reassessment of cartography in many of their most recent literary texts indicates a shift of emphasis away from the desire for homogeneity towards an acceptance of diversity reflected in the interpretation of the map, not as a means of spatial containment or systematic organization, but as a medium of spatial perception which allows for the reformulation of links both within and between cultures.

In this context, the "new spaces" of post-colonial writing in Canada and Australia can be considered to resist one form of cartographic discourse, whose patterns of coercion and containment are historically implicated in the colonial enterprise, but to advocate another, whose flexible cross-cultural patterns not only counteract the monolithic conventions of the West but revision the map itself as the expression of a shifting ground between alternative metaphors rather than as the approximate representation of a "literal truth." This paradoxical motion of the map as a "shifting ground" is discussed at length by the French post-structuralists Gilles Deleuze and Félix Guattari. For Deleuze and Guattari, maps are experimental in orientation:

> The map is open and connectable in all its dimensions; it is detachable, reversible, susceptible to constant modification. It can be torn, reversed, adapted to any kind of mounting, re-worked by an individual, group, or social formation. It can be drawn on the wall, conceived of as a work of art, constructed as a political action or as a meditation. (Deleuze and Guattari 12)

The flexible design of the map is likened by Deleuze and Guattari to that of the rhizome, whose "deterritorializing lines of flight" (222) effect "an asignifying rupture against the oversignifying breaks separating structures or cutting across a single structure" (7–9).

As Diana Brydon has illustrated, Deleuze and Guattari's association of the multiple connections/disconnections of the rhizome with the transformative patterns of the map provides a useful, if by its very nature problematic, working model for the description of post-colonial cultures and for the closer investigation of the kaleidoscopic variations of post-colonial discourse (Brydon). Moreover, a number of contemporary women writers in Canada and Australia, notably Nicole Brossard and Marion Campbell, have adapted Deleuze and Guattari's model to the articulation of a feminist cartography which dissociates itself from the "oversignifying" spaces of patriarchal representation but through its "deterritorializing lines of flight" produces an alternative kind of map characterized not by the containment or regimentation of space but by a series of centrifugal displacements.[11] Other implicitly "rhizomatic" maps are sketched out in experimental fictions such as those of Kroetsch and Baillie (in Canada), and

Bail and Murnane (in Australia) where space, as in Deleuze and Guattari's model, is constituted in terms of a series of intermingled lines of connection which shape shifting patterns of de- and reterritorialization. In the work of these and other "new novelists," the map is often identified, then parodied and/or ironized, as a spurious definitional construct, thereby permitting the writer to engage in a more wide-ranging deconstruction of Western signifying systems (one thinks, for example, of Nicholas Hasluck's sly negotiation of the labyrinths of the legal system in *The Bellarmine Jug* or of Yolande Villemaire's playful critique of the semiotics of Western culture in *La Vie en prose*). If the map is conceived of in Deleuze and Guattari's terms as a rhizomatic ("open") rather than as a falsely homogeneous ("closed") construct, the emphasis then shifts from de- to reconstruction, from mapbreaking to mapmaking. The benefit of Deleuze and Guattari's model is that it provides a viable alternative to the implicitly hegemonic (and historically colonialist) form of cartographic discourse which uses the duplicating procedures of mimetic representation and structuralist reconstitution as strategic means of stabilizing the foundations of Western culture and of "fixing" the position (thereby maintaining the power) of the West in relation to cultures other than its own. Thus, whereas Derrida's deconstructive analysis of the concepts of "centred" structure and "interested" simulacrum engenders a process of displacement which undoes the supposed homogeneity of colonial discourse, Deleuze and Guattari's rhizomatic map views this process in terms of a processual transformation more pertinent to the operations of post-colonial discourse and to the complex patterns of de- and reterritorialization working within and between the multicultural societies of the post-colonial world.

As Stephen Slemon has demonstrated, one of the characteristic ploys of post-colonial discourse is its adoption of a creative revisionism which involves the subversion or displacement of dominant discourses (Slemon). But included within this revisionary process is the internal critique of the post-colonial culture (or cultures), a critique which takes into account the transitional nature of post-colonial societies and which challenges the tenets both of an essentialist nationalism which sublimates or overlooks regional differences and of an unconsidered multiculturalism (mis)appropriated for the purposes of enforced assimilation rather than for the promulgation of cultural diversity. The fascination of post-colonial writers, and of Canadian and Australian writers in particular, with the map topos can be seen in this context as a specific instance of creative revisionism in which the desystematization of a narrowly defined and demarcated "cartographic" space allows for a culturally and historically located critique of colonial discourse while, at the same time, producing the momentum for a projection and exploration of "new territories" outlawed or neglected by dominant discourses which previously operated in the colonial, but continue to operate in modified or transposed forms in the post-colonial, culture. I would suggest further that, in the cases of the contemporary Canadian and Australian literatures, these territories correspond to a series of new or revised rhetorical spaces occupied by feminism, regionalism and ethnicity, where each of these items is understood primarily as a set of counter-discursive strategies which challenge the claims of or avoid

circumscription within one or other form of cultural centrism.[12] These ter-
ritories/spaces can also be considered, however, as shifting grounds which are themselves subject to transformational patterns of de- and reterritorialization. The
proliferation of spatial references, crossing of physical and/or conceptual boundaries
and redisposition of geographical coordinates in much contemporary Canadian and
Australian writing stresses the provisionality of cartographic connection and places
the increasing diversity of their respective literatures in the context of a post-colonial
response to and/or reaction against the ontology and epistemology of "stability"
promoted and safeguarded by colonial discourse. I would conclude from this that the
role of cartography in contemporary Canadian and Australian writing, specifically,
and in post-colonial writing in general, cannot be solely envisaged as the reworking
of a particular spatial paradigm, but consists rather in the implementation of a series
of creative revisions which register the transition from a colonial framework within
which the writer is compelled to recreate and reflect upon the restrictions of colonial
space to a post-colonial one within which he or she acquires the freedom to engage in
a series of "territorial disputes" which implicitly or explicitly acknowledge the
relativity of modes of spatial (and, by extension, cultural) perception. So while the
map continues to feature in one sense as a paradigm of colonial discourse, its
deconstruction and/or revisualization permits a "disidentification"[13] from the procedures of colonialism (and other hegemonic discourses) and a (re)engagement in the
ongoing process of cultural decolonization. The "cartographic connection" can therefore be considered to provide that provisional link which joins the contestatory theories
of post-structuralism and post-colonialism in the pursuit of social and cultural change.

NOTES

1. I shall adopt here Peter Hulme's definition of colonial discourse as "an ensemble
    of linguistically based practices unified by their common deployment in the
    management of colonial relationships" (Hulme 2). For a more detailed account,
    see the opening chapter of Hulme's *Colonial Encounters*.

2. For an excellent summary of these strategies, and of the relations between
    cartographic and colonial practices, see J.B. Harley's essay in Cosgrove and
    Daniels (eds.).

3. For a development of this argument, see Mihai Spariosu's introduction to
    Mimesis in Contemporary Theory.

4. The argument is taken up and expanded in Christopher Board's essay in Chorley
    and Haggett. See also Philip and Juliana Muehrcke's discussion of the limitations
    of and distortions within cartographic representation, and Wright's early, but still
    relevant, essay.

5. For an investigation of the multiple implications of the term "displacement," see
    the essays in, and particularly Mark Krupnick's introduction to, the collection
    Displacement: Derrida and After.

6. Although I am taking issue here with the excessively negative tenor of the recent
    of critiques of Hulme, Felperin and Tiffin of the neo-hegemonic assumptions
    behind Franco-American deconstruction, I would support their general thesis
    that applications of deconstructionist—and other post-structuralist—

methodologies should take account of the ambivalent position of post-structuralist theory within self-privileging Western cultural institutions, and, in particular, of its apparent elevation to the status of a new orthodoxy.

7. For a fictional rendition of this argument see Harris's novella *Palace of the Peacock*. Many of the essays in his collection *Explorations* deal indirectly with maps as metaphors within the wide framework of a "revisioning" of Caribbean (and other post-colonial) cultural history. For essays which explore the implications of Harris's theories for post-colonial writing, see Slemon and Tiffin.

8. Cf. McDougall's comments on Hodgins in "On Location: Australian and Canadian Literature."

9. Cf. Grace's essay on Atwood in Grace and Weir.

10. See Brydon's critique of colonial ethnocentrism in "Troppo Agitato"; see also Dennis Lee's "Cadence, Country, Silence" for a discussion of the problems involved in writing "in colonial space."

11. See also Barbara Godard's introductory essay "Mapmaking" in the collection *Gynocritics*; and Benterrak, Muecke and Roe's reading of Deleuze and Guattari within the context of a post-colonial (more specifically, Aboriginal) critique of Western territorial imperatives.

12. The relevance of counter-discursive formations to post-colonial writing is discussed at length in the essays by Slemon and Tiffin. For a definition of counter-discourse (adapted by Slemon and Tiffin), see Terdiman.

13. The term is Michel Pêcheux's; for a discussion of its implications for post-colonial writing, see Slemon and Tiffin.

WORKS CITED

Atwood, Margaret. *The Handmaid's Tale*. Toronto: McClelland and Stewart, 1985.

Bail, Murray. *Homesickness*. Melbourne: Macmillan, 1980.

Baillie, Robert. *Les Voyants*. Montréal: Hexagone, 1986.

Barker, Francis et al., eds. *Europe and its Others*. 2 vols. Colchester: U of Essex P, 1985.

Barthes, Roland. "The Structuralist Activity." *Critical Essays*. Evanston: Northwestern UP, 1972. 213–20.

Benterrak, Krim, Stephen Muecke and Paddy Roe. *Reading the Country: an Introduction to Nomadology*. Fremantle: Fremantle Arts Centre Press, 1984.

Bhabha, Homi. "Signs Taken for Wonders: Questions of Ambivalence and Authority Under a Tree Outside Delhi; May 1817." Barker, vol. 1. 89–106.

———. "The Other Question: Difference, Discrimination and the Discourse of Colonialism." *Literature, Politics and Theory*. Ed. Francis Barker et al. London: Methuen, 1986. 148–72.

———. "Of Mimicry and Man: The Ambivalence of Colonial Discourse." *October* 28 (1984): 125–33.

Board, Christopher. "Maps as Models." Chorley and Haggett. 671–725.

Bringhurst, Robert. *Pieces of Map, Pieces of Music*. Toronto: McClelland and Stewart, 1986.

Brossard, Nicole. *Picture Theory*. Montréal: Nouvelle Optique, 1982.

Brydon, Diana. "Troppo Agitato: Reading and Writing Cultures in Randolph Stow's Visitants and Rudy Wiebe's *The Temptations of Big Bear*." *ARIEL* 19.1 (1988): 13–32.

Campbell, Marion. *Lines of Flight*. Fremantle: Fremantle Arts Centre Press, 1985.

Chorley, Richard J. and Peter Haggett, eds. *Models in Geography*. London: Methuen, 1967.

Culler, Jonathan. *On Deconstruction: Theory and Criticism after Structuralism*. London: Routledge, 1983.

Deleuze, Gilles and Félix Guattari. *A Thousand Plateaus: Capitalism and Schizophrenia*. Trans. B. Massumi. Minneapolis: U of Minnesota P, 1987.

Derrida, Jacques. *Of Grammatology*. Baltimore: Johns Hopkins UP, 1986.

———. "Structure, Sign and Play in the Discourse of the Human Sciences." *Writing and Difference*. Chicago: U of Chicago P, 1978. 279–93.

Felperin, Howard. *Beyond Deconstruction: The Uses and Abuses of Literary Theory*. Oxford: Clarendon P, 1985.

Godard, Barbara. "Mapmaking." *Gynocritics: Feminist Approaches to Canadian and Quebecois Women's Writing*. Ed. B. Godard. Toronto: ECW Press, 1987. 2–30.

Grace, Sherrill. "Articulating the Space Between: Atwood's Untold Stories and Fresh Beginnings." *Margaret Atwood: Language, Text, and System*. Ed. S. Grace and L. Weir. Vancouver: U of British Columbia P, 1983. 1–16.

Harley, J.B. "Maps, Knowledge and Power." *The Iconography of Landscape*. Ed. D. Cosgrove and S. Daniels. Cambridge: Cambridge UP, 1988. 277–312.

Harris, Wilson. *Explorations: A Selection of Talks and Articles 1966–81*. Mundelstrup: Dangaroo P, 1981.

———. *Palace of the Peacock*. London: Faber, 1968.

Hart, Kevin. "Maps of Deconstruction." *Meanjin* 45.1 (1986): 107–17.

Hasluck, Nicholas. *The Bellarmine Jug*. Ringwood, Victoria: Penguin, 1984.

Hodgins, Jack. *The Invention of the World*. Toronto: Macmillan, 1977.

Hulme, Peter. *Colonial Encounters: Europe and the Native Caribbean: 1492–1797*. London: Methuen, 1986.

Kroetsch, Robert. *Badlands*. Toronto: New Press, 1975.

Krupnick, Mark. "Introduction." *Displacement: Derrida and After*. Ed. M. Krupnick. Bloomington: Indiana UP, 1983. 1–17.

Lee, Dennis. "Cadence, Country, Silence: Writing in Colonial Space." *Boundary 2* 3(1976): 151–68.

Malouf, David. *12 Edmonstone Street*. London: Chatto and Windus, 1985.

McDougall, Russell. "On Location: Australian and Canadian Literature." *True North/Down Under* (1985): 12–42.

Muehrcke, Philip and Juliana. *Map Use: Reading, Analysis and Interpretation*. Madison: JP Publications, 1978.

Murnane, Gerald. *The Plains*. Ringwood, Victoria: Penguin, 1984.

Pécheux, Michel. *Language, Semantics and Ideology*. London: Macmillan, 1982.

Rabasa, José. "Allegories of the Atlas." Barker, vol. 2. 1–16.

Said, Edward. *Orientalism*. Harmondsworth: Penguin, 1985.

Shapcott, Thomas. *Travel Dice*. St. Lucia: U of Queensland P, 1987.

Slemon, Stephen. "Post-Colonial Allegory and the Transformation of History." *The Journal of Commonwealth Literature* 23.1 (1988): 157–68.

———. "Monuments of Empire: Allegory/Counter-Discourse/Post-Colonial Writing." *Kunapipi* 9.3 (1987): 1–16.

Spariosu, Mihai. "Editor's Introduction." *Mimesis in Contemporary Theory: An Interdisciplinary Approach*. Ed. M. Spariosu. Philadelphia: John Benjamins, 1984. i–xxix.

Spivak, Gayatri. "The Rani of Sirmur." Barker, vol. 1. 128–51.

Terdiman, Richard. *Discourse/Counter-Discourse: The Theory and Practice of Symbolic Resistance in Nineteenth Century France*. Ithaca: Cornell UP, 1985.

Tiffin, Helen. "Post-Colonialism, Post-Modernism and the Rehabilitation of Post-Colonial History." *The Journal of Commonwealth Literature* 23.1: 169–81.

———. "Post-Colonial Literatures and Counter-Discourse." *Kunapipi* 9.3 (1987): 17–38.

Van Herk, Aritha. *No Fixed Address*. Toronto: McClelland and Stewart, 1986.

Villemaire, Yolande. *La Vie en prose*. Montréal: Les Herbes Rouges, 1980.

Wright, John. "Map Makers are Human: Comments on the Subjective in Maps." *Cartographica* 19 (1977): 8–25.

What Was Post-Modernism?

JOHN FROW

Th e concepts of the post-colonial and the post-modern are perhaps most consistently defined in terms of their difference from and their difficult and ambivalent resistance to modernity. It is a logic of periodization that ties them together, or more precisely a logic of anti-periodization, defining them emptily through a retrospective negation. Even so open-ended and paradoxical a conception of period, however (the "post"), runs the usual dangers: of reducing a disparate set of political or cultural circumstances to a more or less unified temporality with an ultimately spiritual essence. My concern in this paper is primarily with the concept of the post-modern, but the moral is meant to apply more broadly.

For one of the driving difficulties of any attempt to think post-colonialism and post-modernism as specific epochal structures is the temptation to conflate the cultural and the political with the economic. Jameson does this quite deliberately (post-modernism is "the cultural logic of late capitalism"); others do it almost despite their own better intentions, as in the case of Schulte-Sasse, who, after carefully distinguishing "social" modernity and post-modernity from "cultural" modernism and postmodernism, then casually adds that "postmodernity and postmodernism refer to qualitative changes in society and their cultural manifestations" (6). The word "manifestations" gets the idea quite wrong because it sets up a mechanically causal relation between a primary and a derived realm, and thereby leaves no room for discontinuity or any more complex causality.

The problem lies both with the exclusion of the cultural from the social or the socio-economic, and with the expressive logic that then reduces it to a simple function of the more powerful pole. This creates a problem in part because it then becomes an easy matter to attribute some of the effects of complex social movements to the more limited cultural or political realm.

In order to clarify matters you might want to distinguish between three conceptual moments: *modernism* (a bundle of cultural practices, some of them adversarial); *modernization* (an economic process with social and cultural implications); and *modernity* (which overlaps with the modernization process, but which I understand as a philosophical category designating the temporality of the post-traditional world). The same distinction of ontological levels holds good, *mutatis mutandis*, for post-modernism, post-modernization, and post-modernity. The point is not to grant autonomy to these moments but to make possible their more complex and contradictory articulation.

Of these, the crucial and most powerful moment is that of modernization. This is the force that has torn apart our world, given it the shape of a modernity without precedent, and imposed upon it a relentless universality.

Contemporary accounts of modernization are dominated by the Weberian concept of rationality (this is as true of the modernization theory developed in the postwar period by empiricist social science as it is of Adorno and Horkheimer's *Aufklärung*, Habermas's *Zweckvernunft*, and Foucault's *discipline*). In broad terms, and allowing for significant theoretical differences, modernization is conceived as a more or less systemic process with some of the following components:

- the formation of a homogeneous economic domain through the extension and integration of commodity production and exchange;
- a shift from the closed time of feudalism to the open-ended, dynamic, and godless time of capitalism (specifically, the future-directed temporality of the return on capital and thus of capital accumulation);
- the gridding of space and time into calculable units, and the restructuring of work through the agency of decentralized disciplinary systems;
- the elaboration of mediated rather than direct relations of exploitation of surplus value, and the autonomization of the ethical self as the basis of contract;
- a movement from ascriptive and localized groupings based on kinship and community to highly differentiated social and economic roles performed within functional groupings and supported by a developed education system;
- the increasingly central role of the national state and its bureaucracy in the regulation of the market, the provision of infrastructure support, and the administration of social relations;
- extensive urbanization as part of a shift from agricultural to industrial production, and the extension of the communications and transportation networks;
- the development of machine technology, and the central productive role of scientific knowledge;
- the secularization and autonomization of the spheres of science, art, and morality.

My list is loaded to emphasize that I think modernization can be understood in terms of the forms of instrumental rationality generated by the logic of capital[1]; other lists would put their stress on apparently more autonomous modes of rationality (scientific, ethical, administrative, disciplinary . . .). Most such lists have in common, however, two structural features. The first is the unification of very heterogeneous processes within the concept of the modern, which in itself lacks any unitary logic other than the temporal. The second is that this unification is secured by means of binary opposition to another term, that of "traditional" societies. Here too the apparent unity of the term disappears as soon as we recognize the great variety of social structures classed as pre-modern; the fact that modern and traditional social structures are by no means mutually exclusive; and the extent to which the concept of the "modern" extrapolates from the model of industrially advanced Western societies (cf. Desai).

*   *   *

I have assumed the priority of the socio-economic process of modernization over the cultural and philosophical concepts of modernism and modernity; but it is arguable that this separation, and this priority, are inherent in the structure and the historical force of the concept of the modern itself. For quite precise reasons, which I shall discuss later, the concept of the post-modern seems to me not to be structured in this way. It is, nevertheless, organized in a similar manner through a potentially infinite set of binary oppositions. This is to say that it obeys a discursive rather than a descriptive necessity: its function is that of a logical operator, establishing categorical polarities which then allow — in a tautologous and self-justifying circuit — the construction of fictions of periodization and value. These fictions have no content other than the structure of binary opposition itself.

At the same time, however, we must recognize that this discursive necessity has a definite historical location. It responds to the inner contradictions of a modernism which has gone on too long. The temporality of modernism requires its own obsolescence: a modernism that failed to age, that didn't demand to be superseded, would be a contradiction in terms. Hence the necessity of a successor to modernism, but hence also its definition solely in a chronological form ("post") which refuses all indications of content. The paradoxical result of this is that, since this "post" must be a real *alternative* to modernism, it must be based upon a different temporality: not that of novation but that of stasis. It must be the end of history (hence the post-modern preoccupation with apocalypse). In its determination to *succeed* modernism, however, it corresponds entirely to a modernist logic. Habermas writes that, since the nineteenth century, "The distinguishing mark of works which count as modern is 'the new' which will be overcome and made absolute through the novelty of the next style" (4). In this sense post-modernism is precisely a moment of the modern, a "next style." Its founding gesture is a modernist destruction of the modern, a destruction which is logically entailed by the modernist programme itself.[2] As Lyotard notes, we may suspect today that this "break" is more like a repression (that is, a repetition) of the past than it is an overcoming of it (121).

Another way of putting this would be to say that the concept of the post-modern responds to a *narrative* necessity. This is what modernist artistic production looks like in Lyotard's heroic formulation — it is "a sort of long, persistent, and deeply responsible labour directed towards enquiry into the presuppositions implicit in modernity" (124–25) — a salvational project. Modernism, that is to say, is a *rigorous* programme which leads to a predetermined end; it has the pathos of a necessary trajectory. The modernist artist (Duchamp, Mies and Corbusier, Schoenberg and Webern, Mallarmé, Joyce, Kafka) is the one who explores the given material with absolute commitment and to the point of silence or madness. But this narrative continues, not with a simple succession but with a dialectical reversal: having reached the point of absolute aporia, having taken the exploration of the material to its end, the modernist project becomes both complete and irrelevant. The intervention of post-modernism at this point would involve not a linear succession but a change of ground. Losing faith in both the purity and the futility of modernist practice, post-modernism takes up the discarded or marginalized materials of modernism (figure and representation, for example, or humour and directness of enunciation), and exploits them with a quite different kind of rigour. The parallel with the strategies we associate with the post-colonial is, I hope, clear.

The problem with such an account is that it continues to reduce the heterogeneity of modernism to a paradigm of closed epochal unity. Positing a marked break between epochs, it reinforces the ideal-typical opposition between non-contingent historical unities, and thus cannot deal with the possibility that so-called post-modernist texts remain centrally within the "sentimental" aesthetic of modernism. Following Paz's definition of modernism as a "tradition against itself," Calinescu argues that post-modernism therefore *by definition* cannot escape this paradigm: "Even the 'post' in post-modernism appears to be an unconscious tribute to modernism and to its dialectic of transitoriness and negativity. Insofar as modernism always aspires toward its own dissolution, post-modernism should be seen as one of the most typical products of the modernist imagination" (168). Were it to be qualitatively different, post-modernism would have to be grounded in a quite different temporality, and would thus have to be the paradoxical reversal of its own act of rupture. It would have, not to initiate but to find itself within a stasis which would perhaps be that of a neo-classicism (and in this case its most representative form would be the advertisement, the genre which is most fully reconciled to the order of things and reads it as utopia), or else that of a frenzied renewal which, in a parody of modernist *ostranenie*, occurs in such short waves that it negates itself. This is to say that the post-modern is caught between contradictory imperatives:

to change/to be still;
to be historical/to be the end of history.

* * *

Much of the imprecision of the concept of *post*-modernism stems, then, from the difficulty of assigning temporal limits to cultural modernism, and — to complicate matters — from the different datings used in different cultural spheres. The beginnings of *literary* modernism are usually dated from around 1900 or a bit later. Roberts puts the decisive break in 1914, and describes it in terms of the transformation of the cultural market ("High art since 1914 is no longer bourgeois but produced by and for intellectuals"[54]). Certainly it seems clear that the moment of literary modernism had passed by about 1930, to be replaced by forms of writing whose relation to the modernist moment is still in need of clarification. Levin's essay of 1960, "What Was Modernism?" could speak confidently of modernism as a thing of the past, just as Trilling could speak in *Beyond Culture* (1965) of a fully accomplished and entrenched institutionalization of modernism. In the visual arts, however, a quite different periodization obtains: here the term modernism tends in current usage to mean the period from the late 1940s to the mid-1960s, associated with the dominance of the New York School and with Greenberg's "formally reflexive" conception of modernism. It is arguable that this dating corresponds to the institutionalization of the "critically reflexive" art of the modernist avant garde: as Newman (from whom I borrow this opposition) argues,

> Many of the arguments which assume Greenberg's theory of modernism and assert a postmodernism using post-structuralist categories may in fact be retheorizing a pre-Greenbergian modernism. This is an attempt to maintain a reflexive radicality, a questioning of the institution of art, and an emancipatory ethic — art as a contribution to knowledge and social self-awareness; but without a utopian conception of historical development and, in most but not all cases, without any commitment to a specific political project. Looked at critically, this might be seen as an attempt to maintain the stance of a modernist avant-garde in conditions where this is no longer possible or appropriate, and to do so through critical discourse. (32)

In architecture, finally, modernism refers to the more monolithic structure of the International Style, which has a quite different, non-oppositional relation to the culture of corporate capitalism, and which has undergone a more continuous development from the 1920s through to the 1970s. Indeed, it is in the case of architecture, which has been the privileged domain for the theorization of post-modernism, that these two problems, that of exemplification and that of periodization, most dramatically converge. The difficulty lies in the very terms of the opposition between the modern and the post-modern that is established here — that is, with the assumption of its generalizability. Does architectural Modernism in fact have anything to do with the other modernisms, does it share a common problematic or even a common temporality, or does it have a quite different rhythm and dynamic?

One way of establishing a correlation between architectural Modernism and other domains of aesthetic production would be in terms of a conflation of modernism with modernity. The central categories in such a model would be a certain mode of rationality and a certain complicity with the modernization process. Adorno's is perhaps the most explicit account we have of both of these features: the modernist work of art is characterized by its rigorous commitment to the inherent rationality of its material (however "irrational" this might be in another sense) and to the progressive development of this rationality through a critique of obsolescent forms. The more or less advanced state of the material is directly correlated with the more or less advanced state of the forces of capitalist production. And the dynamic of the work of art is that of an exploration of the autonomous domain in which the material is elaborated (cf. Bürger). An extrapolation of these features to architecture would describe architectural Modernism in terms of a claim to atemporal universality; a self-reflexive relation to architectonic space, including exposure of the materials and especially of the skeleton; an expressive ("functional") relation between inside and outside; and a willed autonomy with respect to the urban context. This formal separateness of the Modernist style is what Portoghesi calls a "dam carefully built around the pure language elaborated *in vitro* on the basis of the rationalist statute" (10).

Similarly, Krauss's description of the function of the *grid* in modernist art could be directly transposed into a description of Modernist architecture:

> In the spatial sense, the grid states the autonomy of the realm of art. Flattened, geometricized, ordered, it is antinatural, antimimetic, antireal. It is what art looks like when it turns its back on nature. In the flatness that results from its coordinates, the grid is the means of crowding out the dimensions of the real and replacing them with the lateral spread of a single surface. In the overall regularity of its organization, it is the result not of imitation, but of aesthetic decree. Insofar as its order is that of pure relationship, the grid is a way of abrogating the claims of natural objects to have any order particular to themselves; the relationships in the aesthetic field are shown by the grid to be in a world apart and, with respect to natural objects, to be both prior and final. The grid declares the space of art to be at once autonomous and autotelic. (9–10)

In their reliance on this principle, the organisation of artistic and of architectural space display clear structural parallels. On the other hand, however, it seems to me important to stress the very marked differences between the two domains. Modernist architecture is integrated into the capitalist mode of production and into a capitalist rationality in a way that is simply not true of other domains, which remain at once complicit with and deeply antagonistic to the logic of modernity. This is in part a question of the different functional relationship of architecture to capital, but it does suggest the difficulty of imposing a universal historicity on distinct and unevenly developed domains of the social.

*   *   *

It is post-modern architecture that constitutes the central exemplificatory instance in Jameson's 1984 essay on the cultural logic of late capitalism. Portman's Bonaventure Hotel in Los Angeles doesn't exactly exemplify the populist and vernacular thrust of post-modernism, since, rather than opening itself to the "tawdry and commercial sign-system of the surrounding city" (81), it withdraws into its own self-contained space, recreating the outside city in miniature. In this one might think that it resembles the aloof disjunction of the High Modernist tower from its surrounding cityscape, but Jameson argues that it corresponds, instead, to a new kind of collective practice and to a new (refusal of) politics: the Bonaventure "is content to 'let the fallen city fabric continue to be in its being' (to parody Heidegger); no further effects, no larger protopolitical Utopian transformation, is either expected or desired" (81).

This "peculiar and placeless dissociation of the Bonaventure from its neighbourhood" (82) is emphasized not only by the occlusion of entrances but by the way the building's glass skin repels its surrounding (giving back only "distorted images" in a deliberate play of illusion). We are confronted here not only with a refusal of relationship but with a turning inwards of signification. The escalators and elevators, for example, function in the first instance as self-regarding symbols: they "replace movement but also and above all designate themselves as new reflexive signs and emblems of movement proper"; and in this they represent "a dialectical intensification of the autoreferentiality of all modern culture, which tends to turn upon itself and designate its own cultural production as its content" (82). In the same (self-referential) movement the operation of reference is foiled: as the elevators rise "the referent, Los Angeles," is spread out beneath; but once you get to the cocktail lounges at the top the city is "now transformed into its own images by the glass windows through which you view it" (83).

In all this, and in the creation of the "hyperspace" of the atrium, the Bonaventure offers "something like a mutation in built space itself" (80), to which the human sensorium is as yet inadequate: the organicist metaphor, which derives ultimately from the passages on the historicity of the five senses in Marx's *1844 Manuscripts* by way of Benjamin's meditations on the experience of the modern city and of modern warfare, defines post-modernity as an evolution which bears strong marks of also being a fall.

There are two major problems with Jameson's discussion. The first is the assumption that there *is* a general "logic" of late capitalism, and that architectural post-modernism thus represents a definite break both with Modernist architecture and (which comes to the same thing) with the logic of an earlier phase of capitalism. This totalizing assumption is disputed by Davis (amongst others), who suggests a different periodization of the urban "renaissance" in relation to the rise of new international circuits of speculative and rentier capital; and a different context for buildings like the Los Angeles Bonaventure in the relationship between a highly capitalized downtown and surrounding urban decay.[3]

The second problem has to do with Jameson's choice of a *signed masterpiece* (Portman's Bonaventure Hotel) as his main example — an unusual choice, given the claim that post-modernism is subversive of the signature and of authorial originality. To emblematize the monumental is as problematic a procedure when you're talking about the built environment as it is in discussing literary texts, and it has the effect of marginalizing other kinds of building. Now, it seems true that the aestheticization of city space, and especially decayed inner-city space, has been one key feature of "post-modern" urban transformation (and it has to do with certain interesting transformations in the structure of late capitalism and of contemporary class formations: that is, it has to do with new, "culturalized" forms of marketing). But, as Zukin notes (440), it is already characteristic of architectural *modernism* to treat urban space in the aestheticizing terms of signature and saleable creation. It is within a modernist framework that "the marketing of design as both a spatial and a cultural commodity" begins, and "the production of superstar architecture derives from the same speculative building activity that generated high modernism." Indeed, if the paradigmatic shift from modernism to post-modernism is seen to consist only in certain stylistic transformations in the form of modelling of the signed monument then very little would seem to have changed.

The more meaningful shift is one of focus. The concept of post-modernism takes on life when it becomes a way of disrupting the hierarchical distinctions between important and routine architecture, between architecture and the rest of the built environment, and between spatiality and social structure. In this altered perspective (one which has particularly marked the discipline of geography in the last decade) it becomes possible to ask questions about the urban infrastructure as a whole,[4] and perhaps especially to ask questions about the construction of architectural *series*: that is, about the intensification of the "modernist" derealization of place through the building of non-localized environments. Much of the literature here (Relph's concept of "placelessness," Boorstin's "pseudo-place," Baudrillard's "hyperreality") is moralistic in tone, but it should in fact be possible to use a fairly neutral vocabulary to describe the form of spatiality of the shopping mall, the resort, the air terminal, the theme park, the motel.

*   *   *

But once you speak of such non-localized spatial series it becomes difficult to separate the "real" places (or the real non-places) from the representations of places that are coextensive with them: the "locales" of film and television, for example, or the self-contained world of advertising. Equally, it becomes impossible to detach the description of place from the description of the forms of social organization that sustain post-modern spatiality: the feminization and casualization of low-paid work, the increased reliance on migrant labour, deindustrialization and the shift of production to the Third World, the commodification of information and the rise of a new class of information-industry workers, the replacement of human by non-human labour and so on. The force of the concept of post-modernism here lies simply in its imperative to conceptualize both a new configuration of the cultural domain (in particular the blurring of boundaries between high and low culture and between commercial and non-commercial art) and a changed relation between culture and economic production.

The most interesting attempts to theorize the changed economic conditions which might, in one sense, be said to underpin post-modernist cultural production, but which in another sense have transformed the relationship of apparent exteriority between the cultural and the economic, are the recent elaborations of a cluster of roughly overlapping concepts describing a shift in capitalist production: the "post-Fordism" of the Regulation School (Aglietta, Billaudot and Gauron, Piore and Sabel, Boyer, Lipietz); Harvey's "flexible accumulation"; Lash and Urry's "disorganized capitalism"; and the more dispersed concepts of post-modernization and flexible specialization. With varying degrees of assuredness these concepts attempt to construct the terms of a general shift — Harvey dates it precisely from 1972 — in the regime of capital accumulation and regulation. A summary of these terms would look something like this:

- with the massively increased productivity of information technologies, capital becomes "hypermobile and hyperflexible, tending towards deterritorialization and delocalization" (Robins 149). This process accentuates the uneven geographical and sectoral development of production and of the division of labour;[5]

- there is a consequent tendency towards the disaggregation of large-scale industrial production and a move to dispersed production units to take account of local political and market circumstances, especially the price and conditions of labour;

- none of this implies a decentralization of economic power; rather there is a paradoxical combination of dispersed production, on the one hand, and on the other of centralized control of capital accumulation and of the circulation of information. New patterns of corporate organization are developed, in which monopolistic integration is complemented by the fragmentation and specialization of laterally linked units;

- the achievement of economies of scale is progressively abandoned in favour of the achievement of economies of scope; the diversification of demand in highly segmented and rapidly changing mass markets is met by the emphasis on "niche" markets, by increased product differentiation, and by a more rapid modification of product ranges (in contrast to the standardization of production in a Fordist regime);

- the new service classes of professionals and information workers acquire increased industrial prominence and increasing political and ideological influence;

- a substantial informal sector (a black economy based on casual work performed by non-union labour, sweatshops, migrant workers, and a feminization of low-paid work) develops over the last two decades; the model of welfare capitalism is in decline, and politically engineered transfers of wealth articulate an increasing gap between the poor and the rich (cf. Cooke);

- the flexibility of international capital and the constant threat of withdrawal of capital from politically unstable or hostile regimes, together with the weakening of organized labour in its defensive reaction to the strategic mobilization of capital, impose absolute limits on socialist strategy;
- inter-urban competition, developed as a response to the increased mobility of corporations, gives rise to the subsidization of corporate presence and to the renovation of the cities as centres of consumption and culture; there is an upsurge in the renovation and gentrification of inner-city areas;
- the "aestheticization of everyday life" is realized as a practice of differentiation of commodities and of places (with place now increasingly marketed as a commodity on the basis of its specific difference and/or its "authenticity"); Zukin (438) speaks of "an increasing commercialization of the social category of design."

This list is problematic in its agglomeration of economic, political, and cultural aspects of post-modernization, and there are important qualifications that must be made to the generality of the model. Robins, noting that accounts of post-Fordism are "increasingly congealing into a new orthodoxy of optimism" (147), cautions both against the assumption of an organic epochal transition and against a disregard of the fact that "so-called flexible specialization combines organizational and functional disintegration or disaggregation with the continued integration of control and co-ordination" (153). Rustin questions the model's adequacy to account for survivals of "mass production" modes and indeed for regressions to apparently superseded strategies (he cites the use of unskilled labour in the hotel industry, and the return to mass formula programming in the television industry). What seems to be emerging, he argues,

> is not one "progressive" mode of information-based production, but a plethora of co-existing and competing systems, whose ultimate relative weight in the system is impossible to predict. Since socio-technical systems do not develop completely autonomously, but only in response to cultural definition, conflicts of social forces, and political decision, it is dubious in principle and possibly misleading in fact to make linear extrapolations from what might seem to be "leading instances," or current trends, to the shape of the whole system. (58)

For my purposes it is crucial to refuse the deduction of post-modernist cultural practice from the economic categories elaborated here,[6] whilst recognizing that the relation of the cultural to the economic has nevertheless significantly changed.

In these terms, the key aspect of post-modernization is the last one listed, which describes the increasing integration of the aesthetic (in the form especially of advertising and design, but also of architecture, of music and Muzak, and indeed of all the arts from the "highest" to the "lowest") into the marketing of commodities. Zukin takes as emblematic of this process the totalizing strategies adopted by Benetton and

MacDonalds in developing "a total 'look' that merges product, production methods, a specialized consumption experience, and an advertising style" (437). But the integrating tendencies of a regime of flexible specialization affect not only the relations between cultural and economic production, but also the spatial ordering of production.

The salient features of a post-Fordist regime are in this respect those which concern the rapidity of motion of capital between nations and sectors, its ability to set nations and regions in competition against each other, and its ability to undercut the price and conditions of labour by means of extraterritorialization. A prominent example is the establishment in the 1970s of sweatshops in Taiwan, Korea, Singapore, and Hong Kong which directly competed with or displaced the First World base factories operated by the same corporations; but against this movement should be balanced the reverse process by which sweatshops and outworking systems based on migrant and female labour are established in the heart of the metropolitan society.

The result of this new speed and flexibility of capital is neither a colonial order of direct domination nor a neo-colonial order of indirect domination of one nation-state by another, but a world system — which we might call precisely "post-colonial" — in which dominance is exercised by international capital through the agency of dominant nation-states and regions but in large part independently of their control. It is in something like these dimensions that I think it is possible to frame — without reducing them to a singular temporality — the concepts of post-modern and post-colonial cultural production.

NOTES

1. I would also want to stress that the systemic nature of modernization has to do with the systemic logic of capitalism. Harvey describes it this way:
   > The transition to a capitalist mode of production was signaled by a shift from the production of capital and labour surpluses by process external to the circulation of capital to an internalization of surplus production within the circulation of capital itself. That shift was also signaled . . . by a role reversal in which rent, interest, merchants' profit, state powers and functions, and the production of built environments became servants of capital accumulation and subservient to its dominant logic. (*Urbanization* 195)

2. Cf. Rosen, 92: "Modernity arises as a 'project' . . . The subsequent rejection of modernity is then simply a re-enactment of the institution of modernity."

3. Davis, 106–13. Jameson mounts a defence of the concept of totality in "Marxism and Postmodernism."

4. The final two chapters of Edward Soja's *Postmodern Geographies*, for example, mention the Bonaventure as a "concentrated representation of the restructured spatiality of the late capitalist city," and then analyse the spatiality of Los Angeles in terms of financial and industrial agglomoration and the internalization of the local economy; large-scale immigration and the growth of an informal economy; deindustrialization and a post-Fordist reindustrialization accompanied by a

savage disciplining of labour; reliance on defence technology; the recompostion of the labour market through deskilling and an increased reliance on low-paid, non-unionized immigrant and female labour; and spatial restructuring through disagglomeration and decentralization, but also through renewed urban concentrations — the "downtown renaissance": and the rise of the "outer city." Cf. Dear.

5. Cf. Massey and Smith.
6. Harvey, for example, speaks of (cultural) post-modernity as "nothing more than the cultural clothing of flexible accumulation" ("Flexible Accumulation" 279).

WORKS CITED

Adorno, Theodor W. *Philosophy of Modern Music*. Trans. Anne Mitchell and Wesley Bloomster. London: Sheed and Ward, 1973.

Aglietta, Michel. *A Theory of Capitalist Regulation: The U.S. Experience*. London: Verso, 1979.

Billaudot, Bernard and Gauron, Andr. *Croissance et crise: Vers une nouvelle croissance*. 2nd ed. Paris: La Dcouverte, 1985.

Boyer, Robert. *Capitalismes: Fin de siècle*. Paris: PUF, 1986.

———. *La Théorie de la régulation: Une Analyse critique*. Paris: La Découverte, 1986.

Bürger, Peter. "The Decline of the Modern Age." Trans. D. Parent. 1984–85. *Telos* 62: 117–30.

Calinescu. "Ways of Looking at Fiction." *Romanticism, Modernism, Postmodernism*. Ed. Harry R. Garvin. Lewisburg: Bucknell UP, 1980.

Cooke, Philip. "The Postmodern Condition and the City." *Comparative Urban and Community Research, Vol I: Power, Community and the City*. Ed. Michael Peter Smith. New Brunswick, N.J.: Transaction Books, 1988.

Davis, Mike. "Urban Renaissance and the Spirit of Postmodernism." *New Left Review* 151 (May-June 1985): 106–13.

Dear, Michael. "Postmodernism and Planning." *Environment and Planning D: Society and Space* 4 (1986): 367–84.

Desai, A.R. "Need for Revaluation of the Concept." *Comparative Modernization: A Reader*. Ed. E. Black. New York: Free Press, 1976.

Habermas, Jürgen. "Modernity—an Incomplete Project." Trans. Seyla Ben-Habib. *The Anti-Aesthetic: Essays on Postmodern Culture*. Ed. Hal Foster. Port Townsend: Bay Press, 1983. 3–15.

Harvey, David. "Flexible Accumulation Through Urbanization: Reflections on 'Post-Modernism' in the American City." *Antipode* 19.3 (1987): 260–86.

————. *The Urbanization of Capital: Studies in the History and Theory of Capitalist Urbanization*. Baltimore: Johns Hopkins UP, 1985.

Jameson, Fredric. "Marxism and Postmodernism." *New Left Review* 176 (July-Aug. 1989): 31–45. Reprinted From: *Postmodernism/Jameson/Critique*. Ed. Douglas Kellner. Washington: Maisonneuve, 1989.

————. "Postmodernism, or the Cultural Logic of Late Capitalism." *New Left Review* 146 (July-Aug. 1984): 53–92.

Krauss, Rosalind E. *The Originality of the Avant-garde and Other Modernist Myths*. Cambridge, Mass.: MIT P, 1986.

Lash, Scott and Urry, John. *The End of Organized Capitalism*. Cambridge: Polity, 1987.

Levin, Harry. "What Was Modernism? (1960)." *Refractions*. London and New York: Oxford UP, 1966.

Lipietz, Alan. *The Enchanted World*. London: Verso, 1985.

————. *Mirages and Miracles: The Crisis of Global Fordism*. London: Verso, 1987.

Lyotard, Jean-Franois. *Le Postmoderne expliqué aux enfants*. Paris: Galileé, 1986.

Massey, Doreen. *Spatial Divisions of Labour: Social Structures and the Geography of Production*. New York and London: Methuen and Macmillan, 1984.

Newman, Michael. "Revising Modernism, Representing Post-modernism: Critical Discourses of the Visual Arts." *ICA Documents 4 (Postmodernism) and 5*. London: Institute of Contemporary Arts, 1986. 32–51.

Piore, Michel and Sabel, Charles. *The Second Industrial Divide: Possibilities for Prosperity*. New York: Basic, 1984.

Portoghesi, Paolo. *Postmodern: The Architecture of the Postindustrial Society*. New York: Rizzoli, 1983.

Roberts, David. "Marxism, Modernism, Postmodernism." *Thesis 11* 12 (1985): 53–63.

Robins, Kevin. "Reimagined Communities? European Image Spaces Beyond Fordism." *Cultural Studies* 3.2 (1989): 145–65.

Rosen, Stanley. "Post-modernism and the End of Philosophy." *Canadian Journal of Political and Social Theory* 9.3 (1985): 90–101.

Rustin, Michael. "The Politics of Post-Fordism: Or, the Trouble with 'New Times' " *New Left Review* 175 (May-June 1989): 54–77.

Schulte-Sasse, Jochen. "Introduction—Modernity and Modernism, Postmodernism and Postmodernism: Framing the Issue." *Cultural Critique* 5 (1986–87): 5–22.

Smith, Neil. *Uneven Development: Nature, Capital and the Production of Space.* Oxford: Basil Blackwell, 1984.

Soja, Edward. *Postmodern Geographies: The Reassertion of Space in Critical Social Theory.* London: Verso, 1989.

Trilling, Lionel. *Beyond Culture.* Harmondsworth: Penguin, 1965.

Zukin, Sharon. "The Postmodern Debate Over Urban Form." *Theory, Culture and Society* 5.2–3 (1988): 431–46.

Being there, being There:
Kosinsky and Malouf

GARETH GRIFFITHS

The accidental, the apparently contingent, the less (or more) than logical, the fact refusing to be contained, the fortuitous occurrence, the "random" event, the unplaceable object (in time or in space): all these seem to be features which the post-colonial text continually engages with and seeks to bring out from behind the silencing effect of imperialist discourse.

It is this concern with the extra-real, the "magical" and the illogical to which J.S. Alexis called attention in his brilliant and innovative address to the first Congress of Negro Writers and Artists in September 1956. In this address Alexis argued, amongst other things, that order, beauty, logic, controlled sensitivity have all been received, but will be surpassed in Haitian art which presents the "real" along with its accompaniment of "the strange and fantastic, of dreams and half-light, of the mysterious and the marvellous" (267).

In making this assertion that the post-colonial text would seek to push down the false barriers to the full experience imposed on post-European expression by the hidden universalist assumptions of "objective" realism Alexis was also careful to insist on the political dimension of the new claims of his "marvellous realism" and to distinguish it from what he called the "cold-blooded surrealistic researches" and "analytical games" of Europe. Along with his mentor Césaire he wanted to insist that the art which he sought to encourage would "lead always to man, to the fight for hope and not to free art and the ivory tower" (268).

Post-modern texts, too, concern themselves with the accidental, the apparently contingent, the less (or more) than logical, the fact refusing to be contained, the fortuitous occurrence, the "random" event, the unplaceable object (in time or in space) that is to say, the post-modern text and its concerns overlap considerably with those of the post-colonial in these respects. Yet, as Alexis's address seems to suggest, and as Césaire before him had asserted, the post-colonial critic and author have sought to resist the tendency of the post-modern to incorporate their project and subsume it into a concern which lays claim to being wider, more pervasive and less "provincial" (it is the term often used) in its provenance and aims (cf. Brydon). Above all they have expressed concern at the degree to which post-modernism has seemed to them to be at odds with the social and political aims of their projects, and the degree to which seemingly it has wedded itself to apolitical goals, stressing the individual existential impasse and answering it not even with the *angst* of modernism but with the black humour and *jouissance* of contemporary post-structuralist theories of "powerful" play.

It is in the light of these aims and distinctions that I want to speculate on the similarities and differences which underlie and are made apparent in the texts of those two modern projects, post-modernism and post-colonialism. To prevent the speculation from becoming totally diffuse and abstract, and to allow the arguments to encounter the particular densities and colorations of specific texts I have used the texts of two writers as examples, the Lebanese-descended Australian writer David Malouf and the Polish expatriate American writer Jerzy Kosinsky. The selection of these two writers itself incorporates something of the questioning of fixed causality, of overarching and determining extra-textual logic inherent, it seems to me, in the texts of both projects. It embraces contingency, chance, in the final sense, openness, as a dominant feature of both kinds of text, and, in a playful sense, in the selection of these particular writers. Finally, of course, like any selection it engages with the question of what qualifies or disqualifies a text for inclusion in either of these two very diffuse and disputed categories, and why.

Malouf's work, especially the text I want to concentrate on, *An Imaginary Life*, dealing as it does with the final part of the life of the poet Ovid and his death in exile from Rome in a remote and "barbarous" province at the edge of the known world, clearly offers a challenge to the conventional idea of what a post-colonial text ought to be about. Malouf's novel is post-colonial in provenance, as an Australian work, though to complicate matters, one written like most of his recent work from a voluntary partial "exile" in Italy. It is not, however, overtly concerned with the post-colonial experience, or place. Nevertheless, it can be cited as a work central to the view that post-coloniality of a text depends not on any simple qualification of theme or subject matter, but on the degree to which it displays post-colonial discursive features. What these features may be is again open to interpretation as are those of any discourse which seeks to constitute itself as discrete, but I might suggest that such concerns as linguistic displacement, physical exile, cross-culturality and authenticity or inauthenticity of experience are among the features which one might identify as characteristically post-colonial.

Yet it is arguable that Jerzy Kosinsky's work shares many of these features. Novels like the early work *The Painted Bird* deal with exile (internal exile at least), with linguistic dislocation and traumatic silencing, with marginalization and prejudice in cross-cultural encounters and so forth. Later novels repeat and develop these themes, and add to them the theme of exile in the external sense. In this sense they illustrate the argument frequently advanced recently that the project identified as characteristically post-colonial is really no more nor less than a local version of the wider twentieth-century projects associated with the term post-modern. Post-modernism, it is argued, also rejects the simple closures of realism and the ideological factors such closures hide; it embraces a radical openness which emphasizes itself in the text at the level of theme as well as formal feature. Post-modern texts, too, the argument continues, characteristically concern themselves with the ideological falsity of universal values, with the results of linguistic dislocation, with exile in its various manifestations (physical and spiritual, external and internal) and with the inability of modern life to authenticate itself without simultaneously revealing the "authentic" as merely reflexive and self-constructed. Both then are also, it is argued, characteristically subversive projects, founded in counter-discursive processes, often working either by direct and violent confrontation with expected norms of language or form, or, conversely, by parody or appropriation, by the re-incorporation of the classic and normative and by the juxtaposition of widely diffuse and contrasting styles and modes. Texts which share such features fall, so the argument goes, on both sides of the fence and have been claimed, at various times, by both groups. To quote Voltaire, for such texts "Te Deums have been sung in both camps." Examples of texts variously claimed in this way might include Salman Rushdie's *Midnight's Children*, Margaret Atwood's *Surfacing* or many of the recent South American novelists; for example, Gabriel García Márquez *One Hundred Years of Solitude* or Augusto Roa Bastos's *I, the Supreme*.

Of course, just as Malouf from one perspective may be regarded as only marginally central to the immediate concerns of post-colonialism, so arguably Kosinsky is only marginally post-modern in so far as his texts do not display the most obvious kinds of reflexivity; though the fragmented structure, the disconnected and episodic narrative, the absence of closure, and the displacement of concern from the author to the reader (insofar as the reader is clearly challenged, indeed at times it seems virtually threatened, to risk avoiding responding to the horrific activities of the text) may be held to be post-modern in a wider and, I believe, more telling way.[1] The texts, especially *The Painted Bird* and the six less well-known texts which have followed, challenge the reader to reject a world peopled with figures whose boundaries are limited morally by an ethic of personal revenge, whose sexuality is at best distorted and at worse bestial, and whose final judgement on their action resolves itself in the words of the rapist from one of Kosinsky's most violent texts into a decision as to whether the activity serves effectively "man's obligation to himself" (*Blind Date* 61). This philosophy of brutal amorality is defended, in the only full-length study of Kosinsky's work to have emerged so far, as a strategy of moral displacement:

> the charge is often made that Kosinsky's characters and situations are marginal and exaggerated. Kosinsky would reply that we are being naïve, that violence and disarray are the experience of many and the expectation of most: "It depends, I think primarily on your outlook. If you look upon the incidents in *The Painted Bird* and *Steps* and *Being There* as peripheral and insane and not too common, then you are bound to have a shock almost every day; but if you will see yourself as part of the larger community, if you will not keep yourself in a locked compartment marked 'for sane only', then you won't be very surprised when confronted by murder, persecution, or old age. Perhaps such an attitude would make you less 'sensitive' — but, conversely, that

would mean that the least aware, the most provincial among us, is also the most
sensitive."

Kosinsky's writing is aimed directly at eliminating our provincial "sensitivity." The
longer we blandly assume that death and pain is the experience of the other guy, the
marginal image on television, but no part of our own lives, the less we will be able to
cope with those things when they do enter our lives. (Lavers 154–55)

Such a defence seems to me to be peculiar, seeking to reimport some of the
containing strategies of realism back into what is surely the more radically subversive
project of Kosinsky's text, which is to make the text in effect an act of terrorism, an
act which by its very randomness, its inconsequentiality and its lack of purpose
radically questions the claims of normal society to order and coherence by refusing at
the fundamental ontological level to participate in the normative process of logic and
reason. The nature of this "terrorism" is, interestingly, the concern too of Malouf's
short novella, *Child's Play*,[2] in which the young terrorist protagonist about to assas-
sinate the ageing great writer speculates thus:

The crime becomes real because it is reported, because it is called an *act of terrorism*,
an *assassination*, because it threatens *mindless violence* and *anarchy*, because it
breaks into the mind of the reader as a set of explosive syllables. These are the language
murders we are committing. What more appropriate victim, then, than our man of
letters? And what more ironical, or more in his line of deadly playfulness, than this
subjection of his being to the most vulgar and exploitive terms, this entry into the heart
of that reality (that un-reality) that is the war of words. (91)

The sentiment, of course, is that of Conrad's secret agent, the target similarly
selected for its symbolic rather than its "real" value. Blowing up the site of Greenwich
Mean Time, like shooting the great liberal humanist writer, is an act of aggression
against the idea that stable authorized and universal values exist outside the social and
political forces which underpin them, forces which, from the terrorist perspective
constitute that deeper and more permanent violence embedded in society itself. The
act of terrorism is an act, then, of unmasking, of forcing into the open the arbitrary
nature of signification, and the false representation of power as natural process. It is
at this level that the projects of the two texts share certain similarities.

The fortuitous moment which made me yoke these two writers together in this
arbitrary fashion in a critical essay stems, however, from the similarity between the
images at the end of Malouf's *An Imaginary Life* and Kosinsky's *Being There*. Or, in
more specific terms, between the Malouf novel and an amalgam of the written text of
Being There and the film version (of which Kosinsky wrote the script) .

Let me set the two endings side by side for comparison; first the Malouf:

The Child is there.

He turns for a moment to gaze at me across his shoulder, which is touched with sunlight, then stoops to gather another snail from the edge of the stream. He rises and goes on. The stream shakes out its light around his ankles as he wades deeper, then climbs onto a smooth stone and balances for a moment in the sun, leaps, leaps again, then wanders upstream on the other bank which is gravel, every pebble of it, white, black, gray, picked out and glittering in the late sunlight as in a mosaic, where he pauses, gathers one, two, four snails, and with the stream rippling as he steps in and out of it, walks on, kicking at the gravel with his toes and lost for a moment in his own childlike pleasure at being free.

I might call to him. I have the voice for that. But do not. To call him back might be to miss the fullness of this moment as it is about to be revealed, and I want so much, at the very end here, to be open to all that it holds for me.

The fullness is in the Child's moving away from me, in his stepping so lightly, so joyfully, naked, into his own distance at last as he fades in and out of the dazzle of light off the water and stoops to gather — what? Pebbles? Is that what his eye is attracted by now, the grayest, most delicately veined of them? Or has he already forgotten all purpose, moving simply for the joy of it, wading deeper into the light and letting them fall from his hands, the living and edible snails that are no longer necessary to my life and may be left now to return to their own, the useless pebbles that where they strike the ground suddenly flare up as butterflies, whose bright wings rainbow the stream.

He is walking on the water's light. And as I watch, he takes the first step off it, moving slowly away now into the deepest distance, above the earth, above the water, on air.

It is summer. It is spring. I am unmeasurably, unbearably happy. I am three years old. I am sixty. I am six.

I am there. (*Life* 151–52)

Here, by contrast, is Kosinsky's ending:

Chance pushed his way through the throng of dancing couples toward the exit. In his eyes there lingered yet a faint, blurred image of the grand ballroom, of the trays of refreshments at the buffet, the multicoloured flowers, brilliant bottles, rows upon rows of shining glasses on the table. He caught sight of EE as she was embraced by a tall, heavily decorated general. He passed through a blaze of photographers' flash-guns as though through a cloud. The image of all he had seen outside the garden faded.

Chance was bewildered. He reflected and saw the withered image of Chauncey
Gardiner: it was cut by the stroke of a stick through a stagnant pool of rain water. His
own image was gone as well.

He crossed the hall. Chilled air streamed in through an open window. Chance pushed
the heavy glass door open and stepped out into the garden. Taut branches laden with
fresh shoots, slender stems with tiny sprouting buds shot upward. The garden lay calm,
still sunk in repose. Wisps of clouds floated by and left the moon polished. Now and
then, boughs rustled and gently shook off their drops of water. A breeze fell upon the
foliage and nestled under the cover of its moist leaves. Not a thought lifted itself from
Chance's brain. Peace filled his chest. (*Being There* 135-36)

It is, perhaps, necessary to add that in the film the final image is of Chance walking
out to the foreshore of a lake and beginning to walk across its surface, into which he
delicately thrusts, with a child-like experimentation, the end of his umbrella before
strolling across towards the far bank.

Let me begin by drawing some relatively crude distinctions, distinctions which
in practice might be modified by many readers but which seem to me to have
nevertheless a certain force. Both texts are concerned to delineate the thin line between
the real and the marvellous, to graphically, but not conclusively, dramatize how the
mythic, the imaginary, the transfiguring idea interweaves with and creates the world
we speak of usually as being there in some real, objective sense. Yet within this shared
purpose Kosinsky's text stresses the existential and Malouf's the material elements in
this exchange of levels of perception. If you like, Kosinsky's text is more concerned
with the "being" and Malouf's with the "there," though neither to the exclusion of the
other term in the whole equation. Malouf's text is grounded (the metaphor is an
appropriate one) in a sense of the materiality of the conditions under which the
perception of his narrator (the aged, dying Ovid) is formed. Kosinsky's narrator,
significantly undramatized in the text, a "free-floating" and omniscient narrator, is not
involved in the process of creating the final image in the same direct way. In Malouf's
text we are concerned with the coming into being of this perception, and its significance in terms of Ovid's physical (and so cultural) displacement in a geography of
perception. In Kosinsky's we are more concerned with the role of Chance and his
radical innocent detachment from purpose or consequence, from here and now,
concerned with it, that is, as a metaphor for the function of contingency in creating the
ever-present, existential choice, arguably the major concern of Kosinsky's text.

Kosinsky has maintained (though this, too, as we shall see has in practice resolved
itself into a form of fiction) that the writer ought not to speak by commentary or in any
other way to directly intervene between the completed text and the reader. Significantly Malouf, on the other hand, provides us with an Afterword, a device which resists
the more decisively "open" claims of Kosinsky's text. This Afterword, as one might
expect, throws light on the text to which it is appended. In many ways it forms the real

"final chapter" of the book, even though it is couched in an "objective" even "academic" style.[3]

In the Afterword Malouf tells us that his project has been to "make this glib fabulist of 'the changes' live out in reality what had been, in his previous existence, merely the occasion for dazzling literary display" (154).

The image Malouf employs here picks up the contrastive force of material and transcendent elements which divide themselves out in the image Ovid applies to the Child as they journey out from the remote settlement across the endless steppe.

> It is as if he moved simultaneously in two separate worlds. I watch him kneel at one of his humble tasks, feeding me, or cleaning up my old man's mess. And at the same time when I look up, he is standing feet away, as when I first saw him in the pinewood, a slight, incandescent figure, naked against the dusk, already moving away from me in his mind, already straining forward to whatever life it is that lies out there beyond our moment together, some life I have not taken into account, and which he will be free to enter only when our journey together is done. (149–50)

Even here at what appears to be a moment of perception in which the absolute categories by which Ovid has lived are radically and irrevocably disrupted by his experience of the Child's alienness and by the conditions and displacements of his own exile, a moment which, perhaps, not too fancifully, might be described as the abrogative moment, corresponding with that moment of denial common to early writing in the post-colonial world (the moment of colonial discourse [Griffiths]), the perception is still locked into the essentially Eurocentric opposition, that binary polarity on which Wilson Harris has commented so well and extensively (Harris). This moment contrasts powerfully with the final section of the text when, coming at last to "it, the place" (150), Ovid loses the ability to characterize this either exclusively as the end of time (the place of his death) or as exclusively the end of the world (the furthest place he reaches on his [life's] journey). At this point in the text such distinctions (or rather the meaningfulness of them) breaks down. Without any preciousness of reference, or any specific invocation or allusion, we are in a discourse in which the post-colonial and post-European categories invoked have at least as much in common with pre-colonial and pre-European formulations such as Aboriginal dreaming or pre-Columbian cyclical notions of time and space as with the space-time coordinates of a contemporary European physics. At such a textual point something very central to post-colonial discourse seems to me to be in the process of being created, a refusal of the privileging of certain categories over others in the establishing "evidence" for reality and meaningfulness.[4] If a privileging, though, does occur, and I believe it does at least as a form of negative discrimination against the dominance of the category of time (history) in Eurocentric formulations, then place, space, landscape dominate time, and obliterate it, at least insofar as they claim the transcendence of objective history. The insistence on the "there" of place reveals time at a personal and historical level to be a persistent and yet hidden construction in the Eurocentric picture of "reality."

Paradoxically, the post-colonial text (in this case, specifically, Malouf's) achieves this not by setting up "landscape" (space) as a sealed alternative but by revealing this, too, as a construct, by placing the narrator in a place where all signs (which are conceivable as always already there, as it were) are obliterated. Geography, like history — landscape, like time — is shown to be "imaginary," and so empowered not to fixity but to change. It is this imaginary life which Malouf constructs through his displaced narrator, cut adrift from the anchoring historicity of a fixed "Roman" geographical context by his journey beyond the known and so "real" world. Here in the text's final paragraphs he is pictured as cut adrift too from the identifiable features of a world in which he can categorize even the elements in a neat and stable way, as earth, as water, or as air.

Of course the perception of the narrator in the final section of the book has, for an Australian readership, a peculiar and local habitation. In Ovid's final description of the Child walking through the stream and up the bank into the mirage of water on which he seems to be balanced and beyond it into, seemingly, thin air, the Australian reader recognizes the physical accuracy of this depiction of perception in the endless flat country of his homeland, and in the distorting heat hazes of the Australian climate; recognizes them, that is, not as unique categories of experience (the setting here is, we presume, the steppes of what is now southern Russia, a landscape with just such features and perceptual possibilities) but as modes which displace the assumptions of immutability in Eurocentric discourses and taxonomies of place and of time, indeed, of even such discourses as the relationship of the "fixed" and "stable" elements themselves in which "to walk on water" or to "fly through the air" is to leave the world of the real for the imaginary, the world of truth for that of fiction, the world of the adult for that of the child whose categories, however appealing, are not those of the "real."[5]

Kosinsky's appropriately named Chance is a beguiling figure, who, at least insofar as the written text is concerned, is not (as represented by the actor Peter Sellers in the film) an intellectual defective or a mental retard but an innocent. Chance's thought processes are, as the text shows, complex and subtle, they simply do not relate to the cultural expectations around him since for decades since he was a very young child his world has been restricted to that of the house and garden within which his mind has been exclusively formed. In this sense he is like Malouf's Child who, brought up in the wild before his capture, is the last in a long line of representations of the *enfant sauvage*, amongst which, of course, the most famous is also a post-colonial example, Kipling's Mowgli. Yet for Kosinsky the circumstances of the child, the specific cultural formations which bring his innocence into being and which simultaneously disable and empower him through the radical difference of his perceptive mode is of little concern. This is borne out by his lack of resistance to the very different characterization brought to the character by Sellers in the film version (Kosinsky was also the scriptwriter for the film version), a difference which by stressing the source of Chance's innocence as inherent rather than cultural profoundly altered the significance of the original character and text. For Kosinsky the perception of Chance is directed towards the confirmation of his belief that above and beyond all such conditionings, finally, contingency operating through the random and fortuitous individual instance and action is all that we can know.[6] That this is his position we can surmise from text after text. It is stated as clearly as anywhere in *The Devil Tree* when the protagonist, the young multi-millionaire playboy J.J. Whalen, is being initiated into a secret governing order of rich and powerful men dedicated to the proposition that "the individual comes first, along with his virtues: honorable ambition, fair speech, pure thoughts, and straightforward action." Whalen, challenged as to whether he objects to the proposition, can only recall the words spoken by the minister over the grave of the young adventuress with whom he has had one of his numerous brutalized affairs in Rangoon, and who has died as a result of the opium addiction to which he has introduced her. The words are, that "[o]f all living creatures, only the human being carries in himself the ultimate threat to his vital existence: the freedom to say yes or no to it, to reaffirm or to transcend the boundaries set for us by the indifferent world" (197).

Apart from the difficulty of imagining what kind of minister in Rangoon would be likely to make such an existential statement at the grave of a young drug-addict, it seems inadequate to argue that this sort of detached, existential philosophy stated time after time in the text is not finally a close approximation to the position of Kosinsky himself. This is borne out in those non-fictional essays which, disingenuously, he has published from time to time, always after an elaborate excuse that they had been previously pirated and so his speaking out in contradiction to his stated belief that the author has no control or connection with the text once it has left his desk is the result of his being forced to do so. In *The Art of the Self: Essays à propos 'Steps,'* the first of these forced confessions, Kosinsky produces an incredibly narcissistic version of Sartrean Self-Other definition. Defining the role of the protagonist in this novel as being to find out who he is, what self is his, and to avoid the loss or dilution of self into some larger whole, he argues that his fiction seeks to avoid the restriction of such larger wholes not only by its attack on collective institutions of all kinds but also by avoiding imagination itself as one such institution. In the words of Kosinsky's most energetic critic and supporter, Norman Lavers, he seeks to show that imagination itself

> can be one of the many enemies of selfhood, because imagination comes between the narrator and "reality" and it is only in reality that the self exists: "for the narrator reality becomes a prerequisite of consciousness of the self." Partly this is because the imagination can tie us to past memory, and reality exists only in the present instant. . . . Modern art attempts to break down the blocks of perception in order to create a reality of pure perception, reality before it is formed into episodes. It objects to the imposing on the present a form of the past, an episode, since it claims that original perception precedes all forms. (73)

This demonstrates very clearly the great gap between a post-modern text such as Kosinsky's and a post-colonial text, despite the similarities of theme and formal structures I have outlined. For Kosinsky the possibility of undoing the control of the oppressive aspects of social and cultural institutions is addressable only at an immediate existential level. He seeks as his project to go behind and beyond cultural formation into some pure existential activity free from all controlling agencies of past or future. Detaching himself from any philosophy which embraces a future project except that of the Heideggerian project of forfeiture, escapable only through the *angst-voll* authentication brought into our present by a contemplation of our future death, he nevertheless in practice stresses a dependency on the fact of existence which if not transcendent in its philosophic credentials is exactly that in its effect. As Lavers points out, Kosinsky is strongly influenced by Heidegger; the Heideggerian term for Being (self-hood), Dasein, was, in fact, the working title for the novel *Being There* (125–26). The paradoxical position Kosinsky's text articulates is precisely that of post-modernism as a whole, and of the post-structuralist philosophical positions which underpin it. Claiming that only by scrupulously avoiding the "grounding" of any moment in a larger project can the tyranny of institutionalization and of "foreshadowing" be avoided in practice, the texts end by endorsing the most tyrannous of instrumentalities and political conditions. The *angst-voll* position, arms thrown up and mouth open in a silent scream, has proved a very ineffective response to the continuing brutalities of personal and institutional violence.

Despite the invocation of freeing the text from oppressive institutions and the "foreshadowed" conclusions involved in any project (such as religion or Marxism), which suggests that "man's destiny is spelled out in the central plot of life" (*Blind Date* 86), the politics of the text is finally to refuse the existence of any determining social or cultural formations, and to postulate for the artist, as for the individual, an absolutely free realm of existential choice beyond any such determinants. Whatever its credentials, in the late twentieth-century world this is to walk on water indeed.

The project of the post-colonial text, on the other hand, can never lose sight of the determining cultural factors which bring it into being, since it is grounded in a perception of how Self and Other are constituted within a discursive matrix which includes the material forces and institutions of cultural production and reproduction, as well as the social and political institutions which give rise to these and to which they lend their support.

Kosinsky's view of Self-Other relations is, as Lavers notes, grounded for the most part in a positive depiction of the establishment and preservation of selfhood by domination of the other. As Kosinsky says:

> The only truly satisfying relationship, then, is one of growing domination, one in which the narrator's experience — a certain form of the past — can be projected onto the other person. Until this hold is gained (assuming that the 'prey' has some

awareness of the protagonist's purpose), the 'prey' maintains some superiority over the protagonist and remains his rival. (Lavers 73)

Lavers, who characterizes this response as "almost admirable, valiantly preserving his selfhood against all hazards" (sic), is forced, reluctantly, to admit that Kosinsky does seem to show a slight acquaintance with Sartre's preference in *Being and Nothingness* for Self-Other relations which display mutuality, and in which as Kosinsky notes there is the attempt to be "simultaneously subject and object, and [in which] the willing relinquishment of the single subject to a new subject created from two single ones, each subject enhanced into one heightened self" (Lavers 74) is achieved. It is significant that such relations appear in the fiction only as negatives, that is, represented to the reader by the depiction of their opposite (in this case, in the sado-masochistic relationship of the ski-instructor in *Steps* with the moribund sanatorium patients). Such representation is again justified by the argument that it is a strategy of moral displacement (as I tried above to characterize it). However that may be, it is certainly a strategy which leads away from any conviction that the Self and its "survival" (read also for this understanding, comprehension and growth) is at the very least dependent upon a network of such mutualities, and that in any meaningful world these must involve the larger constructions of group, of culture, and of society. It leads, that is, away from any belief that the perceived and influential existential crisis of twentieth-century man has itself any limitation or fixedness in a specific historically determined and geographically limited cultural crisis, and that it is itself corrigible, able to be fruitfully and successfully negotiated. It leads away from even the most limited optimism beyond that vested in the vision of the capacity of each person to survive in the most basic way and to discover any such mutualities beyond the most fleeting present instants. It is precisely against this minimalist and pessimistic vision that the post-colonial text speaks out, perceiving as it does that what is again offered as a universal truth, the negative *angst-voll* vision of post-Heideggerian European thought, is in fact one spoken from a very specific historical and geographical position in the world (Meyer 39–50).

Kosinsky's Chance at the end of *Being There* walks out into a world of absolute negation; in the novel to an absolute mindless peace; in the filmscript to a deliberately tongue-in-cheek and ironically presented non-world of miracle and flim-flammery. Malouf's Child, on the other hand, walks out of the limitations of Ovid's perception, out of the restrictive defining contexts of either the crude society Ovid now inhabits or the false sophistication of that from which he has been exiled, into a possibility of endless alternatives, the formation in different times and places of radically new possibilities for humankind. The optimism of the latter is grounded not in any romantic, apolitical vision but in the directly material perception that human possibility is created and denied not only by the discourses within which it is produced but by the material practices which these discourses express, practices which include the physical world whose landscape and character may form a profound resistant substratum to the discourse which seeks to incorporate it into some transcendent cultural "geography."

As one recent critic has argued, the origin of works of art from "New" worlds such as America or any other post-colonial society "can never arise from the de-construction of any historical tradition of bibles/texts but only from the Emersonian command 'Forget the past!' or the Whitmanian transformation of 'pray without ceasing' into 'look for me under your boot-soles' " (Meyer 49). In this sense the site of post-colonial texts is seen to be like the place which, for Malouf's Ovid, is both the end and the beginning of his journey and of the possibilities of his discourse, finally both undeniably there and absolutely boundless.

NOTES

1. Kosinsky's texts form what must be one of the most unrelievedly brutal expositions of modern life, studded as they are with scenes of gratuitous brutality, sexual and non-sexual violence, as well as extreme physical and emotional behaviour. Their characters exist frequently on the far edge of "normal" society and behaviour, and often overlap with popular genre types such as young playboys, secret agents, assassins and so forth. In fact so much so that, republished in lurid covers they have, despite their difficulty as "texts," had a signal success as popular "soft-core" pornography, and in this slightly disguised condition can, occasionally, be encountered plying their trade at airport bookshops and other such venues.

2. In fact it is in the spirit of coincidence that once embarked on the comparison of the two writers I was, of course, forced to perceive endless abutments between their texts from their frequent incorporation of the personal and autobiographical into the texture of their fictions to specific concerns and themes such as this.

3. We have learned, of course, to distrust such fictive objective commentators ever since the pronouncements of that early Nabokovian mask, John Ray, Jr., Ph.D., of Widsworth, Mass.

4. In fact, of course, some writers on post-modernism, such as Jean-François Lyotard, acknowledge precisely the inadequacy of the privileging of scientific discourses over customary discourses and distinguish this as one of the primary modes by which imperialist discourses have come into being. Even though their interest in this is displaced to a concern with the "wider" issue of contemporary ways of "knowing" the world and their limitations, it raises a fascinating point for post-colonial theorists, who may feel that precedences of various kinds flow from this perception.

5. That European discourses are still profoundly resistant to anything but the most qualified acceptance of such alternative modes of conceiving the world can be seen daily in the Australian press in the way in which Aboriginal claims to a perception of a timeless and physically limitless and indissoluble bond between a spirit presence and a physical site is dealt with in regard to the current Lands Rights issues and the Aboriginal claim to the traditional "sacred sites" of the Dreaming. The well-meaning liberalism (even where this exists) of the journalists and commentators breaks down in the pragmatic way in which they seek to articulate their understanding of the inhabitation of a site by a being whose always and eternal significance is vested in the there-ness of the site, not in some specific appearance or "sighting." Such limitations of the perceptual apparatus

of European discursive categories means that even the most liberal commentator seems sometimes to be equating such Aboriginal beings as the Waggyl or the Kunapipi with the yeti or big-foot (themselves, of course, creatures whose "reality" certainly does not depend for the Tibetan or the North American Indian as it seems to do for the European on the existence of so-called objective, scientific proof, i.e., a dead carcass which alone can constitute the incorporation of the being into the category of "specimen" necessary to precede their proper and permanent classification).

6. Kosinsky has embraced this both extra- and intra-textually with his long exposition of the philosophy of Jacques Monod in the critical texts and with the introduction of Monod as a character in the novel *Blind Date*.

WORKS CITED

Alexis, J.S. "Of the Marvellous Realism of the Haitians." *Présence Africaine* 8–10: 260–68.

Atwood, Margaret. *Surfacing*. Toronto: McClelland and Stewart, 1972.

Bastos, Augusto Roa. *I, The Supreme*. New York: Knopf, 1986.

Brydon, Diana. "The Thematic Ancestor: Joseph Conrad, Patrick White and Margaret Atwood." *WLWE* 24.2 (1984): 386–96.

Griffiths, Gareth. "Imitation, Abrogation, and Appropriation: the production of the post-colonial text." *Kunapipi* 9.1 (1987): 13–20.

Harris, Wilson. *The Womb of Space: the Cross-Cultural Imagination*. Westport, Conn.: Greenwood, 1983.

Kosinsky, Jerzy. *The Painted Bird*. Boston: Houghton Mifflin, 1965.

———. *Steps*. New York: Random House, 1968.

———. *Being There*. London: Bodley Head, 1971.

———. *The Devil Tree*. 1979. Rev. New York: St. Martin's Press, 1981.

———. *Blind Date*. London: Hutchinson, 1978.

Lavers, Norman. *Jerzy Kosinsky*. Boston: Twayne, 1982.

Malouf, David. *An Imaginary Life*. London: Chatto and Windus, 1978.

———. *Child's Play*. Ringwood, Victoria: Penguin, 1983.

Márquez, Gabriel García. *One Hundred Years of Solitude*. New York: Harper, 1970.

Meyer, William H. "Emerson vs. Heidegger: the Case for a New World Aesthetic." *New Literature Review* 16 (1988): 39–50.

Rushdie, Salman. *Midnight's Children*. London: Cape, 1981.

"Circling the Downspout of Empire"

LINDA HUTCHEON

The subject of Daphne Marlatt's phrase "circling the downspout of Empire" is "[C]anadians," and she is not alone in seeing Canada as still caught up in the machinations of Empire and colony, imperial metropolis and provincial hinterland (see Monk 14). Irving Layton once defined "Anglo-Canadian" in these terms:

> A native of Kingston, Ont,
> — two grandparents Canadian
> and still living
>
> His complexion florid
> as a maple leaf in late autumn,
> for three years he attended
> Oxford
>
> Now his accent
> makes even Englishmen
> wince, and feel
> unspeakably colonial.
> (Scott and Smith 75)

Whatever truth there may be in these accusations of *neo*-colonialism, there are many others who are coming to prefer to talk about Canada in terms of *post*-colonialism, and to place it in the context of other nations with which it shares the experience of colonization. In much recent criticism, this context has also come to overlap with that of post-modernism. Presumably, it is not just a matter of the common prefix or of the contemporaneity of the two enterprises. In literary critical circles, debates rage about whether the post-colonial *is* the post-modern or whether it is its very antithesis (see Tiffin, "Post-Colonialism").

Part of the problem in deciding which camp to belong to is that in many of these debates the term post-modernism is rarely defined precisely enough to be more than a synonym for today's multinationalist capitalist world at large. But it *can* have a more precise meaning. The architecture which first gave aesthetic forms the label "post-modern" is, interestingly, both a critique of High Modern architecture (with its purist ahistorical embracing of what, in effect, was the modernity of capitalism) and a tribute to its technological and material advances. Extending this definition to other art forms, "post-modern" could then be used, by analogy, to describe art which is paradoxically both self-reflexive (about its technique and material) and yet grounded in historical and political actuality. The fiction of writers like E.L. Doctorow, Graham Swift, Salman Rushdie, Michael Ondaatje, Toni Morrison, and Angela Carter might provide examples. I have deliberately included here writers who would be categorized by others as either post-colonial or feminist in preference to the label "post-modern." While I want to argue here that the links between the post-colonial and the post-modern are strong and clear ones, I also want to underline from the start the major difference, a difference post-colonial art and criticism share with various forms of feminism. Both have distinct political agendas and often a theory of agency that allow them to go beyond the post-modern limits of deconstructing existing orthodoxies into the realms of social and political action. While it is true that post-colonial literature, for example, is also inevitably implicated and, in Helen Tiffin's words, "informed by the imperial vision" ("Post-Colonialism" 172), it still possesses a strong political motivation that is intrinsic to its oppositionality. However, as can be seen by its recuperation (and rejection) by both the Right and the Left, post-modernism is politically ambivalent: its critique coexists with an equally real and equally powerful complicity with the cultural dominants within which it inescapably exists.

Those cultural dominants, however, are shared by all three forces. As Gayatri Spivak notes: "There is an affinity between the imperialist subject and the subject of humanism" (202). While post-colonialism takes the first as its object of critique and post-modernism takes the second, feminists point to the patriarchal underpinnings of both. The title of a recent book of essays on colonial and post-colonial women's writing pinpoints this: *A Double Colonization* (Petersen and Rutherford). Feminisms have had similar impacts on both post-modern and post-colonial criticism. They have redirected the "universalist" — humanist and liberal — discourses (see Larson) in which both are debated and circumscribed. They have forced a reconsideration of the nature of the doubly colonized (but perhaps not yet doubly de-colonized) subject and its representations in art (see Donaldson). The current post-structuralist/post-modern challenges to the coherent, autonomous subject have to be put on hold in feminist and post-colonial discourses, for both must work first to assert and affirm a denied or alienated subjectivity: those radical post-modern challenges are in many ways the luxury of the dominant order which can afford to challenge that which it securely possesses.

Despite this major difference between the post-modern and the post-colonial — which feminisms help to place in the foreground and which must always be kept in mind — there is still considerable overlap in their concerns: formal, thematic, strategic. This does not mean that the two can be conflated unproblematically, as many commentators seem to suggest (Pache; Kröller, "Postmodernism"; Slemon, "Magic"). Formal issues such as what is called "magic realism," thematic concerns regarding history and marginality, and discursive strategies like irony and allegory are all shared by both the post-modern and the post-colonial, even if the final uses to which each is put may differ (cf. During 1985, 369). It is not a matter of the post-colonial *becoming* the post-modern, as one critic has suggested (Berry 321), but rather that the manifestations of their (different, if related) concerns often take similar forms; for example, both often place textual gaps in the foreground but their sites of production differ: there are "those produced by the colonial encounter and those produced by the system of writing itself" (Slemon, "Magic" 20), and they should not be confused.

The formal technique of "magic realism" (with its characteristic mixing of the fantastic and the realist) has been singled out by many critics as one of the points of conjunction of post-modernism and post-colonialism. Its challenges to genre distinctions and to the conventions of realism are certainly part of the project of both enterprises. As Stephen Slemon has argued, until recently it has been used to apply to Third World literatures, especially Latin American (see Dash) and Caribbean, but now is used more broadly in other post-colonial and culturally marginalized contexts to signal works which encode within themselves some "resistance to the massive imperial centre and its totalizing systems" (Slemon, "Magic" 10; also "Monuments"). It has even been linked with the "new realism" of African writing (Irele 70–71) with its emphasis on the localized, politicized and, inevitably, the historicized. Thus it becomes part of the dialogue with history that both post-modernism and post-colonialism undertake. After modernism's ahistorical rejection of the burden of the past, postmodern art has sought self-consciously (and often even parodically) to reconstruct its relationship to what came before; similarly, after that imposition of an imperial culture and that truncated indigenous history which colonialism has meant to many nations, post-colonial literatures are also negotiating (often parodically) the once tyrannical weight of colonial history in conjunction with the revalued local past. The post-modern and the post-colonial also come together, as Frank Davey has explained, because of the predominant non-European interpretation of modernism as "an international movement, elitist, imperialist, 'totalizing,' willing to appropriate the local while being condescending toward its practice" (119).

In post-modern response, to use Canadian examples, Margaret Atwood rewrites the local story of Susanna Moodie, Rudy Wiebe that of Big Bear and Louis Riel, George Bowering that of George Vancouver. And in so doing, all also manage to contest the dominant Eurocentric interpretation of Canadian history. Despite the Marxist view of the post-modern as ahistorical — because it questions, rather than confirms, the process of History — from its roots in architecture on post-modernism has been embroiled in debates and dialogues with the past (see Hutcheon). This is where it overlaps significantly with the post-colonial (Kröller, "Politics" 121) which, by definition, involves a "recognition of historical, political, and social circumstances" (Brydon 7). To say this is not to appropriate or recuperate the post-colonial into the post-modern, but merely to point to the conjunction of concerns which has, I think, been the reason for the power as much as the popularity of writers such as Salman Rushdie, Robert Kroetsch, Gabriel García Márquez, and so many others.

At this thematic and structural level, it is not just the relation to history that brings the two *posts* together; there is also a strong shared concern with the notion of marginalization, with the state of what we could call ex-centricity. In granting value to (what the centre calls) the margin or the Other, the post-modern challenges any hegemonic force that presumes centrality, even as it acknowledges that it cannot privilege the margin without acknowledging the power of the centre. As Rick Salutin writes, Canadians are not marginal "because of the quirkiness of our ideas or the inadequacy of our arguments, but because of the power of those who define the centre" (6). But he too admits that power. The regionalism of magic realism and the local and particular focus of post-modern art are both ways of contesting not just this centrality, but also claims of universality. Post-modernism has been characterized as "that thought which refuses to turn the Other into the Same" (During 1987, 33) and this is, of course, where its significance for post-colonialism comes in. In Canada, it has been Québecois artists and critics who have embraced most readily the rhetoric of this post-colonial liberation — from Emile Borduas in 1948 to *Parti Pris* in the 1960s. However real this experience of colonization is in Québec, there is a historical dimension here that cannot be ignored. Québec may align itself politically with francophone colonies such as Algeria, Tunisia and Haiti (Kröller, "Politics" 120), but there is a major political and historical difference: the pre-colonial history of the French in Québec was an imperialist one. As both Leonard Cohen's *Beautiful Losers* and Hubert Aquin's *Trou de mémoire* point out, the French were the first imperial force in what is now Canada and that too cannot be forgotten — without risking bad faith. This is not to deny, once again, the very real sense of cultural dispossession and social alienation in Québec, but history cannot be conveniently ignored.

A related problem is that post-modern notions of difference and positively valued marginality can themselves be used to repeat (in a more covert way) colonizing strategies of domination when used by First World critics dealing with the Third World (see Chow 91): the precise point at which interest and concern become imperializing appropriation is a hotly contested one. In addition some critics, of course, see post-modernism as itself the dominant, Eurocentric, neo-universalist, imperial discourse (Brydon 5; Tiffin, "Post-Colonialism" 170–72). There are no easy solutions to any of these issues raised by the perhaps uncomfortable overlap of issues between the post-modern and the post-colonial, but that in itself is no reason not to explore that problematic site of interaction.

Besides the formal and thematic areas of mutual concern that I have already mentioned, there is what could be called a strategic or rhetorical one: the use of the trope of irony as a doubled or split discourse which has the potential to subvert from within. Some have seen this valorization of irony as a sign of the "increasing purchase of post-structural codes of recognition in Western society" (Slemon, "Post-Colonial" 157), but post-structuralism can also be seen as a product of the larger cultural enterprise of post-modernism (see Hutcheon). In either case, though, as a double-talking, forked-tongued mode of address, irony becomes a popular rhetorical strategy for working within existing discourses and contesting them at the same time. Its inherent semantic and structural doubleness also makes it a most convenient trope for the paradoxical dualities of both post-modern complicitous critique and post-colonial doubled identity and history. And indeed irony (like allegory, according to Slemon) has become a powerful subversive tool in the re-thinking and re-addressing of history by both post-modern and post-colonial artists.

Since I would like to discuss this point in more detail with particular reference to Canadian art, I must first make what might seem a digression, but which is, I believe, crucial: one of the lessons of post-modernism is the need to respect the particular and the local, and therefore to treat Canada as a post-colonial country seems to me to require some specification and even explanation. This is not to deny in any way that Canada's history and what have been called the "psychological effects of a colonial past" (Keith 3) are not both very real and very important. Indeed, parts of Canada, especially the West, still feel colonized (see Harrison 208; Cooley 182). It is almost a truism to say that Canada as a nation has never felt central, culturally or politically; it has always felt what Bharati Mukherjee calls a "deep sense of marginality":

> The Indian writer, the Jamaican, the Nigerian, the Canadian and the Australian, each one knows what it is like to be a peripheral man whose howl dissipates unheard. He knows what it is to suffer absolute emotional and intellectual devaluation, to die unfulfilled and still isolated from the world's centre. (Mukherjee Blaise 151)

But to say this is still not the same as equating the white Canadian *experience* of colonialism, and therefore of post-colonialism, with that of the West Indies or Africa or India. Commentators are rather too quick to call Canada a Third World (Saul 53) and therefore post-colonial culture (Slemon, "Magic" 10). Yet, they have behind them the weight of the famous pronouncement of Margaret Laurence that Canadians are Third World writers because "they have had to find [their] own voices and write out of what is truly [theirs], in the face of an overwhelming cultural imperialism" (17). While this may be true and while certainly Canadian literary "models remained those of Britain and more recently of America" (18), I cannot help feeling that there is something in this that is both trivializing of the Third World experience and exaggerated regarding the (white) Canadian. Of course Canada was politically a colony; but the consequences for white (not Native) writers today of that past are different from those for writers in Africa, India, or the Caribbean. The structural domination of Empire (see Stam and Spence 3–4) — not to mention the racial and cultural — differs considerably, as even thinking about something as obvious as economic "under-development" (Dorsinville, *Pays* 15) would suggest.

As Helen Tiffin and Diana Brydon have pointed out, there are different types of colonial conditions even within the British Empire. On the one hand, in countries like Africa and India, the cultural imposition associated with colonialism took place on "the homeground of the colonized people" (Tiffin, "Comparison and Judgement" 31;

Brydon 3). On the other hand, in countries like Canada, Australia, and New Zealand, the English language and culture were transplanted (by settlers, convicts, slavemasters) to a foreign territory "where the indigenous inhabitants were either annihilated or marginalized" (Brydon 3). If Canada is any example, these settler colonies meant the near destruction of the indigenous culture (and people): it is one thing to impose one culture upon another; it is another thing practically to wipe out what existed when the colonizers appeared on the scene. From this perspective, it could be said that the British relation to the Native peoples in Canada and their culture was almost more destructive than that relation of imposition that took place in Africa or India. To relegate a culture to secondary status is not the same as making it illegal. But when Canadian culture is called post-colonial today the reference is very rarely to the Native culture, which might be the more accurate historical use of the term. The culture referred to most frequently is the English-language one of the descendants of the whole colonial settlers. (The fact that this is not quite accurate is important — given Canada's pluri-ethnicity — but I will return to that later.) Native and Métis writers are today demanding a voice (Cuthand; Armstrong; Campbell) and perhaps, given their articulations of the damage to Indian culture and people done by the colonizers (French and British) and the process of colonization, theirs should be considered the resisting, post-colonial voice of Canada. Or perhaps the best model is that of Helen Tiffin: the aboriginal writing should be read as standing in what Richard Terdiman calls a counter-discursive relation to the settler literature, just as that settler literature stands counter-discursively against the imperial culture (Tiffin, "Post-Colonialism" 173; "Post-Colonial Literatures" 20). Nevertheless, there is still a difference in the degree and even kind of colonization endured. As Coral Ann Howells puts it:

> Colonization of the prairie was in the deepest sense a power struggle between whites and Indians over possession of the land complicated by the clash of irreconcilable values, for possession of the land meant very different things to the two parties in conflict. In [Rudy Wiebe's novel, *The Temptations of*] *Big Bear* the process of colonization is presented in precisely these terms of cultural clash and eventual imperial domination. To the whites land ownership meant exclusive possession of the prairies through the signing of land treaties with the Indians which "forever extinguished, as the Prime Minister like [*sic*] to say it, all native rights". . . . For them land spelt economic and political power, an extension of the British Empire. For the Indians however the land was life itself, necessary to their physical, cultural and spiritual survival. (149)

This is not quite the genocide of the Caribs or Arawaks in the West Indies, but it is still something which must be considered when dealing with the specificity of *Canadian* post-colonialism (see Pons and Rocard on the Canadian Native as an issue of colonization).

This important difference in the various histories of colonialism can be seen clearly if we extend even briefly this comparison of the Canadian experience with that of the West Indies, which some also see as examples of settler colonies (although to others slavery or "exile in conditions of bondage" [McDonald 78] remains the dominant heritage). Both the Caribbean countries and Canada shared that European colonization which more or less effectively destroyed certain Amerindian cultures. In Wilson Harris's words: "this aboriginal conquest exists like a ruin of psychological premises and biases in our midst" (3). But Canada had no imported African slave labour and no indentured workers from India or China to replace them after Abolition (though the usually ignored Chinese railway workers in Canada might be a close approximation). The racial composition of the two countries has therefore been different, and so too has been the different races' sense of belonging. Indentured labourers, unlike slaves or settlers, were always considered itinerant; they never belonged to where they worked and lived. In the West Indies, the fact that these Indian servants were often poor and caste-bound contributed to the ease with which their own culture could be suppressed. While culturally a hybrid, like all post-colonized nations (Tiffin, "Post-Colonial Literatures" 17), Canada has experienced no actual "creolization" which might have created something new out of an adaptation process within a split racial context (see Brathwaite). Without this racial mixing, Canada's colonial culture lacked some of the sense of a "civilizing" mission, but still defined itself in terms of values which can, today, be seen as British, white, middle-class, heterosexual, and male, and it passed on these values most obviously in its educational system. In her novel, *Cat's Eye*, Margaret Atwood offers a child's view of what was learned in Canadian schools in the middle of the twentieth century:

> In countries that are not the British Empire, they cut out children's tongues, especially those of boys. Before the British Empire there were no railroads or postal services in India, and Africa was full of tribal warfare, with spears, and had no proper clothing. The Indians in Canada did not have the wheel or telephones, and ate the hearts of their enemies in the heathenish belief that it would give them courage. The British Empire changed all that. It brought in electric lights. (79)

The irony of the child's perspective underlines the politics of colonialism — in Canada and in the rest of the Empire. Singing "The Maple Leaf Forever," thinking it is the Canadian content to balance singing "Rule Britannia," the young girl notices that it too is really about England: "Wolfe, the dauntless hero, came / and planted firm Britannia's flag / On Canada's fair domain" (80).

As David Arnason explains the history of this neo-colonialism, Canada was settled by "immigrants who did not regard themselves as Canadians, but as Englishmen living in a new land. The sense of history of this first generation of immigrants is the sense of history of the mother country, not of Canada" (54). As writers, these immigrants, not surprisingly, wrote in the tradition of Britain — at least until the reality of the Canadian experience began to force alterations in the inherited forms. The influx of British Loyalists at the time of the American Revolution further enforced the values of Empire. According to one view, Loyalist myths have encouraged us Canadians to honour colonial symbols instead of adopting our own, and to substitute for nationalism a peculiar form of coattails imperialism. Loyalist myth-makers have never been able to imagine a Canada disentangled from Britain. Perhaps this is why, for a long time after Confederation, few Canadians could think of Canada as a nation, and no longer as a mere colony. (Bell and Tepperman 79)

The nostalgia for the British Empire which was inculcated in Atwood's character has its echo in another typical cultural irony pointed out by Arun Mukherjee: the equestrian statue of King George which sits in Toronto's aptly named "Queen's Park" was brought to Canada from India "after the latter decided to discard all visual reminders of its colonial masters" (88). This example only confirms the long history of colonialism in Canada: from the *British* North America Act (passed in Westminster, not Ottawa) to the very recent repatriation of the Constitution itself. After all, until 1947, Canadians were defined as "British subjects."

This perhaps long, seeming digression is intended to make the point that one can certainly talk of post-colonialism in Canada, but only if the differences between its particular version and that of, especially, Third World nations is kept in mind. Two other distinctions must be made, however, which further condition the use of the term in a Canadian context. The first is the pluri-ethnic (and lately more multiracial) nature of Canadian society. Some of the immigrants who populate this country are not from colonized societies and they often consciously resist being labelled post-colonial. Filippo Salvatore, an Italian Canadian writer living in Québec and writing in French, states: "the defeat of the Plains of Abraham and that of the Patriotes in 1837 did not leave indelible psychic scars on me. Psychologically I am not part of a colonized people" (203). For him and others, the immigrant experience can even be seen as a reverse of that of colonization, a conscious decision to change culture (Caccia 164).

But there are other immigrants who do not share this element of choice, who come to Canada from the West Indies, Asia or Latin America and see it as "a necessarily occupied territory because land was denied somewhere else" (Davies 33). This is largely non-European immigration, and the historical and political contexts of post-colonization cannot usually be ignored, as they might in an Italian or other European perspective. The specificity of *Canadian* post-colonial culture today is being conditioned by this arrival of immigrants from other post-colonial nations. To be educated, as Atwood described, in a British-inspired school system in Canada is still different from being so educated in Jamaica, where the system is seen, by black writers who were trained in it, as even more obviously and "proudly geared towards the needs of the British economy" and as clearly maintaining "the social stratification" that denigrates the living language of the people (Allen 66). Immigrants with this experience, who then come to Canada, bring with them an extra-acute sense of colonialism which is bound to change the nature of post-colonialism in Canada itself.

Witness Cyril Dabydeen's poem, "Sir James Douglas, Father of British Columbia," which opens with

> You were born where I was born.
> Demerara's sun in your blood,
> Guiana's rain on your skin.
> You came from Creole stock
> taking a native wife. (41)

The Guyanese Canadian poet addresses Douglas as "part of my heritage too / despite colonialism. The piece ends with the poet pouring (demerara) sugar into his tea and "thinking if you were more Scottish / I'd be less of the tropics" (42). This is the doubled sense of post-colonialism that is part of some of the writing we now call Canadian.

There is yet one other specific factor of Canadian experience which cannot be separated from the notion of what post-colonial means to it. For years now (see Morton 150), Canadians have felt that they are being "colonized" by American capital. The use of the term "colonization" is not totally metaphoric, for Albert Memmi defined it as "above all, economic and political exploitation" (149), and there are many Canadian economic nationalists who would claim that this is precisely what the United States is doing to Canada. Even if one does not agree with the extremity of such an evaluation, it is still the case that Canadians often feel at least culturally colonized by American mass media. They also often feel somehow politically threatened by the constant reminders of the power and imperialist impulses of our neighbour to the south (for a classic Canadian view of American power, see Grant). And speaking the same language as both the real historical colonizers and the present-day would-be colonizers has created problems for Canadian writers trying to hear their own "English" tongues (Kroetsch 1; Haberly). With these additional issues of the often doubled post-colonial focus of many Canadians and the sensitivity to American imperialism, the very use of the word "post-colonial" cannot help but be a complex issue in a Canadian context.

The fact that post-modernism is alternately claimed as an invention of either Latin America or the United States (cf. Tiffin, "Post-Colonialism" 170) is interesting in this light, for it indirectly points to the intersection of the concerns of post-modernism and post-colonialism that interests me here. Both terms, whatever their geographic origins, are tethered to earlier entities — colonialism and modernism, respectively. Some Canadian artists have addressed this double tethering, most notably photographer Geoff Miles in his *Foreign Relations: Re-W/riting a Narrative in Parts*. A series of texts and photographic images "about" colonial relations, this work offers a view of Canada, not as the Third World, but certainly also not as the First. In his catalogue, Miles notes that to discuss the photograph as a post-modern art object in Canada is "to do so within the confines of colonialism and the colonising power of the gaze of the other(s). For is it not true that we are in the unique position of being colonised by three gazes all at once; that of France, Britain, and the United States" (2). Neither post-modernism nor post-colonialism can go backwards; both by definition contest the imperialist devaluing of the "other" and the "different." But Miles feels that the discourse of photography in Canada is still very much caught within the limits of the colonial and the modernist. But in a way this also describes *any* post-colonial or post-modern art, insofar as both (as the very semantic composition of the adjectives suggests) operate in terms of that which they oppose: both contest from within. The question Miles asks himself is one which has a number of possible answers: "How do we construct a discourse which displaces the effects of the colonising gaze while we are still under its influence?" (3) These answers include, as he notes, deconstructing existing myths which support the discourses of colonialism (including modernism) and constructing different ones to take their place. They would also include irony — that strategic trope that allows a work to address a culture from within, while still articulating some challenge.

When I began this discussion of irony as a discursive strategy of both post-modern-ism and post-colonialism, I suggested that, not unlike allegory, irony is a trope of doubleness. And doubleness is what characterizes not just the complicitous critique of the post-modern, but, by definition, the twofold vision of the post-colonial — not just because of the obvious dual history (Slemon, "Magic" 15) but because a sense of duality was the mark of the colonial as well. Doubleness and difference are established by colonialism by its paradoxical move to enforce cultural sameness (JanMohamed 62) while, at the same time, producing differentiations and discriminations (Bhabha, "Signs" 153). This is the doubleness often represented in the metaphor of Prospero and Caliban (Mannoni; Dorsinville, *Caliban*; for a critique of this see Baker, especially 190–96, and Donaldson). It is the doubleness of the colonial culture imposed upon the colonized (Meyers vii). But it is also the doubleness of the colonized in relation to the colonizer, either as model or antithesis (Memmi 140). As Raymond Williams has argued, however, all national literatures develop in this sort of way — up to a point: from imitation of a dominant pattern to assimilation or internalization of it (see also Marchak 182), but then to a stage of open revolt where what was initially excluded by the dominant pattern gets revalorized (121–28). Is the last one here the post-colonial stage, as most critics suggest? If so, then it can still be argued that its revolt continues to operate within the power field of that dominant culture, no matter how radical its revalorization of its indigenous culture (Tiffin, "Post-Colonialism" 172). This is why irony, the trope that works from within a power field but still contests it, is a consistently useful strategy for post-colonial discourse.

Nevertheless, Homi Bhabha has argued in a series of influential articles that irony and mimicry are the modes of the colonialist, not the post-colonial: "The discourse of post-Enlightenment English colonialism often speaks in a tongue that is forked, not false" and this, he feels, is the strategy of "colonial power and knowledge" ("Of Mimicry" 126). Bhabha sees irony as appropriating the colonized Other, and implicitly therefore as part of the ambivalence and hybridity that characterize the colonial

("Representation" 93; "Signs" 154; "The Other Question" 18) in what both Edward Said and Albert Memmi have seen as its inescapable and complex mutual interrelations with the colonized. In Memmi's words: "The bond between colonizer and colonized is thus destructive and creative" (89). Without denying any of this doubleness of the experience and literature of colonization, it is still possible to see a different and consequent doubleness as characterizing the post-colonial: what has been called its "bicultural vision" (Parameswaran 241) or "metaphysical clash" (Tiffin, "Comparison and Judgement" 32; see, too, "Comparative Methodology" 29). And the way post-colonial critics talk about this literature suggests the potential importance of irony as the subversive force operating from within: "the challenge is to use the existing language, even if it is the voice of a dominant" other — and yet speak through it: to disrupt . . . the codes and forms of the dominant language in order to reclaim speech for itself" (New, *Dreams* x). Irony is one way of doing precisely this, a way of resisting and yet acknowledging the power of the dominant. It may not go the next step — to suggest something new — but it certainly makes that step possible. Often combined with some sort of self-reflexivity, irony allows a text to work within the constraints of the dominant while placing those constraints *as constraints* in the foreground and thus undermining their power.

On the level of language, irony becomes one of the chief characteristics of what Bharati Mukherjee calls the "step-mother tongue" in which post-colonial writers write, "implying as it does the responsibility, affection, accident, loss, and secretive roots-quest in adoptive-family situations" (Mukherjee Blaise 147). Irony is thus one way of creatively modifying (JanMohamed 84; New, "New Language" 363) or even twisting the language so as to signal the "foreignness" of both the user and her/his experience. W.H. New has traced, as one common thread in Commonwealth literature, the *sense* of irony, the sense of being caught between two worlds: "Though dualities abound in the ironist's world, the stances he may take range from parody and innuendo through sarcasm and self-disparagement to absurdity and nihilism. . . . At its best, the ironic stance provokes a serious deliberation into the problems that led to dualities in the first place" (New, *Among Worlds* 3). This involves a re-viewing of colonial and post-colonial history through the doubled lenses of ironic defamiliarization: in Canada, Cohen's *Beautiful Losers* remains perhaps the most powerful example of this process. The contradictions and heterogeneous dualities that make up the post-colonial experience also resonate with the paradoxes and multiplicities of the post-modern and, in both, irony seems to be a preferred trope for the articulation of that doubleness. The post-modern challenges to humanist universals come together with post-colonial contestings provoked by statements like A.J.M. Smith's famous valorization of those Canadian poets who "made an effort to escape the limitations of provincialism or colonialism by entering into the universal civilizing culture of ideas" (xxiv). Such a description can today be seen as pure neo-colonialism, looking as it does to Arnoldian standards for validation, standards which have been argued to be anything but universal — but rather the product of specifically nineteenth-century British, middle-class, white, male values (Belsey).

Because irony is also the trope of the unsaid, it becomes as well a possible way to encode a subtext which will deflect the risks of "[f]ull visibility and accessibility ... [which] constitute an inherent danger for the colonized" (Weir 61). As Lorraine Weir argues, irony

> in the hands of those who exercize genuine power is very different from the same device in the hands of those classified as powerless. Among those whose basic communication may frequently depend upon the skilled use and reception of ironic utterance — that is, among the powerless irony will be all the more powerful. The Irish, as is commonly known, are masters of irony and invective; so is the primary community of women. (67)

Joining women and the Irish here would be ironic post-colonial writers as obvious as Narayan and Rushdie, each in his different way, and others perhaps less immediately obviously: Ruth Prawer Jhabvala (see Gooneratne 65–78) or Ngugi and Tayib Salih (Said 54).

Irony is the trope of the redeployable and the refracted as well as simply of the double, but doubleness seems to provide fertile ground for its usage. This makes Canada — as a post-colonial nation (in the very specific sense offered above) and as part of a general post-modern culture — rich terrain indeed:

> *Canada est omnis divisa in partes duo*: all Canada is divided into two parts. We used to have Upper and Lower Canada, but, with the settling of the plains beyond Ontario, this division is now expressed as East and West. There's also North and South and lots of divisions not based on geography: a political division between the Provincial and Federal governments; an economic one between the have and have-not provinces; a sectorial one between industrial regions and agricultural; a linguistic one between English and French. And so on. (Pechter 291)

But the multiplicity of these dualities does not always make the often resulting ironies easy to interpret, for these are frequently double-directed ironies. For example, James Reaney's poem, "The Royal Visit" (in Barbour and Scobie 58), uses repetition to signal irony: the repeated line that both those in Stratford, Ontario, who were slighted by not being presentable and thus presented to royalty and those who did not manage to see the Queen because the train moved too quickly through the town would remember the event "to their dying day." But is the irony directed against colonial royalists in Canada? against an inculcated neo-colonial mentality? against royalty for not caring enough for those who cared for them? or against all of these simultaneously? What about the subtle, self-reflating Canadian ironies of Miriam Waddington's "Back at York University" (271–72) where the narrator confronts the dual colonization of Canadian culture:

I am walking back
to an English colony,
watch me change into
an American aspiration,
look, I'm whispering into
a Canadian answer-box . . .

But neither Waddington nor Reaney are usually considered post-modern writers, and so it is hard to see from these passing examples where irony actually marks the overlapping of concerns for which I have been arguing. But in order to show that, instead of looking to the writing of Atwood, Ondaatje, Kroetsch or other writers in Canada who are generally seen as both post-colonialist and post-modern, I would like to change media and investigate briefly the intersection of the post-colonial with the post-modern in Canadian visual art and film which are usually labelled as post-modern, but which I think ought to be viewed in the light of post-colonialism as well, especially in their use of irony in the negotiation of the aesthetic and historical heritage within which they work.

Some Canadian artists *do* see themselves as working within the bounds of a historically determined colonialism. London artist Greg Curnoe writes: "the artists who are original, who break out of the colonial mode, are the ones who really affect our culture . . . because they develop out of their whole background" (quoted in Théberge 17). None of Smith's universalism for Curnoe! Post-colonial art, he implies, would be that which derives directly from its own local and particular situation. This too is a tenet of post-modernism, of course. Another example of the kind of artist who might be simultaneously post-colonial and post-modern is Charles Pachter. Like many other Canadians (such as Margaret Atwood and Joyce Wieland), Pachter's time in the United States seems to have sharpened his sense of what constitutes both the historical and current nature of colonialism in Canada. His 1972 series of paintings and prints on the theme of *Queen and Moose* chooses deliberately provocative subjects and forms: the Queen as the symbol of nostalgic neo-colonialism meets the Ur-cliché of the Canadian wilderness experience. His ironic portrayals and situations explode both myths, or rather, he makes them implode under their own accumulated cultural weight.

The entire question of Canadian identity has become a kind of playground — or battlefield — for the post-modern as well as the post-colonial defining of "difference" and value. As Laura Mulvey has written:

The question of Canadian national identity is political in the most direct sense of the word, and it brings the political together with the cultural and ideological issues immediately and inevitably. For the Canada delineated by multinationals, international finance, U.S. economic and political imperialism, national identity is a point of resistance, defining the border fortifications against exterior colonial penetration. Here nationalism can perform the political function familiar in Third World countries. (10)

Mulvey argues that Geoff Miles's work, *The Trapper's Pleasure of the Text*, deconstructs the Canadian identity and reduces it to its male, Anglo-Saxon and capitalist defining essences. And it would seem to be irony that triggers and even enables this deconstruction. The title alone, with its incongruous juxtaposition of a well-known work by Roland Barthes and the notion of a trapper, sets up the possibility for irony. The trapper here is the original European, white, male traveller, exploiting nature for financial gain, who made colonization possible in Canada. But in conjunction with the photograph (of a street scene devoid of people except for the shadow of the photographer), the person who captures the visual image is also a trapper: also a white male, he has just returned from studying in England; he too exploits external reality for potential financial gain (if he can sell his photographs). Like the trapper of old, he not only captures "reality" but fixes it and in that sense destroys its "life." This too is a form of metaphoric colonization, a taking over through representations. As Mulvey writes: "the metaphor ironizes and parodies the way that photographic aesthetics have apotheosized the decisive moment (the kill) and consequently the 'Trapper' himself as hero" (10). Further ironies result from the text which accompanies the visual image: one, positioned near the photographer's shadow, reads "Standing above it all / he sensed the power / of his position." The preying and the voyeuristic are clearly not absent from this awareness of position. On the other side, away from the shadow, we read: "The text needs its shadow! / This shadow is a bit of ideology, / a bit of representation, a bit of subject." And, of course, a shadow can, by definition, only ever be a bit of a subject and a bit of a representation. Without a shadow, that is, without a self-reflexively revelatory doubling, the text is in danger of replacing the photograph as a transparent realist medium presuming direct access to the "real." The deliberate echoing of Barthes, from the title to these texts, also recalls Barthes's own autobiographical and complex ironic use of photographs and text in both *Roland Barthes by Roland Barthes* and *Camera Lucida: Reflections on Photography*. In Miles's work too, the viewer must respond actively to decipher ironies and construct meanings in the relation of text to image. The post-colonial "Trapper" and the post-modern "Pleasure of the Text" overlap within the problematics of ironic doubleness.

The same dualities or perhaps, more accurately, the same unreconciled and unresolved contradictions that characterize both the post-modern and the post-colonial can be seen in Joyce Wieland's political film trilogy, *True Patriot Love*, a title whose echo of "O Canada" immediately places in the foreground the significance of her Canadianness to her exploration of the intersection of the aesthetic and the political in these films. The first, *Rat Life and Diet in North America*, was made when Wieland was living in New York in 1968. But it is also subtly concerned with historical as well as current colonialism, for it is a loving parody of Beatrix Potter narratives. It is about the rebellion of a group of rats (actually gerbils in the film) against the oppression of New York and the Vietnam War. These "political prisoners" escape to Canada where they live on an organic co-op farm. Some critics have argued that this idealistic and naïve view of Canada shows Wieland to be "removed from the political mainstream"

(Magidson and Wright 39), but perhaps it depends on *whose* political mainstream. What such a view misses are the ironies that perhaps only Canadians would notice: ironies of disjunction between the real and the ideal Canada, and ironies resulting from the view that, for a Canadian, even a less than ideal Canada might be preferable to the United States — a point American critics might be forgiven for missing.

The second film, *Reason over Passion* (1967–69) is an ironic reworking of the conventions of the travel documentary. It portrays the Canadian landscape as recorded by a hand-held camera through the windows of trains and cars. There are also freeze-frame pictures of the face of Pierre Trudeau, the man who uttered the rationalist statement that gives Wieland her title. This material is rephotographed from a moviola to get a grainy effect that self-reflexively serves to introduce an immediately noticeable visible mediation between the recording and the recorded. The images are accompanied by a variety of machine noises, a female voice, and 537 printed permutations of the title's letters, as selected by reason's instrument — a computer. This reappropriation of the landscape of Canada as the subject of art is a political and cultural statement of the value of the local and the particular over the universal and the eternal. It is not, as some critics have suggested, a nostalgic move, but a post-modern and post-colonial challenging that both contests nostalgia and post-modernly mixes elegy with exaltation in the viewing of the land. And it is the ironic juxtaposition of the title, the Trudeau shots, and the soundtrack with the landscape, as well as the self-reflexive mode of recording, that makes this double contesting possible.

The third film, *Pierre Vallières*, is the most overtly political, as its title suggests, for it is a parody of the documentary portrait. Its three parts link Québec colonization and search for liberation with that of women. The fixed camera frames the Québec revolutionary Vallières's mouth from which come the words we hear: thirty-three minutes of monologue with subtitles. After a while the moustached mouth with its crooked, discoloured teeth goes beyond suggesting the paradoxical revolutionary folk hero and working-class victim imaged as one (see Rabinovitz, "Films" 168–69) to imply almost a kind of sex-inverted, ironic *vagina dentata*, the terror of which informs the messages of women's liberation as well as Québec decolonization in the soundtrack.

Many of these same national and gender ironies are picked up in her 1971 National Gallery retrospective, also called *True Patriot Love/Véritable Amour Patriotique*. The entire show was set up to feel like a country fair, perhaps in itself signalling a feminist subversion of the honorific retrospective format. She even sold bottles of a perfume she created, called "Sweet Beaver: The Perfume of Canadian Liberation." The beaver as sweet here suggests more than a "nostalgic longing for a Canadian wilderness past" (Rabinovitz, "Issues" 40). As a symbol of Canada, the beaver is "sweet" because it is both pleasurable and innocent, but also because it was an appealing lure to European fur-traders and colonizers, first, and then to American capital. As medievalists also know well, the beaver (*castor*) has traditionally in the West represented a gentle (male)

beast and the secretions of its scent glands were considered important to medicine —
while serving the beaver as a mode of sexual attraction. In various versions of myth,
when hunted, the beaver is said to bite off its own testicles (mistaken for scent glands)
and thus escape with its life. Wieland's Canadian beaver may also be self-mutilating
but safe, attracting but medicinal. The link between castration and *castor* is also an
evident one, offering another form of safety, this time from sexual vices and sins. But,
as a number of critics have noted, *today* this image also cannot help connoting
pornographic reductions of women as well: "Canada's history as a land raped and
colonized by England and then by the United States parallels women's history of
oppression" (Rabinovitz, "Issues" 40). Moreover, by ironically, if indirectly, pointing
to the capitalist and patriarchal representations of women (in both pornography and in
advertising — she did make the perfume a commercial object), Wieland adds another
level of irony: perfume here is the very femininely coded medium that delivers a
message which defies the trivialization it seems to invite. Perfume has traditionally
been used to enhance women's sexual attraction to men, but here the "sweet" lure is
loaded! The feminist, the environmentalist and the Canadian nationalist ironies here
are at one and the same time post-modern and post-colonial.

Such is also the case in Fastwürms's installation, *Father Brébeuf's Fugue State*.
According to medical psychology, a "fugue state" is a state wherein awareness of
identity seems to disappear. This work politicizes and historicizes — and thereby
ironizes — this term in relation to the spiritual conquest of North America, which was
the first step in the French colonization of Canada's aboriginal peoples and the
destruction of their identity. Using industrial materials to create post-modern ironic
incongruities in the representation of historical objects, this work suggests the juxtaposition of the colonizing quest of the Jesuit missionaries with the resistance of the
Native peoples, including their torture of Father Jean de Brébeuf in 1649. Tarpaper
walls and fluorescent lights implicitly signal the loss and indeed the total destruction
of one culture, the one close to nature; a charred wooden cross suggests the survival,
despite many trials, of the other. As one commentator describes another part of the
installation: "Heaped onto a pile of consumer kitsch and junk goods of Western culture
are a few cobs of Indian corn and a complete deer skeleton, the leg bones of which
prop up a barbecue grill topped with a steak — the stake of colonization" (Fischer 12).
But it is also, most ironically and horrifically, the stake at which Brébeuf was burned
— or barbecued. Yet the cross remains, however charred, and all that is left of the
Native culture is bones. This is the loss of identity suggested by the title's fugue state:
Brébeuf's loss of the memory of the act of colonization and its subsequent destruction
of the identity of *others*.

The art of Geoff Miles, Joyce Wieland and Fastwürms, each in its own way,
confronts the amnesia of colonialism through the memory of post-colonialism. And
all three use the discursive strategy of irony to underline the political dimension of that
confrontation. But in each case, the contesting is done from within the dominant
discourse, as may be inevitable given the structure of the trope of irony. The post-

colonial is therefore as implicated in that which it challenges as is the post-*modern*. Critique may always be complicitous when irony is its primary vehicle. For this reason, I would disagree with one important part of Simon During's particular definition of post-colonialism as "the need, in nations or groups which have been victims of imperialism, to achieve an identity uncontaminated by universalist or Eurocentric concepts and images" (1987, 33). Most post-colonial critics would oppose this as an essentialist, not to say simplifying, definition, and I would have to agree with them that the entire post-colonial project usually posits precisely the impossibility of that identity ever being "uncontaminated": just as the *word* post-colonialism holds within it its own "contamination" by colonialism, so too does the culture itself and its various artistic manifestations, in Canada as elsewhere. Colonies might well speak "unreflectingly," as Dennis Lee has suggested (163), but the *post*-colonial has at its disposal various ways of subverting from within the dominant culture — such as irony, allegory, and self-reflexivity — that it shares with the complicitous critique of post-modernism, even if its politics differ in important ways. I return to this last point once again to emphasize the difference that the use of irony by both underlines. The post-colonial, like the feminist, is a dismantling but also constructive political enterprise insofar as it implies a theory of agency and social change that the post-modern deconstructive impulse lacks. While both "post-"s *use* irony, the post-colonial cannot *stop* at irony, as Ihab Hassan's exposition of the trope's post-modern features in the end suggests:

Irony. This could also be called, after Kenneth Burke, perspectivism. In the absence of a cardinal principle or paradigm, we turn to play, interplay, dialogue, polylogue, allegory, self-reflection — in short, to irony. This irony assumes indeterminacy, multivalence; it aspires to clarity, the clarity of demystification, the pure light of absence. We meet variants of it in Bakhtin, Burke, de Man, Jacques Derrida, and Hayden White. And in Alan Wilde we see an effort to discriminate its modes: 'mediate irony,' 'disjunctive irony,' and 'postmodern' or 'suspensive irony' 'with its yet more racial vision of multiplicity, randomness, contingency, and even absurdity.' Irony, perspectivism, reflexiveness: these express the ineluctable recreations of mind in search of a truth that continually eludes it, leaving it with only an ironic access or excess of self-consciousness. (506)

WORKS CITED

Allen, Lillian. "A Writing of Resistance: Black Women's Writing in Canada." Dybikowski et al. 63–67.

Arnason, David. "Icelandic Canadian Literature." Balan 53–66.

Armstrong, Jeannette C. "Writing from a Native Woman's Perspective." Dybikowski et al. 55–57.

Atwood, Margaret. *Cat's Eye.* Toronto: McClelland & Stewart, 1988.

Baker, Houston A., Jr. "Caliban's Triple Play." *Critical Inquiry* 13.1 (1986): 182–96.

Balan, Jars, ed. *Identification: Ethnicity and the Writer in Canada.* Edmonton: Canadian Institute of Ukrainian Studies, University of Alberta, 1982.

Barbour, Douglas and Stephen Scobie, eds. *The Maple Laugh Forever: An Anthology of Comic Canadian Poetry.* Edmonton: Hurtig, 1981.

Bell, David and Lorne Tepperman. *The Roots of Disunity: A Look at Canadian Political Culture.* Toronto: McClelland & Stewart, 1979.

Belsey, Catherine. *Critical Practice.* London and New York: Methuen, 1980.

Berry, Reginald. "A Deckchair of Words: Post-colonialism, Post-modernism, and the Novel of Self-projection in Canada and New Zealand." *Landfall* 40 (1986): 310–23.

Bhabha, Homi K. "Of Mimicry and Man: The Ambivalence of Colonial Discourse." *October* 28 (1984): 125–33.

———. "The Other Question—the Stereotype and Colonial Discourse." *Screen* 24.6 (1983): 18–36.

———. "Representation and the Colonial Text: A Critical Exploration of Some Forms of Mimeticism." *The Theory of Reading.* Ed. Frank Gloversmith. Brighton: Harvester P, 1984. 93–122.

———. "Signs Taken for Wonders: Questions of Ambivalence and Authority Under a Tree Outside Delhi, May 1817." *Critical Inquiry* 12.1 (1985): 144–65.

Brathwaite, Edward Kamau. *The Development of Creole Society in Jamaica 1770–1820.* Oxford: Oxford UP, 1978.

Brydon, Diana. "The Myths that Write Us: Decolonising the Mind." *Commonwealth* 10.1 (1987): 1–14.

Caccia, Fulvio. "The Italian Writer and Language." Trans. Martine Leprince. Pivato 153–67.

Campbell, Maria. *Halfbreed.* Halifax: Goodread Biographies, 1973.

Chow, Rey. "Rereading Mandarin Ducks and Butterflies: A Response to the Postmodern Condition." *Cultural Critique* 5 (1986-87): 69–93.

Cooley, Dennis. *The Vernacular Muse: The Eye and Ear in Contemporary Literature.* Winnipeg: Turnstone P, 1987.

Cuthand, Beth. "Transmitting Our Identity as Indian Writers." Dybikowski et al. 53–54.

Dabydeen, Cyril. *This Planet Earth.* Ottawa: Borealis P, 1979.

Dash, J. Michael. "Marvellous Realism: The Way Out of Negritude." *Caribbean Studies* 13.4 (1974): 57–77.

Davey, Frank. *Reading Canadian Reading*. Winnipeg: Turnstone P, 1988.

Davies, loan. "Senses of Place." *Canadian Forum* 727 (April 1983): 33–34.

Donaldson, Laura E. "The Miranda Complex: Colonialism and the Question of Feminist Reading." *Diacritics* 18.3 (1988): 65–77.

Dorsinville, Max. *Caliban Without Prospero: Essay on Quebec and Black Literature*. Erin, Ont.: Press Porcépic, 1974.

————. *Le Pays natal: essais sur les littératures du Tiers Monde et du Québec*. Dakar: Nouvelles Editions Africaines, 1983.

During, Simon. "Postmodernism or Postcolonialism?" *Landfall* 39.3 (1985): 366–80.

————. "Postmodernism or Post-colonialism Today." *Textual Practice* 1.1 (1987): 32–47.

Dybikowski, Ann, Victoria Freeman, Daphne Marlatt, Barbara Pulling, Betsy Warland, eds. *In the Feminine: Women and Words/Les femmes et les mots (Conference Proceedings 1983)*. Edmonton: Longspoon P, 1985.

Fastwürms. Father Brébeuf's Fugue State (1983). Canada Council Art Bank, Ottawa.

Fischer, Barbara. *Perspective 88: Fastwürms*. Catalogue, AGO, 17 August – 26 October 1988.

Gooneratne, Yasmine. *Diverse Inheritance: A Personal Perspective on Commonwealth Literature*. Adelaide: Centre for Research in the New Literatures in English, 1980.

Grant, George. "Canadian Fate and Imperialism." *Technology and Empire: Perspectives on North America*. Toronto: Anansi, 1969. 61–78.

Haberly, David T. "The Search for a National Language: A Problem in the Comparative History of Postcolonial Literatures." *Comparative Literature Studies* 11.1 (1974): 85–97.

Harris, Wilson. "The Phenomenal Legacy." *The Literary Half-Yearly* 11.2 (1970): 1–6.

Harrison, Dick. *Unnamed Country: The Struggle for a Canadian Prairie Fiction*. Edmonton: U of Alberta P, 1977.

Hassan, Ihab. "Pluralism in Postmodern Perspective." *Critical Inquiry* 12.3 (1986): 503–20.

Howells, Coral Ann. "Re-Visions of Prairie Indian History in Rudy Wiebe's *The Temptations of Big Bear* and *My Lovely Enemy*." Pons and Rocard. 145–54.

Hutcheon, Linda. *A Poetics of Postmodernism: History, Theory, Fiction*. London and New York: Routledge, 1988.

Irele, Abiola. "Parables of the African Condition: A Comparative Study of Three Post-Colonial Novels." *Journal of African and Commonwealth Literature* 1 (1981): 69–91.

JanMohamed, Abdul R. "The Economy of Manichean Allegory: The Function of Racial Difference in Colonialist Literature." *Critical Inquiry* 12.1 (1985): 59–87.

Keith, W.J. *Canadian Literature in English.* London and New York: Longman, 1985.

Kroetsch, Robert. "A Canadian Issue." *boundary 2* 3.1 (1974): 1–2.

Kröller, Eva-Marie. "The Politics of Influence: Canadian Postmodernism in an American Context." *InterAmerican Literary Relations.* Ed. M.J. Valdes. Vol. 3. New York: Garland, 1985. 118–23.

———. "Postmodernism, Colony, Nation: the Melvillean Texts of Bowering and Beaulieu." *University of Ottawa Quarterly* 54.2 (1984): 53–61.

Larson, Charles R. "Heroic Ethnocentrism: The Idea of Universality in Literature." *The American Scholar* 42 (1973): 463–75.

Laurence, Margaret. "Ivory Tower or Grassroots?: The Novelist as Socio-Political Being." *A Political Art: Essays in Honour of George Woodcock.* Ed. William H. New. Vancouver: U of British Columbia P, 1970. 15–25.

Lee, Dennis. "Cadence, Country, Silence: Writing in Colonial Space." *boundary 2* 3.1 (1974): 151–68.

McDonald, Avis G. "How History Hurts: Common Patterns in Australian and West Indian Fiction." *Queen's Quarterly* 96.1 (1989): 78–93.

Magidson, Debbie and Judy Wright. "True Patriot Love." *Art and Artists* 8.7 (1973): 38–41.

Mannoni, O. *Prospero and Caliban: The Psychology of Colonization.* 1950. New York: Praeger, 1964.

Marchak, Patricia. "Given a Certain Latitude: A (Hinterland) Sociologist's View of Anglo-Canadian Literature." *In Our Own House: Social Perspectives on Canadian Literature.* Ed. Paul Cappon. Toronto: McClelland & Stewart, 1978. 178–205.

Marlatt, Daphne. *How Hug a Stone.* Winnipeg: Turnstone P, 1983.

Memmi, Albert. *The Colonizer and the Colonized.* 1957. New York: Orion P, 1965.

Meyers, Jeffrey. *Fiction and the Colonial Experience.* Totowa, N.J.: Rowman and Littlefield, 1973.

Miles, Geoff. *Foreign Relations: Re- W/riting a Narrative in Parts.* Catalogue, Gallery 44.

Monk, Philip. "Colony, Commodity and Copyright: Reference and Self-Reference in Canadian Art." *Vanguard* 12.5–6 (1983): 14–17.

Morton, W.L. *The Canadian Identity*. 1961. Toronto: U of Toronto P, 1972.

Mukherjee, Arun P. "South Asian Poetry in Canada: In Search of a Place." *World Literature Written in English* 26.1 (1986): 84–98.

Mukherjee Blaise, Bharati. "Mimicry and Reinvention." *The Commonwealth in Canada*. Ed. Uma Parameswaran. Calcutta: Writers Workshop Greybird, 1983. 147–57.

Mulvey, Laura. "Magnificent Obsession." *Parachute* 42 (1986): 6–12.

New, William H. *Among Worlds: An Introduction to Modern Commonwealth and South African Fiction*. Erin, Ont.: Press Porcépic, 1975.

———. *Dreams of Speech and Violence: The Art of the Short Story in Canada and New Zealand*. Toronto: U of Toronto P, 1987.

———. "New Language, New World." *Awakened Conscience: Studies in Commonwealth Literature*. Ed. C.D. Narasimhaiah. New Delhi: Sterling, 1978. 360–77.

Pache, Walter. "The Fiction Makes Us Real: Aspects of Postmodernism in Canada." *Gaining Ground: European Critics on Canadian Literature*. Ed. Robert Kroetsch and Reingard H. Nischik. Edmonton: NeWest P, 1985. 64–78.

Parameswaran, Uma. "Amid the Alien Corn: Biculturalism and the Challenge of Commonwealth Literary Criticism." *World Literature Written in English* 21.1 (1982): 240–53.

Pechter, Edward. "Of Ants and Grasshoppers: Two Ways (or More) to Link Texts and Power." *Poetics Today* 9.2 (1988): 291–306.

Petersen, Kirsten Holst and Anna Rutherford, eds. *A Double Colonization: Colonial and Post-Colonial Women's Writing*. Mundelstrup, Denmark: Dangaroo P, 1986.

Pivato, Joseph, ed. *Contrasts: Comparative Essays on Italian Canadian Writing*. Montréal: Guernica, 1985.

Pons, X. and M. Rocard, eds. *Colonisations: Rencontres Australie-Canada*. Toulouse: Université de Toulouse-Le Mirail, 1985.

Rabinovitz, Lauren. "Issues of Feminist Aesthetics: Judy Chicago and Joyce Wieland." *Women's Art Journal* 1.2 (1980-81): 38–41.

———. "The Films of Joyce Wieland." *Joyce Wieland*. Toronto: AGO; Key Porter Books, 1987. 117–20, 161–79.

Said, Edward W. "Intellectuals in the Post-Colonial World." *Salmagundi* 70–71 (1986): 44–64.

Salutin, Rick. *Marginal Notes: Challenges to the Mainstream*. Toronto: Lester and Orpen Dennys, 1984.

Salvatore, Filippo. "The Italian Writer of Quebec: Language, Culture and Politics." Trans. David Homel. Pivato 189–206.

Saul, John Ralston. "We Are Not Authors of the Post-Novel Novel." *Brick* (Winter 1988): 52–54.

Scott, F.R. and A.J.M. Smith, eds. *The Blasted Pine: An Anthology of Satire, Invective and Disrespectful Verse*. Rev. ed. Toronto: Macmillan, 1967.

Slemon, Stephen. "Magic Realism as Post-Colonial Discourse." *Canadian Literature* 116 (1988): 9–23.

———. "Monuments of Empire: Allegory/Counter-Discourse/Post-Colonial Writing." *Kunapipi* 9.3 (1987): 1–16.

———. "Post-Colonial Allegory and the Transformation of History." *Journal of Commonwealth Literature* 23.1 (1988): 157–68.

Smith, A.J.M., ed. *The Oxford Book of Canadian Verse in English and French*. Toronto: Oxford UP, 1960.

Spivak, Gayatri Chakravorty. *In Other Worlds: Essays in Cultural Politics*. New York and London: Routledge, 1988.

Stam, Robert and Louise Spence. "Colonialism, Racism, and Representation." *Screen* 24.2 (1983): 2–20.

Théberge, Pierre. *Greg Curnoe*. Ottawa: National Gallery of Canada, 1982.

Tiffin, Helen. "Commonwealth Literature and Comparative Methodology." *World Literature Written in English* 23.1 (1984): 26–30.

———. "Commonwealth Literature: Comparison and Judgement." *The History and Historiography of Commonwealth Literature*. Ed. Dieter Riemenschneider. Tübingen: Günter Narr, 1983. 19–35.

———. "Post-Colonial Literatures and Counter-Discourse." *Kunapipi* 9.3 (1987): 17–34.

———. "Post-Colonialism, Post-Modernism and the Rehabilitation of Post-Colonial History." *Journal of Commonwealth Literature* 23.1 (1988): 169–81.

Waddington, Miriam. *Collected Poems*. Toronto: Oxford UP, 1986.

Weir, Lorraine. "Toward a Feminist Hermeneutics: Jay Macpherson's *Welcoming Disaster*." *Gynocritics: Feminist Approaches to Canadian and Quebec Women's Writing/-*

Gynocritiques: Démarches feministes à l'écriture des Canadiennes et Québecoises. Ed. Barbara Godard. Toronto: ECW P, 1987. 59–70.

Wieland, Joyce, dir. *Rat Life and Diet in North America.* 1968.

———. dir. *Reason Over Passion.* 1967–69.

———. dir. *Pierre Vallières.* 1972.

Williams, Raymond. *Marxism and Literature.* Oxford: Oxford UP, 1977.

The White Inuit Speaks:
Contamination as Literary Strategy

DIANA BRYDON

My title is inspired by the coincidental appearance of the Inuit as symbolic figure in two important Canadian novels published in 1989, Kristjana Gunnar's *The Prowler* and Mordecai Richler's *Solomon Gursky Was Here*. By echoing the influential American ethnographic text *Black Elk Speaks*, I mean to highlight the assumptions about cultural purity and authenticity that post-modernism and post-colonialism, and these two texts, both use and challenge. *Black Elk Speaks* itself is now being recognised as a white man's construct, fusing traditional Lakota with Christian philosophy — a hybrid rather than the purely authentic of the anthropologist's dreams (Powers). Unlike those who deplore a perceived loss in authenticity in Black Elk's cultural contamination, Gunnars and Richler explore the creative potential of such cross-cultural contact. For them, as for the bilingual Canadian poet Lola Lemire Tostevin, "the concept of contamination as literary device" would seem to be appealing. Tostevin argues that "Contamination means differences have been brought together so they make contact" (13).

Such a process defines the central activities of post-modernism and post-colonialism — the bringing of differences together into creative contact. But this is also where they part company. For it is the nature of this contact — and its results — that are at issue. For post-colonial writers, the cross-cultural imagination that I am polemically calling "contamination" for the purposes of this article, is not just a literary device but also a cultural and even a political project. Linda Hutcheon ("Circling the Downspout") in this collection points out that post-colonialism and feminism have "distinct political agendas and often a theory of agency that allow them to go beyond the post-modern limits of deconstructing existing orthodoxies into the realms of social and political action." In contrast, she argues, "post-modernism is politically ambivalent" (168). At the same time, however, she concludes that the post-colonial is "as implicated in that which it challenges as is the post-*modern*" ("Downspout" 183). This assertion depends on a leap from the recognition that the post-colonial is "contaminated" by colonialism (in the word itself and the culture it signifies) to the conclusion that such "contamination" necessarily implies complicity. It is this notion I would like to explore more fully in the rest of this paper.

If we accept Hutcheon's assertion that post-modernism is politically ambivalent, what are the implications of such a theory? There are at least two that interest me here.

Firstly, what enables this ambivalence? Post-modernism takes on a personality; it becomes a subject, human-like in its ability to express ambivalence. The functions of the author, declared dead by post-structuralist theory, resurface in post-modernism and in the post-modernist text through the concept of ambivalence. The authority of the post-modernist text comes from this ambivalence, this ability to see all sides, to defer judgement and to refuse agency. Secondly, what are the effects of this ambivalence? It would seem to suggest that action is futile; that individual value judgements are likely to cancel each other out; that one opinion is as good as another; that it would be futile and dishonest to choose one path above any other; that disinterested contemplation is superior to any attempt at action. In effect, then, ambivalence works to maintain the status quo. It updates the ambiguity so favoured by the New Critics, shifting their formalist analysis of the text's unity into a psychoanalysis of its fissures, and their isolation of text from world into a worldliness that cynically discounts the effectiveness of any action for social change.

To refer to contradictions instead of a fundamental ambivalence places the analysis within a political rather than a psychoanalytical framework. Post-modernism and post-colonialism often seem to be concerned with the same phenomena, but they place them in different grids of interpretation. The name "post-modernism" suggests an aestheticising of the political while the name "post-colonialism" foregrounds the political as inevitably contaminating the aesthetic, but remaining distinguishable from it. If post-modernism is at least partially about "how the world dreams itself to be 'American' " (Stuart Hall quoted in Ross xii), then post-colonialism is about waking from that dream, and learning to dream otherwise. Post-modernism cannot account for such post-colonial resistance writing, and seldom attempts to.

Much of my work over the past decade has involved documenting the contradictions of Canadian post-colonialism. Reading Canadian literature from a post-colonial perspective, recognizing Canadian participations in empire and in the resistance to empire, one quickly encounters some of the limitations of post-modernist theory in accounting for Canadian texts, even for those apparently post-modernist in form. Because Linda Hutcheon is one of Canada's preeminent theorists of the post-modern, this essay engages with her work first of all as a way of posing some of the problems I see when the post-colonial and the post-modern are brought together.

Despite post-modernism's function as a problematising mode, several assumptions central to imperial discourse survive unchallenged in the work of its defenders. These include an evolutionary model of development, a search for synthesis that relies on a revival of the notion of authenticity, and an insistence on judging a work on its own terms alone as if there were only one true reading. A post-colonial reading would reject such assumptions; post-modernist readings affirm them under the guise of a disinterested objectivity.

I am aware here of entering disputed territory. The quarrels over the meaning of post-modernism are well documented elsewhere in this book and in numerous others. Post-colonial criticism has its own disputes, with a scantier and more recent documentation. I would distinguish the post-colonial criticism developed by Ashcroft, Griffiths and Tiffin in *The Empire Writes Back* from that developed by the U.S.-based Jameson, Gates and Spivak, which to my mind suffers from some of the same assumptions as does post-modernism.

1. *The Evolutionary Model*

In "Circling the Downspout" Hutcheon writes that "[t]he current post-structuralist/post-modern challenges to the coherent, autonomous subject have to be put on hold in feminist and post-colonial discourses, for both must work first to assert and affirm a denied or alienated subjectivity: those radical post-modern challenges are in many ways the luxury of the dominant order which can afford to challenge that which it securely possesses." (168) There are several problems with this statement. The first is the notion that there is a single evolutionary path of literary development established by the European model. Secondly, there is the idea of a norm of subjectivity also established by the European model. Thirdly, there is the implied assumption that political commitment (to the liberation of nation or women), even in non-European countries, must necessarily express itself through a literary realism that presents a unified subject along the nineteenth century European model. And finally, it seems to demean literary criticism as a "luxury," something nonessential that not all societies really need, as if critique is not a necessary component for culture or identity building.

These assumptions are so strongly embedded in our western culture that even texts challenging such notions are read to confirm them. Consider Jamaica Kincaid's *Annie John*, a complex metafictional work challenging notions of a unified subjectivity that is often read as a traditional *bildungsroman* consolidating a simple achievement of just such a selfhood. Yet as Simon Gikandi argues in these pages, "Caribbean women writers are concerned with a subject that is defined by what de Laurentis calls 'a multiple, shifting, and often self-contradictory identity, a subject that is not divided in, but rather at odds, with language.' " (14) This is the kind of subject whose exploration Hutcheon argues must be "put on hold" in feminist and post-colonial writing, yet in fact we find it in many of these texts, if we read them with the openness we bring to European fictions.

2. *The Search for Synthesis*

In expressing her unease with the use of post-colonial to describe the settler and multicultural contemporary cultures of Canada, Hutcheon suggests that perhaps Native culture "should be considered the resisting, post-colonial voice of Canada." (172) This search for the authentic Canadian voice of post-colonialism mirrors the title of her book on post-modernism in Canada, *The Canadian Postmodern*. Just as we saw a unitary subjectivity being affirmed in the evolutionary model, so we see a unified voice or style being advocated here. Although Hutcheon here identifies Robert Kroetsch as "Mr Canadian Postmodern" (*Postmodern* 183), I would argue that there are several Canadian post-modernisms just as there is more than one Canadian post-colonial voice. A term may have multiple, subsidiary meanings without losing its usefulness in indicating a general category.

Hutcheon's assumption that the post-colonial speaks with a single voice leads her to belabour the necessity of resisting the totalising application of a term that in her analysis would blur differences and deny the power relations that separate the native post-colonial experience from that of the settlers. Certainly turning to the post-colonial as a kind of touristic "me-tooism" that would allow Canadians to ignore their own complicities in imperialism would be a serious misapplication of the term. Yet, as far as I know, discussions of Canadian post-colonialism do not usually equate the settler with the native experience, or the Canadian with the Third World. The kind of generalisations that Richard Roth criticises in Abdul JanMohammed's work do tend to totalise in this way, but this kind of work always ignores countries like Canada. To my mind, Hutcheon gets it backwards when she writes: "one can certainly talk of post-colonialism in Canada but only if the differences between its particular version and that of, especially, Third World nations is kept in mind" (174). The drawing of such distinctions is the whole point of talking about post-colonialism in Canada. The post-colonial perspective provides us with the language and the political analysis for understanding these differences. The danger is less that Canadians will rush to leap on the victim wagon than that they will refuse to recognize that they may well have some things in common with colonised people elsewhere.

Hutcheon's argument functions as a sort of straw man that misrepresents the post-colonial theoretical endeavour as practised in relation to Canada, deflecting attention away from its radical potential. Her argument demonstrates that in our care to respect the specificity of particular experiences we run another risk, that of a liberal pluralism which uses the idea of different but equal discourses to prevent the forming of alliances based on a comparative analysis that can perceive points of connection. Consider the following statement from *The Canadian Postmodern*: "If women have not yet been allowed access to (male) subjectivity, then it is very difficult for them to contest it, as the (male) post-structuralist philosophers have been doing lately. This may make women's writing *appear* more conservative, but in fact it is just *different*" (5–6). By positing female writing as "just different" from the male norm, Hutcheon erases the power differential she has been trying to establish, while reaffirming the male as the norm and the experimental as more advanced than and superior to the conservative. It sounds like special pleading for the second-rate, while on the surface it reaffirms the liberal myth of society formed from a plurality of equal differences.

Her assertion of Canadian difference from other post-colonial experiences functions in a similar way. The focus on uniqueness denies us the insights to be derived from careful comparison. Far from separating it from other post-colonial nations, Canada's pluri-ethnic composition allows for points of connection with some experiences elsewhere which when analysed comparatively may yield insights into how power operates, other than by sheer force, in our own fairly comfortable world. Far from totalising, a post-colonial analysis can identify structural patterns of oppression and the moves that coopt difference to maintain oppression as well as the strategies for resisting it.

Hutcheon suggests in "Circling the Downspout" that "Canada has experienced no actual 'creolization' which might have created something new out of an adaptation process within a split racial context" (173). What about the Metis, and the literature now being created by Metis writers? What about a writer like Tostevin, equally at home in English and French? At a less literal level, what about the metaphorical creolization of novels like *The Prowler* and *Solomon Gursky Was Here?* Most of the rest of this essay concerns itself with challenging this claim.

3. The Cult of Authenticity

Paul Smith suggests that post-modernist discourse replaces the "conflictual view and the comic view of the third world" with a "cult of authenticity" (142). This seems to be what is happening with Hutcheon's assertion that only Canada's native peoples may claim to speak with an authentic post-colonial voice. Such an assertion connects her approach to post-colonialism to that of Fredric Jameson which produces a first world criticism respectful of a third world authenticity that it is believed his own world has lost. But what are the effects of such a "cult of authenticity"? Meaghan Morris concludes her analysis of *Crocodile Dundee* with the statement that "[i]t is hardly surprising, then, that the figure of the colonial should now so insistently reappear from all sides not as deprived and dispossessed by rapacity but as the naive spirit of plenitude, innocence, optimism — and effective critical 'distance' " (124). The postmodernist revisionings of the colonial and post-colonial that Smith and Morris discuss function to defuse conflict, denying the necessity of cultural and political struggle, and suggesting that tourism is probably the best model for cross-cultural interaction.

Hutcheon's argument that Canada's native peoples are the authentic post-colonial voice of the nation, with its implication that descendents of settlers and immigrants represent at best a contaminated post-coloniality, conforms to this post-modernist model. To challenge it, as Hutcheon knows, is fraught with difficulties because authenticity has also been used by colonial peoples in their struggles to regain power over their own lives. While post-colonial theorists embrace hybridity and heterogeneity as the characteristic post-colonial mode, some native writers in Canada resist what they see as a violating appropriation to insist on their ownership of their stories and their exclusive claim to an authenticity that should not be ventriloquised or parodied. When directed against the Western canon, post-modernist techniques of intertextuality, parody, and literary borrowing may appear radical and even potentially revolutionary. When directed against native myths and stories, these same techniques would seem to repeat the imperialist history of plunder and theft. Or in the case of *The Satanic Verses*, when directed against Islam, they may be read as sullying the dignity of a religion that prides itself on its purity.

Although I can sympathise with such arguments as tactical strategies in insisting on self-definition and resisting appropriation, even tactically they prove self-defeating because they depend on a view of cultural authenticity that condemns them to a continued marginality and an eventual death. Whose interests are served by this retreat into preserving an untainted authenticity? Not the native groups seeking land rights and political power. Ironically, such tactics encourage native peoples to isolate themselves from contemporary life and full citizenhood.

All living cultures are constantly in flux and open to influences from elsewhere. The current flood of books by white Canadian writers embracing Native spirituality clearly serves a white need to feel at home in this country and to assuage the guilt felt over a material appropriation by making it a cultural one as well. In the absence of comparable political reparation for past appropriations such symbolic acts seem questionable or at least inadequate. Literature cannot be confused with social action. Nonetheless, these creole texts are also part of the post-colonial search for a way out of the impasse of the endless play of post-modernist difference that mirrors liberalism's cultural pluralism. These books, like the post-colonial criticism that seeks to under-stand them, are searching for a new globalism that is neither the old universalism nor the Disney simulacrum. This new globalism simultaneously asserts local inde-pendence and global interdependencies. It seeks a way to cooperate without cooption, a way to define differences that do not depend on myths of cultural purity or authenticity but that thrive on an interaction that "contaminates" without homogenis-ing.

Darlene Barry Quaife's *Bone Bird* is one of the most interesting of these new creole texts. Aislinn Cleary, part-white and part-native, learns to reach out to others through her initiation into a mixture of local Vancouver Island native spiritual practice and her grandmother's beliefs, brought with her as a refugee from Mexico fleeing the aftermath of Pancho Villa's thwarted rebellion. Her friendship with two tree planters temporarily working in town acquaints her with the stories of other refugees: Hugh's Chinese mother fleeing the Second World War in the Pacific and Ivan's Polish mother fleeing the same war in Europe. Hugh is researching and documenting historical and cultural links between China and the West Coast of America that might explain the similarities he has discovered between certain artistic symbols. He and Aislinn need each other to complete this work. The "bone bird" metamorphoses as a spiritual guide, leading Teodora, Aislinn's grandmother, out of despair into new life and directing Aislinn toward new journeys with Hugh, and as "the scavenger," mascotting the unemployed loggers of Aislinn's town toward new lives elsewhere. The political realities of a colonial economy where a logging operation can first destroy the material bases of the native culture and then that of the settler culture logging the trees by shutting down the single industry company town are at the heart of this narrative. They are at once part of a global system of exploitation and a specifically evoked particular experience, with its own smells, sights, sounds, pleasures and pains. The text records these accurately, with love and anguish, but it directs its quest for spiritual values toward the alliances that can survive, resist, and renew. The only advocate of cultural purity is Aislinn's racist, and very ill, English mother, a war bride who did not know that her Canadian husband was part-Indian until it was too late to turn back.

4. *Judging the Work on its Own Terms*

Hutcheon's conclusion to her *Poetics of Postmodernism* admits the "limited" aims of post-modernism and its "double encoding as both contestatory and complicitous" (230). She acknowledges that "I would agree with Habermas that this art does not 'emit any clear signals'," but adds that its saving grace is that "it does not try to." It cannot offer answers, "without betraying its anti-totalizing ideology" (231). I have suggested that it does surreptitiously offer answers — in ambivalence itself, in the relativity of liberal pluralism, in the cult of authenticity that lies behind its celebration of differences. But is it true that answers necessarily totalise? Are these the only alternatives? Is Hutcheon here asking enough of the post-modernist text? Or is she even asking the most interesting or the most important questions? Isn't the effect of such a conclusion to preserve the status quo and the myth of an objectivity that itself totalizes? Can we legitimately ask more of a text than it asks of itself? Post-colonial criticism suggests that we can.

5. *Reading the White Inuit*

To read Kristjana Gunnars' *The Prowler* and Mordecai Richler's *Solomon Gursky Was Here* is to enter two very different literary experiences. Both nod to post-modernist antecedents (Gunnars to Grass's *Tin Drum* and Richler to Márquez's *One Hundred Years of Solitude*) and employ post-modernist techniques (fragmenting narrative, doubling incidents, metafictional commentary, interrupted chronology, mixing of modes), but in *The Prowler* these techniques are integral to the way the text makes its meaning whereas in *Solomon Gursky* they are entertaining excrescences on a tale almost Dickensian in its fundamental faithfulness to a realist's investment in character and story.

Far from surrendering the author's authority, Richler delights in his control, duplicating it within the text in the story of Solomon Gursky's/Sir Hyman Kaplansky's manipulation of Moses Berger. Here the author plays his reader as a fisherman plays a fish, the fish gladly seizing the hook of narrative in return for the pleasure of the quest. *The Prowler* abandons such myths of control in search of an equal partnership between writer and reader, both prowlers seeking to transgress the boundaries of traditionally delimited territories and seeking to subvert the linearity and predicability of traditional plots with their winners and their losers. *The Prowler* puts as much distance as possible between the writer as prowler and the idea of an author God in control of the story. Prowling the borders, silences and dead ends of stories, reader and writer nonetheless come together to share a point of view, to discern emergent patterns, and to make choices about how we make meaning in the world.

These reading experiences are different in the power they allocate to writer and reader, and in the distance they are willing to travel to question dominant assumptions about the way the world works and whether or not it is possible to change it to make it a better place. Richler's is finally a conservative vision and Gunnars's a radical one. Nonetheless, both texts insist that the reader must move beyond a post-modernist ambivalence into a world of moral decision making. Neither Gunnars nor Richler offer answers, but their texts do make value judgements and encourage their readers to make them too. Although they recognize inevitable complicities, they choose contestation; they discover free spaces for resistance; they introduce love and freedom into worlds of pain and hatred. In their work, post-modernist devices serve post-colonial ends. Although the experience of reading these two books is very different, they offer similar visions of the marginalised, similar questionings of myths of purity and authenticity, similar affirmations of cultural contamination, and similar insistences on the political agency that characterizes the post-colonial. These similarilities, I would suggest, derive from the particular circumstances of a Canadian post-coloniality that is not indigenous but in the process of becoming so.

Just as the North functions for many non-Northerners as a final frontier, so the Inuit can seem a last symbol of cultural integrity. Both Gunnars and Richler explode these myths of North and Northerners. For them the North is an archetypal colony and the people who inhabit the North find their identity in dispute between those committed to maintaining an ideal of cultural purity and those who favour cultural interaction.

The Prowler explains that "White Inuit" are Icelanders, Northerners who survive on a diet of fish in a country with a history of multiple colonisations. As "White Inuit" their identity is already hybrid, privileged by race and underprivileged by location. The narrator's already hybrid identity as white Inuit is further complicated by different parental legacies, by language, by class, and by changes in the power structures governing her island as well as shifts in her geographical location. Her response to such endless discriminations of difference is to multiply the contaminations: "The solution was to study more languages. I would learn French and German, Faeroese and Inuit. I would confuse them all" (Section 133). If language determines identity, multiply the identities; confuse the categorisers; transgress the limits imposed on identity. She will be a boundary-crosser, a border-prowler. Cultural purity, the myth of her homogenous Icelandic society, is not possible even there.

But neither is it possible to be all things to all people. To speak Danish and English is not to betray her Icelandic identity, but to ask questions such as "Why has there been such a long history of starvation?" (Section 44) is to begin to recognise that "it is not possible to sympathize with all sides at once. When you choose your allegiances, I thought, you ally yourself with the one who suffers" (Section 142). Such an alliance entails drawing connections between political realities and private lives, between military occupations and imperial control on the one hand and the shortage of food and shelter on the other, between comfort in Denmark and the United States and suffering in Iceland.

The text's post-modernist celebration of multiplicities — "I imagine a story that allows all speakers to speak at once, claiming that none of the versions is exactly a lie" (Section 68) — is complicated by its recognition that "human psychology is determined by politics. And politics is determined by diet. That is, those who eat best win" (Section 155). Material realities ground the text's utopian desire for surfeit in the remembrance of a manipulated scarcity. Nonetheless, *The Prowler* chooses to end with an image of hope, rewriting the story of Noah's Ark as an Icelandic myth of a new beginning with a communal welcoming after the disaster of the Second World War. This Ark contains the mothers and fathers of future generations, returning Icelanders enriched by their contact with the outside world.

Richler too reappropriates the story of Noah's Ark in multiple rewritings that turn the doomed ship Erebus of the Franklin expedition into an ark that enables the survival of his mythical Jewish explorer Ephraim Gursky. Gursky takes as his emblem the raven that disappointed Noah on the Biblical ark but that represents a survivor trickster figure for North American Native mythologies. The raven, who "speaks in two voices" (500), provides an alternative creation myth to that of Genesis for Ephraim's grandson Solomon. Solomon's son Henry meets his death on what his neighbours term "Crazy Henry's Ark," and his son Isaac only survives through an act of cannibalism that appears to symbolise Richler's view of father/son relations in this text. Despite the cultural contaminations of Richler's Ark of origins, it remains throughout its transformations a purely masculine process that limits its celebration of cultural hybridity.

Ephraim introduces Jewish customs into Inuit practice, to the confusion of anthropologists and historians seeking cultural authenticity in the far North. Richler's comic invention of "The McGibbon Artifact," the only Eskimo carving of what was clearly meant to represent a kangaroo" (61) makes a serious political point reiterated throughout the text, that the movements of peoples and interactions of cultures that have characterized the twentieth century have taken place as part of the military expansion of capital, but that there is always a space for resistance, for eluding control and surprising the enemy. Ephraim Gursky beats the convict system that built the British empire in the nineteenth century; Solomon Gursky beats the capitalists at their own game in the twentieth. The multiple colonial childhoods that Kaplansky/Gursky/Raven invents to entertain his British guests draw the reader's attention to the structural similarities produced by the expansion of empire even as the stories function for his listeners as isolated instances of a titillating authenticity.

Solomon, the archetypal wandering Jew who survived prohibition in Canada and the Holocaust in Europe "didn't die of old age," Moses suspected, "but in the Gulag or a stadium in Latin America" (550–1). He becomes the spirit of resistance to oppression in all its guises, changing shapes as fast as his enemies, always one step ahead of those who would betray the human spirit. The danger in such tales is the homogenizing of differences into the repetition of a single narrative, and the elimination of collective action in favour of the myth of the superhuman individual whose triumphs can easily be used to justify the continued oppression of the rest of us. Its strength lies in its insistence that individual lives do matter, that each of us can make a difference, a point brought home by the book's title "*Solomon Gursky Was Here.*" The survival of the surprising Mr. Morrie and the rejuvenation of Moses further support such a reading as do other elements in the text.

Using the recurrent post-colonial metaphor of the colony as the empire's garbage dump, both Gunnars and Richler explore what it means to live in a place that is powerless to refuse others' refuse, what others have refused. Iceland is where other countries dump their lepers. "They did not think people on this remote island counted" (Section 41). Canada is where the British dump "the effluvium of their slums" (Richler 81). Both novels affirm, however, that such apparent disadvantages may be turned to advantage. Gunnars' narrator muses on how North America "turns out to be a place where major defects go unnoticed" (Section 149). A weakness elsewhere may be turned into a strength here. (This is a premise explored at more length in Bharati Mukherjee's *Jasmine*.) Similarly, Richler's Moses muses: "If Canada had a soul . . . then it wasn't to be found in Batoche or the Plains of Abraham or Fort Walsh or Charlottetown or Parliament Hill, but in The Caboose and thousands of bars like it that knit the country together from Peggy's Cove, Nova Scotia to the far side of Vancouver Island" (64). In other words, that elusive Canadian essence is not to be found in historic defeats, military battles or the parliamentary process, but in the survival of working class communal culture at the local level throughout the land. The "effluvium" of British slums bring a tough cultural specificity to Canada that Britain rejected but our writers now embrace. This turning the tables on those who think they have you where they want you, this transvaluation of values is part of the post-colonial literary strategy that clears a space for history's silenced ones to speak. Strength comes not from victimhood, from what one has been denied, but from a reevaluation of what one has.

Richler's embrace takes in the ugly racism as well as the moral probity of the Bert Smiths whom he has Solomon see as the "essence" of this country (74). Bert Smith, like Moses's arch enemy Professor Hardy, believes in cultural purity but finds himself defeated as the "true north, strong and free" of the national anthem yields to Richler's celebration of a "mongrelized" nation (79–80). In a delightfully understated ironic reversal, just when Smith and his landlady, Mrs. Jenkins, think they have finally parted company, Richler shows us Mrs. Jenkins unconsciously seeing with Smith's eyes and Smith unconsciously speaking in Mrs. Jenkins' voice (444–5). For all their stubborn opposition to each other's point of view, they have inevitably contaminated one another through the proximity in which they have lived. Despite themselves, their horizons have broadened and they have grown in the process.

Both Richler and Gunnars retain the utopian dream of the quest for a just society, and locate that quest in the contaminations of cross-cultural exploration. Both write out of positions specifically located in the current debate about multiculturalism in Canada: Richler as a male, Canadian-born Jew and Anglophone Quebecker; Gunnars as a female, Icelandic immigrant to the Canadian West for whom English is not a first language. Both vigorously dispute any residual faith in the possiblity of cultural authenticity. Both show how colonial relations permeate some European and North American experiences. It is not possible to postulate a Them and Us based on geography or the nation-state alone. These texts work to "resuscitate" the local referent from "the coma induced by typecasting" (Roth 249), showing how post-modernisms and post-colonialisms are themselves riddled by differences that nonetheless may be understood through a double-pronged analysis that looks for the workings of power in specific conditions.

Perhaps the clearest difference between a post-modernist practice and a post-colonial practice emerges through their different uses of history. As Hutcheon points out, "[h]istoriographic metafiction acknowledges the paradox of the *reality* of the past but its *textualized accessibility* to us today" (*Poetics* 114). Without denying that things happened, post-modernism focuses on the problems raised by history's textualized accessibility: on the problems of representation, and on the impossibility of retrieving truth. Post-colonialism, in contrast, without denying history's textualized accessibility, focusses on the reality of a past that has influenced the present. As a result of these different emphases, post-modern fiction takes liberties with what we know of the facts of the past much more freely than does post-colonial fiction. Richler's improbable introduction of fictional characters into historical narrative has more in common with the methods of a Sir Walter Scott than a D.M. Thomas. Neither he nor Gunnars deny that different versions of specific events will circulate, but they are interested in the effects of historical happenings: the effects of invasion, of military occupation, of food blockades, of revolution.

More than this, they do not hesitate to suggest that some interpretations carry greater validity than others: lies may be distinguished from truths; false values from valid ones. Gunnars writes: "Reading *Morgunbladid*, the Icelandic daily, I saw the population of the island was being reassured. The American Base, it said, is not a nuclear base. Some months later in Canada I happened upon an American military map. Iceland, it showed, *is* a nuclear base" (Section 30). Richler provides a diary entry showing Kaplansky asking his French neighbours who came to the dinner parties put on by the German officers occupying his house during the Second World War. One neighbour sobs in reply: "We had no choice but to accept his invitations. It was awful. His father was a pork butcher. He had no manners. He didn't even know that Pouilly-Fume is not a dessert wine" (515–6). Here Richler relies on our knowledge of the Holocaust to "place" these values. Richler's most sympathetic characters need to believe that a writer should not be bought, that not everything can be turned into a commodity, even in a commodity culture. *The Prowler* believes that "the text desires to be true" (Section 69). Near its end, its narrator admits "That the text has been prowling in the reader's domain. Telling itself and then interpreting itself.... The text is relieved that there are no borders in these matters" (Section 164). In other words, neither author is willing to surrender the agency that Hutcheon sees as characterizing the post-colonial but not the post-modern. Their recognition of complicities does not make them complicit.

As Stephen Slemon points out in this collection, "Western post-modernist readings can so over-value the anti-referential or deconstructive energies of postcolonial texts that they efface the important recuperative work that is also going on within them" (7). Those deconstructive energies are at work in these two novels, but it is the recuperative power, which they seek to energize for their readers and their Canadian culture, that most distinguishes them. And it is this power that a post-colonial reading can help us to understand. The white Inuit are speaking. Who is listening?

WORKS CITED

Ashcroft, Bill, Gareth Griffiths and Helen Tiffin. *The Empire Writes Back: Theory and Practice in Post-Colonial Literatures.* London: Routledge, 1989.

Black Elk, and John G. Neihardt. *Black Elk Speaks.* 1961. Lincoln: U of Nebraska P, 1979.

Gates, Henry Louis, ed. *Race, Writing and Culture.* Chicago: University of Chicago P, 1986.

Gunnars, Kristjana. *The Prowler.* Red Deer: Red Deer College P, 1989.

Hutcheon, Linda. *The Canadian Postmodern: A Study of Contemporary English-Canadian Fiction.* Toronto: OUP 1988.

————. *A Poetics of Postmodernism: History, Theory, Fiction.* London: Routledge, 1988.

Jameson, Fredric. "Third World Literature in an Era of Multinational Capitalism." *Social Text* 15 (1986): 65–88.

Morris, Meaghan. "Tooth and Claw: Tales of Survival and *Crocodile Dundee*." Ross 105–27.

Powers, William. "When Black Elk Speaks, Everybody Listens." *Social Text* 24 (1990): 43–56.

Quaife, Darlene Barry. *Bone Bird.* Winnipeg: Turnstone P, 1989.

Richler, Mordecai. *Solomon Gursky Was Here.* Markham: Viking, 1989.

Ross, Andrew, ed. *Universal Abandon?: The Politics of Post-Modernism,* Minneapolis: U of Minnesota P, 1988.

———. "Introduction." *Universal Abandon?*: vii–xviii.

Roth, Richard. "The Colonial Experience and its Post-Modern Fate." *Salmagundi* 84 (Fall 1989): 248–65.

Smith, Paul. "Visiting the Banana Republic." Ross 128–48.

Spivak, G.C. *In Other Worlds: Essays in Cultural Politics*. London: Methuen, 1987.

Tostevin, Lola Lemire. "Contamination: A Relation of Difference." *Tessera*. (Spring 1989): 13–14.

Notes on Contributors

IAN ADAM is Professor and Head of the Department of English at the University of Calgary. He is the author of *George Eliot* (1969), and has also written two volumes of poetry and articles on Victorian and Post-Colonial Literature. He edited *ARIEL: A Review of International English Literature* from 1980 to 1990.

DIANA BRYDON teaches at the University of Guelph. She is author of *Christina Stead* (1987) and, with Helen Tiffin, *Decolonising Fictions* (forthcoming). She is editor of *World Literature Written in English* and Chair of the Canadian Association for Commonwealth Literature and Language Studies.

ANNAMARIA CARUSI lectures in the Department of Literary Theory at the University of South Africa, Pretoria. Her previous publications include articles on freudo-marxism, especially in the work of Barthes and Kristeva, and in the journal *Tel Quel*. She is presently researching political aspects of post-structuralist theories.

SIMON DURING teaches at the University of Melbourne. His interests include the relation between writing, modernity and colonialism.

JOHN FROW is the author of *Marxism and Literary History* (1986) and Head of the Department of English at the University of Queensland.

SIMON GIKANDI is author of *Reading the African Novel* (1987) and of numerous articles and essays on African and Caribbean literature. He is Assistant Professor in the Department of Black Studies at the University of Massachusetts, Boston, and a 1989/90 Mellon Faculty Fellow at Harvard University.

GARETH GRIFFITHS is Professor of English at the University of Western Australia. He has published a book on African and West Indian literatures, and numerous articles on post-colonial literatures and literary theory.

GRAHAM HUGGAN, a graduate of the University of British Columbia, has recently taken up an appointment in the English Department at Harvard University.

LINDA HUTCHEON teaches English and Comparative Literature at the University of Toronto. She is the author of *Narcissistic Narrative* (1980); *Formalism and the Freudian Aesthetic* (1984); *A Theory of Parody* (1985); *A Poetics of Postmodernism: History, Theory, Fiction* (1988); *The Canadian Postmodern: A Study of Contemporary English-Canadian Fiction* (1988); and *The Politics of Postmodernism* (1989).

HENA MAES-JELINEK is Professor of English and Commonwealth literature at the University of Liege and President of its centre for Commonwealth Studies. Author and editor of several books, including *Wilson Harris* and *A Shaping of Connections: Commonwealth Literature Then and Now* (ed. with Anna Rutherford and Kirstin Holst Petersen), she is a leading authority on Wilson Harris.

STEPHEN SLEMON teaches Commonwealth Literature at the University of Alberta. His articles on post-colonial literature and criticism have appeared in *ARIEL*, *Canadian Literature*, *The Journal of Commonwealth Literature*, and *Kunapipi*.

ARUNA SRIVASTAVA writes on South Asian writing, and has also completed work on Afrikaner South African novels and Canadian ethnic writing, usually from perspectives informed by post-colonial, post-structuralist and feminist theory. She teaches at the University of British Columbia.

HELEN TIFFIN is Associate Professor in the Department of English, University of Queensland. She is the author (with Bill Ashcroft and Gareth Griffiths) of *The Empire Writes Back* (1989) and has written articles on post-colonial literatures and literary theory. She has also co-edited (with Stephen Slemon) a collection of articles on post-colonial literary theory, *After Europe* (1989).

ROBERT RAWDON WILSON is a Professor of English at the University of Alberta. His current interests lie in the areas of narrative theory and Renaissance Literature. His book, *In Palamedes' Shadow: Explorations in Play, Game and Narrative Theory*, was published by Northeastern University Press in 1990.

INDEX

Adam, Ian, xiii, 82, 84
Adorno, Theodor W., 140, 143
Alexis, J. P., xiii, 153
Allen, Lillian, 174
Althusser, Louis, 104
Anderson, Johannes C., 43
Anthony, Michael, 17
Aquin, Hubert, 170
Arac, Jonathan, 8, 111
architecture: modernist, 143–44;
    post-modernist, 144–46, 167–68
Arnason, David, 173
Ashcroft, Bill (W. D.) et al., *The
    Empire Writes Back*, 47, 59, 193
Ashcroft, W. D. (Bill), 88
Atwood, Margaret, 131, 135, 155, 169,
    173–74
authenticity: in *Black Elk Speaks*, 191;
    as cult, 195–97; in dissolution of
    fixed categories in Malouf,
    159–60; as indigenization, 80; as
    indigenization through Peirce's
    semiotic, 79–90 *passim*; in Maori
    culture, 29–42; pre-colonial in
    South Africa, 99–100; and quest
    for tradition in Wilson Harris,
    52–54, 54–60 *passim*; role of
    material practices in establishing,
    163–64. *See also*
    cross-culturalism; identity;
    indigenous cultures
autoreferentiality: *See* intertextuality
Awatere, Donna, 29–30
Awkward, Michael, 90

Bail, Murray, 84, 121, 133
Baillie, Robert, 132
Baker, Houston A., 176
Bakhtin, M. M., 15–16, 61, 110
Barbour, Douglas, 178

Barthes, Roland, 53, 66, 76, 100, 104,
    129, 180
Bastos, Roa, 155
Baudrillard, Jean, 113, 146
Belich, James, 35
Bell, David, 174
Belsey, Catherine, 176, 177
Benjamin, Walter, 145
Bennett, David, 112, 113
Benterrak, Krim, 135
Berry, Reginald, 169
Bertens, Hans, 49, 57, 60
Best, Elsdon, 32, 40
Bhabha, Homi, xiv–xv, 1, 4, 57, 126,
    128, 176
Birney, Earle, "David," 79–90
Black Elk, 191
Board, Christopher, 134
Bonaventure Hotel, 144, 145
Boorstin, Daniel J., 146
Borduas, Emile, 170
Boswell, James, *Journal of a Tour to
    the Hebrides*, 23–26
Bowering, George, 169
Brathwaite, Edward Kamau, 15, 80
Brébeuf, Father Jean de, 182
Bringhurst, Robert, 125
Brossard, Nicole, 132
Brydon, Diana, xii, 10, 132, 135, 153,
    169, 170, 171
Buchler, Justus, 87, 88
Bürger, Peter, 144
Burroughs, Edgar Rice, 6–7

Caccia, Fulvio, 174
Calinescu, Matei, 142
Campbell, Marion, 132
canonicity, 4–5. *See also* universality
Carey, Peter, "Do You Love Me?,"
    79–90

207